The Spectrum of Teaching in Physical Education

This is the first in-depth, practice-focused book to explain 'spectrum theory' and its application in physical education and sports coaching. Spectrum theory identifies 11 distinct teaching styles, with decision making as a central characteristic, and allows teachers to select age and developmentally appropriate styles across social, physical, ethical, emotional and cognitive channels. The book brings together leading thinkers in spectrum theory, to demonstrate how it can be applied to improve teaching and learning in PE and coaching.

Drawing on real-world research in schools and universities, the book considers the history of spectrum theory, and examines its significance across important areas such as physical education teacher education, sport pedagogy, teacher development, models such as Games Sense and Teaching Games for Understanding, skill acquisition and student learning and perception. Every chapter highlights the practical implications of research in real-world settings and considers how spectrum theory can enhance learning experiences.

This book is invaluable reading for all pre-service and in-service school physical education teachers, sports coaches, school pedagogical leaders and college lecturers.

Brendan SueSee is Lecturer at the University of Southern Queensland, Australia.

Mitch Hewitt is Adjunct Lecturer at the University of Canberra and University of Southern Queensland, Australia and works for Tennis Australia.

Shane Pill is Associate Professor in Physical Education and Sport at Flinders University, Australia.

The Spectrum of Teaching Styles in Physical Education

Edited by Brendan SueSee,
Mitch Hewitt and Shane Pill

Routledge
Taylor & Francis Group

LONDON AND NEW YORK

First published 2020
by Routledge
2 Park Square, Milton Park, Abingdon, Oxon OX14 4RN

and by Routledge
605 Third Avenue, New York, NY 10017

Routledge is an imprint of the Taylor & Francis Group, an informa business

First issued in paperback 2021

British Library Cataloguing-in-Publication Data
A catalogue record for this book is available from the British Library

Library of Congress Cataloging-in-Publication Data
A catalog record has been requested for this book

ISBN 13: 978-0-367-35718-4 (hbk)
ISBN 13: 978-1-03-223788-6 (pbk)
ISBN 13: 978-0-429-34134-2 (ebk)

Typeset in Goudy
by Wearset Ltd, Boldon, Tyne and Wear

MIX
Paper from
responsible sources
FSC   FSC™ C013985
www.fsc.org

Printed in the United Kingdom
by Henry Ling Limited

Dedication

We would like to dedicate this book to Muska Mosston and Sara Ashworth for their contribution to not only pedagogy, but the field of education in general. Sara's generosity and patience with us has been so appreciated and supported all our learning. *The Spectrum of Teaching Styles* has allowed the three of us as educators to create learning experiences that have hopefully contributed to the development of students across the five developmental channels. It has also enabled our students to see physical education as not only the physical but also the many other aspects of an individual that can be developed through our choice of teaching styles. Your work lives through not only us but also our students and the students they teach. The Spectrum has also helped the three of us develop as teachers and researchers. We would like to also thank the students we have all taught (both at university level and schools) who have put up with us being learners when we have tried new teaching styles for the first time. The use of the styles was not always as successful as we had hoped but your patience was appreciated as we developed.

Contents

Contributors

Sara Ashworth is Director of the Spectrum Institute for Teaching and Learning, USA.

Stephen Berg is Associate Professor in the Okanagan School of Education at the University of British Columbia, Canada, where he teaches undergraduate courses in physical and health education curriculum and instruction, and graduate courses in educational research methodology. Dr. Berg's research focuses on children's physical activity levels in outdoor early learning environments, psychosocial and sport programming for at-risk adolescent girls and multi-disciplinary approaches to community-based health promotion.

Brent Bradford is Associate Professor in the Faculty of Education at Concordia University of Edmonton, Canada. He teaches an array of education-related undergraduate, after degree and graduate courses. Along with extensive K-9 teaching experiences (2000–2009), Brent has been teaching pre-service teachers since 2009 (CUE, University of Alberta, St. Francis Xavier University, University of British Columbia). Brent, an Erasmus+ and Mobile+ Scholar (University of the Basque Country, 2016), was awarded CUE's 2019 Gerald S. Krispin "President's" Research Award. Brent's research interests include: Physical and Health Education; wellness; effective teaching; and teacher education. Brent's contribution to higher education includes: Board of Directors (PHE Canada); Editor (Runner Journal); Research Advisor (UNICEF Canada); Program Reviewer (SHAPE America); Associate Editor (various academic journals); and Vice President (Education Society of Edmonton).

Mark Byra is Professor in the Division of Kinesiology and Health, College of Health Sciences, University of Wyoming, USA. Between 1979 and 1986, Mark taught physical education and French at the junior high school level in Penticton, British Columbia. He played volleyball as an undergraduate at the University of Victoria, and coached boys' and girls' teams at the regional and provincial levels in British Columbia and Nova Scotia.

At Dalhousie University, Mark was an assistant coach for the men's team. His primary line of research revolves around learner cognition and behaviour as impacted by different Spectrum teaching styles within the context of physical education.

Constantine Chatoupis is Physical Education Teacher at the third secondary school of Chania, Greece. His main research interests lie in the area of teaching effectiveness and instructional methodology. In particular, using Spectrum theory, he investigates the effects of teaching behaviours on elementary school children's learning and achievement. For 11 years, he has been affiliated with the National and Kapodestrian University of Athens, Greece. Apart from his research work, he is involved in literary endeavours as an essayist, novelist, and poet. His work has been published in Greek literary journals and newspapers.

Donetta J. Cothran is Professor at Indiana University in the USA. Her research is devoted to understanding both teachers' and students' beliefs and actions in K-12 education settings. She is a former Associate Editor at both *Research Quarterly for Exercise and Sport* and *Journal of Teaching in Physical Education*. Dr. Cothran is a Fellow of the National Academy of Kinesiology and the Society of Health and Physical Educators.

Matthew Curtner-Smith is Professor of Sport Pedagogy in the Department of Kinesiology at the University of Alabama, USA. He works with undergraduates training to teach physical education and graduate students studying sport pedagogy. His research examines physical education teaching, teachers, teacher education and curriculum.

Nikolaos Digelidis is Professor at the University of Thessaly, Greece, where he teaches physical education sport pedagogy, teaching methods in PE, curriculum design and development and physical activity and health education programs design and interventions. He participated in every significant educational reform in his country like "Olympic Education" (2000–2006) and "Promoting social and gender equality" (2006–2008) nationwide programs, new books for PE (2004–2006), "New School" action (2011–2013), and he was scientific coordinator for the New Curriculum and Teachers' Guidelines for senior high school PE (2014–2015).

Michael Goldberger is Emeritus Professor of Kinesiology at James Madison University, USA.

Clive Hickson is Professor Emeritus at University of Alberta, Canada. During his career, he served as a high school physical education specialist, an elementary school classroom teacher, a vice-principal of a K–7 school, a principal of K–7 and K–12 schools, and Professor and Associate Dean in the Faculty of Education at the University of Alberta, Canada. Clive also served on numerous education committees and worked on provincial curriculum resource development. Clive served on the Board of Directors for Physical and Health Education Canada.

Pamela Hodges Kulinna is Professor in Mary Lou Fulton Teachers College at Arizona State University in the USA. Professor Kulinna's research focuses on changing the culture of schools to healthy and active. She studies teaching, teacher education, and curriculum as they relate to student learning outcomes. Professor Kulinna has served as the co-editor of the *Journal of Teaching in Physical Education* and reviews for several other Physical Education, education and Kinesiology focused journals.

Joss Rankin is Lecturer in Health and Physical Education at Flinders University, Australia. At Flinders University, Joss coordinates and teaches Physical Education studies in initial teacher education, as well as coordinating the suite of Outdoor Education studies for the Bachelor of Sport, Health and Physical Activity. Joss is involved in a range of organisations and continues to connect with schools through a range of partnerships. As a member of ACHPER and OEASA, Joss enjoys sharing his work at a range of conferences and continues to advocate for Health, Physical and Outdoor Education.

Ioannis Syrmpas is a Stavros Niarchos Postdoctoral Research Fellow at the Department of Physical Education and Sport Science, University of Thessaly, Greece. He teaches swimming lessons for beginners, teaching methods in physical education and curriculum and teaching secondary physical education.

Chapter 1

Introduction to The Spectrum

Mitch Hewitt, Brendan SueSee and Shane Pill

This book came about as the editors reflected on the numerous conversations they have had with teachers and academics over the years about The Spectrum of teaching styles. One of the most common questions asked revolved around the fidelity or accuracy with which they were using a style. Questions such as "Is it Practice Style if the feedback is not private?", "Is it still Reciprocal Style if the students do not have a criteria sheet but I have given them criteria verbally?". We realised that many teachers either seemed to embrace The Spectrum or reject The Spectrum based on their perspective. The three perspectives were: you are doing the teaching style as per the text book landmark definition, you were interpretatively pragmatic (Stolz & Pill, 2016) and making it work by leaving parts out (or modifying it), or you were rejecting The Spectrum as the Landmark Teaching Styles were too rigid. Those who thought they were not doing a Landmark Teaching Style often seemed to express views that they were failing and stopped doing it. This made us think that many teachers seemed to hold a classic 'versus' approach!

We wished to highlight the many ways that teachers, sports coaches and academics were using The Spectrum by having a new perspective on The Spectrum published. A publication that was more about cases of using The Spectrum. Many of the examples you will find in this book are examples of using The Spectrum brought about because of a new perspective. While these perspectives are not all the same, the commonality is that the contributing authors wanted to use The Spectrum and have made it 'work' in each of their environments. In these cases, they have made it work by considering the learner at the centre and adapted by modifying the Landmark Style. However, not all chapters in this book are examples of modifying The Spectrum. Some are about how it has been applied in new ways to examine teaching or teach under graduate teachers or coaches.

Readers of this book will have a range of levels of knowledge about The Spectrum of Teaching Styles. This is not a book just for those who have a high level of knowledge about The Spectrum. We hope that it is a book for pre-service teachers, teachers, teacher educators, academics, sports coaches and people who want to learn more about how The Spectrum can help your teaching. It is also intended to engage and raise issues about The Spectrum.

Brief history and changes

In 1966, Muska Mosston first published The Spectrum of Teaching Styles (from this point on referred to as The Spectrum throughout this text). He did not create The Spectrum in the same way that Newton did not create gravity – it was always there waiting to be discovered. Mosston suggested that The Spectrum grew from "how does all this vast accumulation of knowledge from so many disciplines affect teaching behaviour? How does the philosophy of a theoretician affect every act of the teaching experience?" (Mosston, 1972, pp. 1–2). Mosston was contemplating what educators had learnt over time from research and how had it affected or influenced teaching. He noted that there had been research in psychology, cognitive psychology, motor learning and education and many of the concepts overlapped. Mosston felt that the knowledge, although similar, was played off against other concepts as if only one idea could exist or was superior to the other. This observation is evident when he suggested "the great question is not Skinner vs Brunner, creativity vs conformity and so on, along the path of opposing pair; the question is when conformity? When creativity? When individualised instruction? When media?" (Mosston, 1972, p. 5).

The way that ideas and concepts were played off against each other (or the 'versus' approach) asked teachers to abandon ideas (Mosston & Ashworth, 2002) and lead the teacher to applying theories according to his or her personal understanding. This behaviour resulted in "an idiosyncratic approach to the implementation of pedagogical theories" (Mosston & Ashworth, 2002, p. 3); meaning that educational theories are not applied to their full potential. This theorising led Mosston to search for a body of knowledge beyond idiosyncrasies.

The final issue that Mosston was concerned with was what he believed was a lack of consistency or uniformity with common terminology. In his opinion, inconsistency of terminology leads to limits with educational practices as teachers are not always talking about the same thing or there is a lack of agreement. These three issues – a verses approach, idiosyncratic teaching styles, and non-uniformity of terminology, "served as the foundation for Mosston's paradigm shift" (Mosston & Ashworth, 2002, p. 4). It led Mosston to search for the answer to "what is the body of knowledge about teaching that is beyond idiosyncratic behavior?" This question led him to theorise that teaching is a chain of decision making. This theory is the fundamental proposition of The Spectrum. When teaching is examined in this way, a range of teaching styles emerge and are defined according to the decision making and the behaviours of the student and teacher.

Every decision made by a teacher in every act of teaching has the consequence of inclusion and exclusion. These decisions serve as a powerful and sometimes irreversible antecedent to what actually occurs to the learner, for or against the learner.

(Mosston, 1969, p. 6)

To Mosston, "teaching therefore cannot be a one-dimensional form of behaviour. The richer teacher is the one with the larger repertoire of behavioural models" (Mosston, 1972, p. 5). Mosston believed The Spectrum (1966a) accurately presented the repertoire of behavioural models that gave a teacher mobility and freedom to match teaching to learning objectives. He suggested that:

The teacher who is familiar with a variety of teaching styles is ready to cope with new conditions and to interact successfully with various forms of student behaviour-to cope without threat, to experience without fear, and to bring to all his relations with students a contagious spirit of hope.

(Mosston, 1972, p. 6)

This quote embodies one of the crucial points of The Spectrum (2002). The Spectrum (2002) is not just a range of teaching styles that create a learning journey for the student. It is also a journey for the teacher, as they move along The Spectrum (2002), gradually handing the reigns of learning responsibility and decision making, over to the student, so that they can become an autonomous learner when appropriate, or if the learning objective requires. This is not to say that the teacher must move (as one style is more valuable than another) rather the teacher knows when to move and is able to move along The Spectrum. That is, teachers have 'mobility ability'.

In Figure 1.1, we show an example where problem solving and *creativity* are potentially interpreted as having higher value than recall or *reproduction* of knowledge.

This diagram "was inconsistent with the non-versus premise of The Spectrum-that all behaviours contribute to educational objectives, and that no one behaviour is more important than any other" (Mosston & Ashworth, 2008, p. 20). At this early stage of The Spectrum development, Byra (2000) suggested that Mosston was passing value judgements on teaching styles. Learner decision making and independence (Byra, 2000) were better in his opinion than teacher decision making. As you read this text and think of current syllabus documents you may think that this valuing of creativity over recall or memory still exists 53 years later and that a versus approach is still alive and well. Another example of the bias in value towards one approach over another is represented by Mosston, hoping his Spectrum (2002) "will serve as a contribution to more effective teaching of free students and indeed will lead the learner from command to discovery" (Mosston, 1966a, p xiv). According to Professor Ashworth, Mosston's use of the word 'free' is alluding to what he perceived at the time as an overuse of the Command Style and the

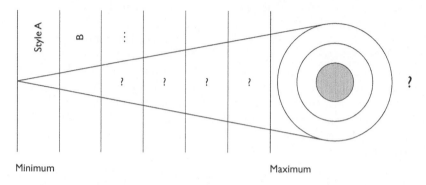

Minimum   Maximum

Figure 1.1 Diagram of Spectrum – 1966

Source: Reprint from Teaching Physical Education First Online Edition, 2008 are used with permission from Dr. Sara Ashworth, Director of the Spectrum Institute. Free Digital Download Available at: https://spectrumofteachingstyles.org/index.php?id=16

desire to free students so that they would experience other styles (personal correspondence, 2011).

At this early stage of Spectrum development Byra argued that Mosston "conceptualised the command style of teaching as having the least amount of value" (Byra, 2000, p. 230) and teaching styles that involved *problem solving* or *creativity* as having the "greatest amount of value" (Byra, 2000, p. 230). However, we argue that Mosston was referring to a hierarchy of the structure of subject matter (Mosston, 1966b, p. 2) and not teaching styles. Mosston goes further when he answers the questions "Is it necessary to experience the entire Spectrum?" Is it necessary to travel from style to style in the order of the Spectrum?" (Mosston, 1966c, p. 4). He addresses these questions by suggesting that one "must move "From Command to Discovery" (the sub-title of The Spectrum) in order to comprehend the intellectual cohesiveness of the Spectrum". However, we argue that this is not the same as saying one style is more valuable than another style nor is it a hierarchy. We suggest that Mosston is saying to understand all of it (The Spectrum) you need to experience all styles. He expands suggesting that teacher's need to know the entire Spectrum so that they are "able to make style-preference decisions whenever it is called upon by the learning style of the student … " (Mosston, 1966c, p. 5). We contend this comment emphasises the need for all styles to be experienced and not the valuing of one style over another. More specifically to the diagram or continuum "The direction of this continuum point to two polarities (the theoretical limits in the Teaching-Learning Transaction) of decision making: Maximum decision by the teacher on one hand and maximum decision by the student on the other; and therefore, the subtitle: "From Command to Discovery", Mosston, 1969, p. 17). We are aware that this notion challenges other beliefs and, as the title of this book suggests, offers a new perspective.

About the chapters

This book brings together leading and innovative thinkers in the field of pedagogy to offer new perspectives on The Spectrum. It begins with Sara Ashworth, 'the mother' of The Spectrum, giving a history and overview of The Spectrum and providing personal insights about Muska Mosston that only she could. She covers the beginning, theory of The Spectrum and its development and the future of where The Spectrum may go.

Those interested in how The Spectrum can be used in Physical Education Teacher Education (PETE) programs will be particularly interested in Chapters 3, 5 and 9. In Chapter 3, Mark Byra explains how he has used The Spectrum at the University of Wyoming and how The Spectrum addresses some of Windshcitl's (2012) dilemmas when implementing teaching styles. In Chapter 9, Matt Curtner-Smith provided ideas on how to implement The Spectrum for those considering including it in their PETE programs. Through the lens of transformative tertiary physical education, Shane Pill and Joss Rankin also explained how they use The Spectrum in the PETE program at Flinders University as a deliberate mechanism to disrupt the common technocratic and sport-as-sport techniques physical education perspective. Chapter 13 by Yannis Syrmpas and Nikolaos Digelidis emphasised the importance of understanding pre-service physical education teachers' mental models of reproduction and production cluster styles so that adoption of new styles may be successful. In Chapter 12, Donetta Cothran and Pamela Kulinna explored research that has been done covering what styles were being used, by whom, and what those individuals believed about the styles. They then draw this research to others work around the central themes in an attempt to capture a more complete picture of The Spectrum decision making chain and to suggest new paths of inquiry regarding The Spectrum and its use.

For those interested in using The Spectrum whether as a teacher or a sports coach will find Chapters 6 and 7 useful. Mitch Hewitt's Chapter 6 positions the coach as an educator and provides a series of practical tennis games and play practices that appeal to the holistic development of tennis players in a variety of learning domains. Brendan SueSee, Shane Pill and Mitch Hewitt' contributed Chapter 7, examining the Constraints Led Approach (CLA) through the lens of The Spectrum. They demonstrated how the CLA can be seen as a range of teaching styles on The Spectrum.

Teachers will find Brent Bradford, Clive Hickson and Stephen Berg's Chapter 14 on the Teaching Continuum – a modified version of The Spectrum, aimed specifically at generalist trained primary school teachers – very helpful. It is not designed to replace The Spectrum, rather to provide a foundational framework that can help build success for non-specialist (GT) teachers' understanding of physical education teaching. In Chapter 4, Brendan SueSee used The Spectrum to interrogate the teaching styles of physical education teachers and how alignment between syllabus aims and goals, and the teaching style/s required to create learning episodes to enable students to meet these goals can be assisted by looking through The Spectrum. Michael Goldberger and Brendan SueSee, in Chapter 11, show how the Reciprocal Style creates a learning episode that improves motor performance, the amount of feedback given and the quality of feedback given by the participants. Staying with Landmark Styles, in Chapter 10, Mark Byra provides a real-world example of using the Inclusion Style in physical education and describes how Inclusion Style relates to the physical, cognitive and affective educational learning domains, and he follows-up with some suggestions for implementation.

Finally, in Chapter 8, Constantine Chatoupis examines The Spectrum research over 20 years, outlining how it has changed and makes some insightful recommendations for those contemplating further research on The Spectrum.

Spectrum development

As The Spectrum (2002) developed based on feedback, research, new insights and reflection, the 'versus approach' of one style versus another transformed. Transformation occurred as Mosston believed "the ideas in education are generally presented *in opposition* to the status quo" (Mosston & Ashworth, 2002, p. 2). He outlines the negativity of such an attitude by suggesting that "because of the 'versus approach', educators are constantly asked to abandon existing theories for the sake of new ones" (Mosston & Ashworth, 2002, p. 2). These changes in thinking lead him to believe that "each style of teaching was not inherently better or more effective than others, but rather each style met a specific set of unique objectives or goals" (Byra, 2000, p. 230). From here a teacher could think of the objectives they wanted to achieve and pick a style that Mosston believed would create the appropriate learning experiences to achieve the desired objectives.

> a Teaching Behavior Theory must not present a situation of Model A vs. Model B, nor a statement that Model A is better than Model B, but needs to construct the relationships among the identified behavioral models. Further, it must show the mobility from one model to another – preferably on a continuum.
>
> (Mosston, 1969, p. 16)

The Spectrum is now represented by the diagram in Figure 1.2, "a continuum with equal spaces and dotted lines representing the incremental, yet cumulative shift of decisions and the design variations that exist between landmark styles" (Mosston & Ashworth, 2008, p. 20).

A	B	C	D	E	F	G	H	I	J	K

Figure 1.2 Current Diagram of The Spectrum demonstrates a non-versus approach and an equal valuing of all teaching styles

Source: Reprint from Teaching Physical Education First Online Edition, 2008 are used with permission from Dr. Sara Ashworth, Director of the Spectrum Institute. Free Digital Download Available at: https://spectrumofteachingstyles.org/index.php?id=16

Over the years the precision with which decisions are analysed to distinguish one behaviour from another has also become more detailed. "This precision in analysing decisions led to the addition of several new landmark teaching-learning behaviours" (and to the previously mentioned elimination of others) (Mosston & Ashworth, 2008, p. 20). While other changes, such as the refinement of decision categories, the expansion of the individual teaching styles and the identification of all styles have taken place over the years, they have been "minimal in comparison to the 'versus' issue" (Byra, 2000, p. 231). While it may be easy to think that The Spectrum is an old theory that would be an incorrect conclusion to draw as the 1966 version has clearly evolved over time.

Criticisms of The Spectrum

Although research has recognised the contributions of The Spectrum to Physical Education pedagogy (Goldberger, 1992; Graber, 2001) the work of Mosston has been the subject of critique, misunderstanding and modification. While some scholars have attempted to elucidate and modify The Spectrum (Crum, 1995; Digelidis, 2006; Hurwitz, 1985; Krug, 1999) others have highlighted what they consider to be problems associated with it. A number of sports pedagogy writers (Hurwitz, 1985; Metzler, 1983; Sicilia-Camacho & Brown, 2008; Williams, 1996) have identified various problematic issues. For instance, Metzler (2005) has indicated that The Spectrum represents a decidedly limited perspective of instruction and fails to "address the full range of theoretical, design, planning, and assessment considerations in Physical Education instruction" (Metzler, 2005, p. 187). Metzler also suggested that The Spectrum places an overemphasis on teacher behaviour by illustrating in detail what the teacher is expected to do when a particular teaching style is being employed. This outcome is believed to result in discounting student process behaviour which largely affects achievement and instructional success (Metzler, 2005). In addition, The Spectrum has been criticised for a distinct lack of sequential description of student and teacher behaviours. In other words, it fails to adequately provide a description of the sequence in which teacher and student behaviour is meant to occur within any teaching style (Hurwitz, 1985). According to Hurwitz (1985), realising the precise sequence in which these behaviours occur is crucial to planning. This critique was based on the 2nd edition of *Teaching Physical Education* (Mosston, 1981). Criticism in relation to neglecting the context of learning has also been levelled at The Spectrum by Williams (1996). Williams claimed that the learning styles of students are not considered and that more effective learning is realised when the teaching style employed is consistent with the favoured learning style of the student.

The Spectrum has also been the subject of misinterpretation. Sicilia-Camacho and Brown commented: "the original Spectrum of teaching styles was made up from a collection of eight commonly observed teaching approaches or styles" (Goldberger et al., 2012, p. 87). This, however, was not how The Spectrum was developed (Goldberger et al., 2012). Mosston did not collect known teaching approaches or methods and organise these approaches into a framework (Goldberger et al., 2012). Rather, he developed the framework "from a premise, to the anatomy, and then to the landmark styles ... it was revealed in a systematic process of logical uncovering" (Goldberger, 2012, p. 272). In another apparent misinterpretation, Sicilia-Camacho and Brown wrote that a paradigm shift occurred from a "versus (opposing) notion of learning and teaching to a non-versus (non-opposing) notion" (2008, p. 85) of learning and teaching, beginning with the second edition of *Teaching Physical Education* (Mosston, 1981). They noted: "While seemingly innocuous, we contend that this shift can be seen in epistemological terms as an advance (back) towards positivism in PE despite years of dialogue from emerging interpretive standpoints" (Sicilia-Camacho & Brown, 2008, p. 85).

Goldberger and others strongly suggested that Sicilia-Camacho and Brown read more into Mosston's 'paradigm shift' than he intended. They suggested that the shift had more to do with a misrepresentation within his original schema than with The Spectrum itself. In Mosston's original schema, the diverging lines "implied directionality, suggesting that teaching should go from Command to Discovery ... it seemed to project a biased hierarchical view of the relationship among the styles and so it needed to be changed" (Goldberger et al., 2012, p. 273). Furthermore, on no occasion did Mosston view individual teaching styles as oppositional to each other as Sicilia-Camacho and Brown (2008) suggested. More accurately, Mosston regarded all the teaching styles as complementary to one another. He perceived the value of each style in relation to the diverse relationships it might possibly establish between the teacher, learner and the content. Ashworth has since provided a robust clarification of this misinterpretation, stating:

> Muska [Mosston] NEVER considered one style more important than another ... unfortunately his first diagram represented a VERSUS point of view but his thinking and presenting of styles has always been from a non-versus perspective-that is the foundation of The Spectrum. He was

fighting an entrenched Command Style system and he was trying to get teachers and coaches to accept the notion that students could produce ideas along The Spectrum and certainly in Divergent Discovery thinking (that style name was not used until later editions). Discovery and Divergent thinking were not common ideas when Muska began promoting The Spectrum ... he pushed the extreme teaching styles in the beginning (called Problem Solving and Going Beyond in the first edition in 1966). Guess you could say that in the beginning Muska's emotions got in his way, he was fighting to educate a profession to accept a Spectrum of alternative teaching approaches and he wanted to show that where these Spectrum ideas could lead to, therefore, he exaggerated the extreme opposing position of Style A. Of course, that was way too extreme for the Command Style system to embrace in the beginning.

(S. Ashworth, personal communication, 2 July 2012)

As a consequence of Mosston's original diagram representation depicting The Spectrum (Mosston, 1966a), many authors incorrectly assumed that Mosston valued teaching styles in the production cluster of The Spectrum more than teaching styles in the reproduction cluster. According to Ashworth (S. Ashworth, personal communication, 2 July 2012) The Spectrum has always been a 'non-versus' theory.

Sicilia-Camacho and Brown (2008) also questioned the use of the reproduction and production clusters on The Spectrum (Mosston & Ashworth, 2008). Goldberger and colleagues noted that in the first edition of *Teaching Physical Education* (Mosston, 1966a) the clusters had not yet been introduced. These categories were not presented until the third edition published in 1986. Furthermore, the development of the *clusters* was not to position teaching styles in opposition as Sicilia-Camacho and Brown (2008) suggested (Goldberger et al., 2012). Rather, the clusters provided more of a navigational reference point along The Spectrum. Sicilia-Camacho and Brown also conveyed concern regarding the potential for teachers to lose their individuality and creativity when utilising The Spectrum. They maintained that, "any pedagogical model that attempts to universalize and objectify will necessarily have to separate personhood from pedagogy, and thereby once again devalue and neglect the important issue of subjectivity" (Sicilia-Camacho & Brown, 2008, p. 87). Further, they described the styles as "neutral, technical instructional devices that reflect no particular value" (Sicilia-Camacho & Brown, 2008, p. 98). However, rather than depersonalising the teacher, The Spectrum has the capacity to provide a comparison between a teacher's intent and behaviour during lessons (Goldberger et al., 2012). Mosston's desire to identify 'universal' pedagogical constructs "was not motivated in the least by a desire to diminish the creativity or individualization of teachers" (Goldberger et al., 2012, p. 274), but rather, to provide them with an adaptable "tool through which they can express their creativity and individuality" (Goldberger et al., 2012, p. 274).

Discussions involving The Spectrum often refer to earlier versions of the pedagogical model that have since been refined. For instance, in their examination of teaching styles, Jones, Hughes and Kingston (2008) refer to Mosston's (1966a) original version of The Spectrum that comprises eight teaching styles – the latest version of the model consists of 11 (Mosston & Ashworth, 2008). Similarly, some authors have simply misinterpreted some aspects of the theory that underpins The Spectrum. For example, Launder (2001) illustrated this point when he stated that "Muska Mosston implied that indirect methods were educationally more valuable than direct methods" (Launder, 2001, p. 22). As stated earlier, this was not the case.

In an attempt to elucidate the theoretical underpinnings of The Spectrum, some authors have adapted certain aspects of Mosston and Ashworth's pedagogical framework. For instance, 30 years after Mosston (1966a) produced the initial version of The Spectrum, Kirk, Nauright, Hanrahan, Macdonald and Jobling (1996) implemented significant modifications to "make it more user friendly" (Cassidy, Jones & Potrac, 2009, p. 31). The subsequent changes consisted of condensing the number of teaching styles from 11 to 5, as well as replacing the term teaching styles to teaching methods. While Kirk and colleagues (1996) failed to provide an explanation for replacing the term styles for methods, Tinning, Kirk and Evans (1993) suggested that the word styles has come to represent "a manner of self-expression peculiar to the individual" (Tinning, Kirk & Evans, 1993, p. 118) and, therefore, potentially subjective. Callcott, Miller and Wilson-Gahan (2012) also presented an abridged version of The Spectrum. This version consisted of six teaching styles. This interpretation also referred to "teacher-centred strategies are at one end moving towards the other end of the spectrum to learner-centred strategies" (Callcott et al., 2012, p. 79). In reference to The Spectrum, according to Sara Ashworth, the terms teacher-centred and student-centred:

> Have been inaccurately applied … the basic and most frequent inaccurate conclusion is that teaching styles A–E are teacher-centred or teacher on-stage and that teaching styles F–K are student-centred or learner on-stage … if teaching is competent and professional all episodes will be student-centred and all styles do focus on the learners as centre stage learners … if the learners' learning is not the focus – then whatever the teacher is doing needs to be re-examined.
>
> (S. Ashworth, personal communication, 30 January 2011)

Coleman (2012) presented a version of The Spectrum in a podcast for students enrolled in a coaching module. In this online seminar, Coleman refers to ten 'coaching styles' from Command to Discovery as opposed to the 11 teaching styles from Command Style-A to Self-Teaching Style-K that constitute the latest version of The Spectrum (Mosston & Ashworth, 2008). Coleman also used the term 'Pre-Discovery coaching styles' to describe the first five teaching styles on The Spectrum. Mosston and Ashworth (2008) employ the term, reproduction cluster when describing this cluster of styles.

In spite of these modifications, misinterpretations and criticisms, The Spectrum has been embraced and implemented by educators in many countries, and widely used as a framework for teaching physical education (Chatoupis & Emmanuel, 2003; Franks, 1992; Krug, 1999). For almost 50 years, The Spectrum has endured as a pedagogical conception for teaching, coaching and research in physical education internationally. It continues to present as a practical framework for the provision of instruction in physical education.

This chapter has described the genesis for this book and its title, *The Spectrum of Teaching Styles in Physical Education*. We have outlined how new perspectives have allowed teachers to use The Spectrum in different ways, sometimes varying from the Landmark Styles described. A brief history of The Spectrum has been provided, along with an alternative view of early Spectrum development. We have also outlined some of the criticisms of The Spectrum over time. This book has brought together leading and contemporary Spectrum researchers who have provided insights into how you may use The Spectrum with your students, athletes, pre-service teachers or teachers.

References

Australian Curriculum, Assessment and Reporting Authority. (2016). *The Health and Physical Education Curriculum*. Version 8.2, Sydney, Australia.

Byra, M. (2000). A review of Spectrum research: The contribution of two eras. *Quest*, 52, 229–245.

Chatoupis, C. (2010). Spectrum research reconsidered. *International Journal of Applied Sports Sciences*, 22(1), 80–86.

Chatoupis, C., & Emmanuel, C. (2003). Teaching physical education with the inclusion style: The case of a Greek elementary school. *Journal of Physical Education, Recreation and Dance*, 74(8), 33–38.

Callcott, D., Miller, J., & Wilson-Gahan, S. (2012). *Health and physical education: Preparing educators for the future*. New York, NY: Cambridge University Press.

Cassidy, T., Jones, R., & Potrac, P. (2009). *Understanding sports coaching: The social, cultural and pedagogical foundations of coaching practice*. (2nd ed.). London: Routledge.

Colella D., Ercolino L., & Morano M. (2012). Teaching Styles, motor performances and physical self-efficacy in primary school. In *Together for Physical Education – Scientific Communication of the 7th European FIEP Congress* (pp. 378–382), Barcelona 7–9 June 2012.

Cothran, D. J., & Kulinna, P. H. (2006). Students' perspectives on direct, peer, and inquiry teaching styles. *Journal of Teaching in Physical Education*, 25, 166–181.

Cothran, D. J., & Kulinna, P. H. (2008). Teachers' knowledge about and use of teaching models. *The Physical Educator. Fall 2008*, 122–129.

Crum, B. (1995, 5–6 March). *Muska's claim reconsidered: The spectrum or a spectrum of teaching styles*. Paper presented at the AIESEP, World Congress Conference:

Windows to the future: Bridging the gaps between disciplines curriculum and instruction. Wingate Institute, Israel.

Cuellar-Moreno, M. (2016). Effects of the command and mixed styles on student learning in primary education. *Journal of Physical Education & Sport*, 16(4), 1159–1168.

Derri, V., & Pachta, M. (2007). Motor skills and concepts acquisition and retention: A comparison between two styles of teaching. *International Journal of Sport Science*, 3(3), 37–47.

Digelidis, N. (2006). Extending the Spectrum: An in depth analysis of the teaching styles taxonomy. *Inquiries in Sport and Physical Education*, 4(2), 131–147.

Franks, D. (1992). The spectrum of teaching styles: A silver anniversary in physical education. *Journal of Physical Education, Recreation and Dance*, 63(1), 25–26.

Goldberger, M. (1992). The spectrum of teaching styles: A perspective for research on physical education. *Journal of Physical Education, Recreation and Dance*, 63(1), 42–46.

Goldberger, M., Ashworth, S., & Byra, M. (2012). Spectrum of teaching styles retrospective 2012. *Quest*, 64, 268–282.

Graber, K. C. (2001). Research on teaching in physical education In V. Richardson (Ed.), *Fourth Handbook of Research on Teaching*, (pp. 491–519). Washington, DC: American Educational Research Association.

Jones, R. L., Hughes, M., & Kingston. K. (2008). *An introduction to sports coaching: From science and theory to practice*. (2nd ed.). London and New York: Routledge.

Kirk, D., Nauright, S., Hanrahan, D., Macdonald, D., & Jobling, I. (1996). *The sociocultural foundations of human movement*. Melbourne, Vic: Macmillan Education Australia.

Krug, D. (1999, 14–15 December). *Mosston's spectrum of teaching styles: A new vision*. Paper presented at the AIESEP World Science Congress, Education for Life, Jyvaskyla, Finland.

Launder, A. G. (2001). *Play practice: the games approach to teaching and coaching sports*. Champaign, IL: Human Kinetics.

Metzler, M. W. (2005). Implications of models-based instruction for research on teaching: A focus on teaching games for understanding. In L.L. Griffin & J.I. Butler (Eds). Teaching games for understanding: theory, research, and practice, 193–198. Champaign, IL: Human Kinetics.

Metzler, M. W. (1983). On styles. *Quest*, 35, 145–154.

Morgan, K., Kingston, K., & Sproule, J. (2005). Effects of different teaching styles on the teacher behaviours that influence motivational climate and pupils' motivation in physical education. *European Physical Education Review*, 11, 257–285.

Mosston, M. (1966a). *Teaching Physical Education*. Columbus, OH: Charles E Merril Publishing. from https://spectrumofteachingstyles.org/assets/files/articles/Mosston_1969_Inclusion_and_Exclusion_In_Education.pdf

Mosston, M. (1966b). The integration of a style of teaching with the structure of the subject matter. Paper presented to the National College Physical Education Association of Men. Retrieved from file:///C:/Users/u1068965/Desktop/shaneFB/Moston1966b_The_Integrationof_a_Style.pdf

Mosston, M. (1969c). *Notes on the Spectrum of Teaching Styles*. Paper presented to the second and third general sessions of the 1969 SAPECW conference. Retrieved from https://spectrumofteachingstyles.org/assets/files/articles/Mosston1969c_Notes_On_The_Spectrum.pdf

Mosston, M. (1969). *Inclusion and exclusion in education – II.* Presented to a Symposium on: Innovations in Curricular Design for Physical Education.

Mosston, M. (1972). *Teaching from Command to Discovery.* Belmont, CA: Wadsworth.

Mosston, M. (1981). *Teaching physical education.* (2nd ed.). Columbus, OH: Merrill.

Mosston, M., & Ashworth, S. (2008). *Teaching physical education.* (1st Online ed.). Spectrum Institute for Teaching and Learning. Retrieved from http://www.spectru mofteachingstyles.org/e-book-download.php

Sanmuga, N. (2008). An investigation into school boys' interest and game situation performances using TGFU model incorporated within styles B, E, and H of Mosston and Ashworth teaching styles as training regimes. Presentation at *Teaching Games for Understanding International Conference*, Vancouver, British Columbia, Canada.

Scottish Qualifications Authority (2012). *National 3 Physical Education Course Specification* (Scotland). Retrieved from www.sqa.org.uk

SHAPE America – Society of Health and Physical Educators. (2014). *National standards and grade-level outcomes for K–12 physical education.* Champaign, IL: Human Kinetics.

Sicilia-Camacho, A., & Brown, D. (2008). Revisiting the paradigm shift from the versus to the non-versus notion of Mosston's spectrum of teaching styles in physical education pedagogy: A critical pedagogical perspective. *Physical Education and Sport Pedagogy, 13*(1), 85–108.

Silverman, S. (1985). Critical considerations in the design and analysis of teacher effectiveness research in physical education. *International Journal of Physical Education, 22*(4), 17–24.

Skolverket. (2011). Curriculum for the compulsory school, preschool class and the leisure-time centre 2011. www.skolverket.se/publikationer

Stolz, S., & Pill, S. (2016). A narrative approach to exploring TGfU-GS. *Sport, Education and Society, 21*(2), 239–261.

Tinning, R., Kirk, D., & Evans, J. (1993). *Learning to teach physical education.* London: Prentice-Hall.

Williams, A. (1996). *Teaching physical education. A guide for mentors and students.* London: David Fulton Publishers.

Chapter 2

History and overview of The Spectrum

Sara Ashworth

The history of The Spectrum is a journey travelled through many years and through multiple perspectives. This journey led to a unifying theory that explains the universality of pedagogy (teaching and learning) called The Spectrum of Teaching Styles. This chapter presents an overview of The Spectrum framework while highlighting several of its critical and inherent components. It is a journey that was started in 1965 by Muska Mosston as he struggled to understand the structure of teaching. In 1969, I joined Muska in this search. It was a partnership that lasted 25 years until Muska's death in 1994, and it is a journey that is still just beginning.

The beginning

Muska Mosston's journey began when he was a confident professor at Rutgers University. One day a student approached him. The following is Mosston's retelling of that conversation:

> "I can't be you!" the student said, "Thank you," I responded – and began to walk away. "Furthermore," the student said, "I don't want to be like you." I was quite stunned. I was upset. It took me some time to recover, but that statement kept gnawing at my mind. Is that what I was doing to my students? Did I demand replication of "me"? ... I kept asking myself: What is the body of knowledge about teaching that is beyond my idiosyncratic behaviour? ... This emotional and cognitive irritation did not subside. The search to understand teaching independent of my idiosyncrasies had begun.
>
> (Mosston & Ashworth, 2008, p. 7)

This student shattered Mosston's perspective of teaching. He realised that teaching must be more than his personal preferences. He needed to search for a different understanding, a new perspective, for thinking about teaching. Three questions guided his search:

- Is teaching independent of one's idiosyncrasies?
- Is there only one or more than one teaching approach?

- And if there are many approaches to teaching, what differentiates one teaching approach from another?

From this beginning, new insights gradually accumulated. Mosston's observed ideas about teaching and learning were typically guided by the following perspectives:

- Versus – meaning ideas are in competition with and pitted against each other no matter how good the idea;
- Idiosyncratic – meaning teachers typically implement ideas guided by their own peculiarities, preferences, biases, idiosyncrasies, and personal opinions; and
- Inconsistent use of terminology – meaning commonly used terms had little consistency or uniformity in the literature.

Mosston observed how limiting these perspectives were to the advancement and development of pedagogy. This led him to propose contrasting *counterpoints* to these perspectives. He proposed the following governing principles:

- A "Non-Versus" approach that embraced diverse and seemingly opposing ideas;
- A unifying theory of teaching that contained a body of knowledge that went beyond the limits of one's idiosyncratic preferences and behaviours; and
- A systemic approach that adhered to a common language with consistent terminology and specific meanings. Terminology is the fundamental and common component that defines a profession.

These governing principles not only led to uncovering The Spectrum, but they also serve as the philosophical pillars that support the unified theory of The Spectrum. These governing principles established and continue to establish the criteria for any new updates, corrections or alterations to The Spectrum theory.

Mosston observed that a cumulative chain of decisions were always being made in every teaching event. This single, universal principle – **teaching is a chain of decision making** – was the beginning point – **the axiom** – from which the unifying framework evolved.

After uncovering the axiom, additional key concepts were revealed which reinforced Mosston's governing principles and supported a universal view of teaching. What were the specific and common sets of decisions that teachers could make in all teaching/learning events? This section identifies the conceivable list of decisions that can be made in any teaching event and is labelled, 'anatomy of any style'. The decisions in the Anatomy are clustered according to their function (Figure 2.1).

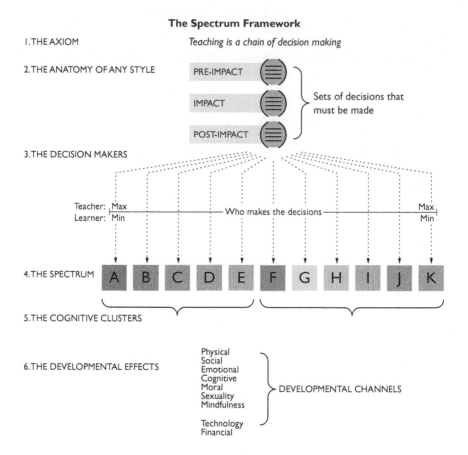

Figure 2.1 The Structure of The Spectrum

Source: Reprint from Teaching Physical Education First Online Edition, 2008 are used with permission from Dr. Sara Ashworth, Director of the Spectrum Institute. Free Digital Download Available at: https://spectrumofteachingstyles.org/index.php?id=16

- Pre-impact – these are planning decisions;
- Impact – these involve decisions made during implementation of the planning decisions; and
- Post-impact – these involve assessment and feedback decisions.

Who can make these decisions? Each decision can be made by either the teacher or the learner. It is this maximum-to-minimum decision-making metric between teacher and learner that establishes the foundation of The Spectrum. Each teaching style on this continuum (Styles A through K) is comprised of a deliberate but different decision configuration for both teacher and learners.

In a disciplined manner, Mosston identified teaching styles by systematically shifting decisions between teacher and learner. A new Landmark Teaching Style emerged and was labelled when a significantly new set of learning opportunities were established by shifting specific decisions.

Landmark Styles (A–K)

Mosston first identified the Command Style (view in Figure 2.1, on the far-left side of The Spectrum). In the Command Style, the teacher makes all decisions, all except one, the learner's one decision is whether to follow the teacher's directions/commands explicitly. What might this look like in reality? If you picture a marching band striding down the street, you have an image of the Command Style in action. All decisions, from dress, to movements, to music played (including pace and rhythm), are made by the leader. The band members follow the leader's commands as precisely as possible. Precision is the power of a marching band and the essence of the Command Style.

It is imperative to understand the Command Style is not inherently good or bad, or an appropriate or inappropriate way to teach. The Command Style is not harsh or vindictive rather, it is what it is, a relationship where the teacher makes all decisions and the learners adhere to those decisions. The learning conditions – or opportunities – produced by this arrangement would seem appropriate for certain purposes or situations. In the marching band example, the behaviour of band members marching and playing their instruments in synchrony could not be achieved without use of the Command Style. Rowing is another example; each member of the crew preforms in total unison to obtain the greatest speed. These precision tasks can be best learned and preformed through the Command Style.

Mosston had identified a distinct teaching style, the Command Style, with a clear set of teacher and learner behaviours, clear learning opportunities produced, and clear potential learning outcomes. In following his plan to uncover teaching styles using the organising principles of decision making, Mosston wanted to identify another teaching style, one that was akin to the Command Style, yet significantly different.

After extensive research and observation, he realised that some decisions within the *Impact Set* (this is when the learner is practicing/performing/doing the task) could be shifted to the learner while still maintaining near maximum teacher control and performance integrity. He identified nine specific decisions within the Impact set – including location, order, starting time, pace and rhythm of performance, stopping time, interval, questions or clarification, and posture during practice that could be shifted. The Practice Style emerged. In Practice Style, the teacher decides on the task(s) to be learned and on the criteria of acceptable performance, but the learner decides the set of nine decisions during practice. This set of nine decisions, made while the learner is engaged in the task, introduces the beginning of independence while not changing the task or the level of expected performance.

In identifying the next teaching style along The Spectrum, the Reciprocal Style, Mosston observed a shift in decisions within the *post-impact* set. Rather than the teacher assessing and providing feedback to learners during their practice, while they are learning the task, in the Reciprocal Style learners are paired/partnered and as one learner – the doer – engages in the teacher-designed task, the other learner – the observer – assesses the action and provides feedback based on criteria provided by the teacher. After the first learner completes the task, they switch roles and reciprocate. Not only is feedback about task performance provided more quickly and personally under these conditions, learners also practice working together by giving and receiving feedback resulting in the enhancement of these aspects of socialisation.

In the next style along The Spectrum, the Self-Check Style, the decision-shift also takes place in the post-impact set. In Self-Check Style, the learner self-assesses task performance based on criteria provided by the teacher. The correct responses must be provided by the teacher to allow the learners to check their own work. Imagine a class with learners working individually on a set of mathematical problems. After the learners complete the task, they individually check their work. If their answers are correct, they are ready to move on. If a learner answers a question incorrectly, they can go back and try again. In this mathematics example the teacher provides instructions for each solution allowing the learner to figure out the correct answer if a mistake was made.

Self-testing is nothing new in education. This approach to teaching/learning has been around long before Mosston called it Self-Check Style. This is true for many of the teaching styles along The Spectrum. However, what The Spectrum provides is a compendium of pedagogical approaches, not presented in an adversarial but a complimentary manner.

Mosston went on to identify seven additional Landmark Teaching Styles in this same deliberative decision-shifting manner. A continuum of teaching styles emerged, each with an individual name, letter designation and decision-making structure capable of producing its own unique conditions for learning. The Spectrum provides the teacher with an incredible array of teaching options. In the future, there may be additional teaching styles revealed and of the ones already identified, there may be modifications or adjustments. The Spectrum is an ever-evolving paradigm.

In the last teaching style along The Spectrum, Self-Teaching Style (the style on the far-right side of The Spectrum), the learner makes all decisions in all three sets of decisions. In fact, there is no teacher in this style. In this teaching style the learner is making decisions in the pre-impact set about everything, including goals, content, and how or if to involve others. The learner works independently during engagement time and evaluates their own performance along the way. As you might expect, the learner who can engage productively in the Self-Teaching Style is self-motivated.

As was mentioned earlier, over the years there have been some changes to The Spectrum. However, the essence of The Spectrum has remained integral. These 11 teaching styles are referred to as Landmark Styles. The term "landmark" is not used in a pejorative sense but rather is intended to provide order, anticipation, and an expectation. Just as landmarks assist travelers along their journey from one point to the next, Landmark Styles provide this same sense of order, anticipation, and expectation in teaching and learning.

Clusters

Each style along The Spectrum initiates within the learner a thinking process and cognitive operations. The Command Style, for example, triggers cognitive processes associated with memory. In contrast, Divergent Discovery Style, activates the learner to think expansively and divergently.

Teaching styles along The Spectrum can be grouped into two clusters according to their cognitive emphasis. Styles A through E are grouped within the reproduction cluster. Styles in this cluster require the learner to engage their *memory* – a thinking process that triggers a variety of cognitive operations which rely on recall and replication. Whereas styles F through K are grouped within the production cluster, styles in this cluster require the learner to engage in *discovery* – a thinking process that engages learners in the production of information that was previously unknown to them. Clusters are simply another way of organising teaching styles along The Spectrum.

Non-Landmark Styles – Canopy Styles

Aside from these 11 Landmark Teaching Styles, do other teaching styles exist? What would it be called if one decision or set of decisions associated with the learner in one style was made by the teacher? In other words, are modifications permitted? What about a non-Spectrum teacher, a person who knows nothing about The Spectrum, could that person's teaching be placed somewhere along The Spectrum?

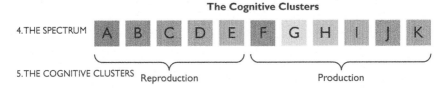

Figure 2.2 Teaching styles are organised into two cognitive clusters; reproduction and production

Source: Reprint from Teaching Physical Education First Online Edition, 2008 are used with permission from Dr. Sara Ashworth, Director of the Spectrum Institute. Free Digital Download Available at: https://spectrumofteachingstyles.org/index.php?id=16

By asking the question, "Who made which decisions and when?", any observed teaching/learning event can be located along The Spectrum based on its decision-making structure. We have done this kind of analysis for years, and in almost every instance the observed teaching/learning event can be associated more closely to one style than another along The Spectrum. We introduced the idea of *Canopy Styles* to explain instances where a Landmark Style could not be identified. A canopy represents the design variations within and between each Landmark Teaching Style. When we say, for example, that a teaching/learning event was 'canopy E' our meaning is that the observed event had the essential decision-making structure of Inclusion Style, but it was not Landmark Style-E. One or more decisions associated with the Inclusion Style were not implemented as prescribed by the Landmark Style specifications.

It is important to understand that canopy styles are not less legitimate or appropriate than a Landmark Style when taught deliberately. The Spectrum is a tool and therefore the user/teacher must be able to use the tool and make adjustments/modifications as necessary. However, modifications need to be made within the framework of the governing principles, 'anything goes' is not acceptable for professional teaching.

When trying to understand The Spectrum it is important to keep in mind that, like many 'elegant' theories, The Spectrum is a duality, both simple and complex. Simple in its logic and progressions, and yet, as one peels back the layers of decision making, it can become very elaborate and intricate. The Spectrum offers an incredible variety of teaching/learning/content/human development options and it helps to transform chaos into order when engaged in dynamic teaching.

Episodic Teaching*

Portions of this section have been adapted from an upcoming book on The Spectrum.

How can teachers deliberately implement in the classroom a variety of alternative teaching and learning behaviours? What is the thinking that supports the inclusion of multiple T-L behaviours? How do teachers move from the current thinking about *lesson planning* to an altered design that incorporates multiple T-L experiences?

One of the simplest and yet most useful concepts we uncovered is the idea of an episode. An *episode* is a unit of time within which the teacher and learner are engaged in the same T-L style, heading towards the same set of objectives. An episode might last a few minutes, an entire period, or longer. Each episode becomes the individual 'unit of measure' (O-T-L-O) for what is happening in the classroom.

Teaching that incorporates a series of planned episodes is called *Episodic Teaching*. Episodic teaching may follow a *multiple objective design*, meaning planned episodes that represent different teaching styles and reinforce

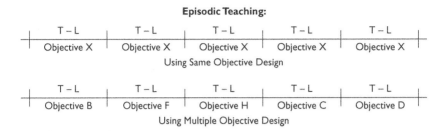

Figure 2.3 Episodic teaching same objective design and multiple objective design

Source: Reprint from Teaching Physical Education First Online Edition, 2008 are used with permission from Dr. Sara Ashworth, Director of the Spectrum Institute. Free Digital Download Available at: https://spectrumofteachingstyles.org/index.php?id=16

different sets of objectives. Or a *same objective design*, meaning they planned episodes that represent the same teaching style and reinforce a similar set of objectives (Figure 2.3).

Variation can exist within episodes. An episode might involve a group of learners, a pair of learners, or an individual learner. Two or more episodes might be conducted at the same time within the same instructional setting. For example, one group of learners might be working in a Practice Style episode while, simultaneously, another group might be engaged in an Inclusion Style episode. Each episode can be viewed for its contributions in supporting or derailing the anticipated overall content, behaviour, developmental, or logistical expectations. Once learners have been introduced to each individual style's learning expectations, engaging in a multiple objective episodic teaching lesson will flow seamlessly. We have found that using episodes for organisation not only benefits teachers and learners, it also makes the role of the supervisor more organised and helpful.

The Spectrum supports maximising student's learning experiences; therefore, a variety of different teaching styles need to be implemented. No single T-L behaviour can accomplish all the intended content and human behaviour goals of education nor can any one set of T-L behaviours meet all students' needs.

Currently, research indicates that although teachers implement a variety of classroom activities that focus on logistical, content, and human developmental needs, they rarely change their predominate T-L interaction. The image of the classroom may vary (such as working individually, in groups, or a whole class); however, these variations generally represent the same set of T-L decision expectations. On the other hand, in our experience, Spectrum teachers generally use different teaching styles all class period.

Episodic Teaching Research

Episodic teaching should be the new frontier in pedagogical research. Research that investigates one teaching style or seeks to compare the superiority of one style *over* another needs to be revisited. Style research that verifies what an individual teaching behaviour theoretically accomplishes is worthwhile but individual style research that pits one behaviour against another is not. Such research does not contribute to the individual worthwhileness of a repertoire of T-L experiences. The styles are not in competition. In fact, each style has its own learning focus; one style does not develop another style's objectives, nor can one episode accomplish all learning objectives. Different styles develop different objectives. Episodic teaching can provide us with new insights about the impact different style combinations have on learning.

O-T-L-O

Each episode has its own objectives, teaching and learning behaviours and outcomes. We abbreviate and call this the O-T-L-O. What is the relationship among these components? This relationship is logical, causative, and organic. The objectives (O) present the intent of the episode. The teaching-learning behaviour (T-L) describes the interaction expectations between teacher and learner during content mastery – the style of teaching. The outcome (O) answers the question, to what degree were the objectives reached?

We refer to these components taken together as the "pedagogical unit". The proposition undergirding The Spectrum is that a teaching style will produce predictable learning opportunities which in turn, will produce expected learning outcomes. Will there be times when an episode does not work in producing expected outcomes? Of course, as is true in most human endeavours, but there are reasons why it didn't work and in most cases the reasons can be determined and with persistence rectified. The key component in the O-T-L-O is the teacher-learner interaction. Teaching is a purposive activity. There is a purpose undergirding and driving the activity. But, regardless of the purpose, it is the teacher's behaviour and expectations that drive the learners' responses. The Spectrum helps to bridge the gap between teacher intent and teacher behaviour.

Developmental Channels*

Portions of this section have been adapted from the upcoming book on The Spectrum.

The more we studied and implemented The Spectrum in different situations, the more we realised each teaching style produces distinctively different conditions and opportunities for learning. Our perspective of what each style developed expanded. These varied conditions and opportunities in each style provide the essential circumstances for development of a cadre of decision-making skills, cognitive variety, content flexibility, and diversity of human attributes (characteristics). Each style has a unique effect on learning that occurs within specific Developmental Channels. The various Developmental Channels represent the areas through which all students progress and develop. Additionally, each channel is comprised of an infinite number of human attributes that define our character and our humanity. These intrinsic and universal channels are physical, social, emotional, cognitive, moral/ethical, mindfulness, and sexual, with two extrinsic categories of technology and financial. The attributes within these channels are the diverse characteristics which we can chose from to guide our thoughts and everyday behaviour, establishing the code for our individual daily conduct. Attributes are ubiquitous; they may be beneficial or harmful to an individual or others.

The literature states that, in the classroom, attributes are learned when teachers use diversified teaching approaches (2000, Learning to Learn). The Spectrum identifies diversified, non-versus teaching and learning approaches that deliberately trigger different attributes allowing different learning intents from Command to Discovery to be experienced. The decisions in each Landmark Style establishes a significantly different developmental code of conduct that guides the episodes' learning focus.

There is an infinite number of human attributes, such as: Patience, tolerance, intolerance, respect for others, impulsiveness, empathy, mood management, compromise, reliability, social interaction, ability to manipulate facts, acknowledge others, maintain safe *and* healthy habits, sharing, curiosity, truthfulness, etc. Each attribute can be woven into the behaviour expectations of the task; therefore, these attributes are not separate characteristics that are studied or implemented in isolation or that are independent of the task expectations. Rather, attributes are imbedded and support the learning expectations of the task, becoming part of the behaviour expectations while engaged in the task.

Although each channel has its unique attributes, there is an assortment of attributes that can be experienced in all channels such as: compromise, accepting consequences, exhibiting empathy, resisting peer pressures, dependability, etc. Attributes represent the humanity in teaching.

Note that the list of channels in the first cluster represent the intrinsic Developmental Channels. These channels always guide our development – they are intrinsic to our being a human being. Note: Technology and Finances have been added in this edition – with a space that separates them from the intrinsic Developmental Channels. These two channels are extrinsic categories that are profoundly and fundamentally influencing the way we develop and behave as human beings on each of the Developmental Channels. Therefore, they cannot be ignored. In fact, technology has and will continue to profoundly alter the way we think about the Developmental Channels and the myriad list of attributes in each channel. Many of the current attributes will and have become obsolete and new, yet unknown, attributes will guide our daily conduct because of the prevalent role of technology. Technology has already altered the way we think about socialising, emotional impulses, ethical parameters, physical development, sexual expressions and financial expectations. Gradually, and, at times with incredible speed, technology is changing our behaviour and belief systems. Therefore, technology has been added as a supplemental, external category to the Developmental Channels.

Financial Developmental Channel

Our individual dependence and reliance on finance requires people to examine the role finances play to the future advancement of a society. A society's development is stalled if there is not minimum independence and competence by its citizens to make basic life skill decisions. Without minimum competence in decision making, employment, and thus the opportunity for financial independence is impossible. The nine decisions of the Practice Style are the entry point to a path that develops competence in those decisions allowing for the development of independence. Work environments require a variety of relationships and each relationship requires a different set of decision-making skills. Each Spectrum teaching style emphasises a different skill level of independence which is needed in various work environments. A healthy society needs citizens who are decision makers so they can begin a journey to personal and financial independence and avoid becoming the responsibility of the society. Although there are external factors that affect financial independence, it is imperative that individuals seeking independence develop adequate decision-making skills and competence in various attributes along the *Developmental Channels*.

The role of the Developmental Channels is new pedagogical territory that needs to be researched.

Center on Teaching

From 1972 through 1980, we developed and administered the Center on Teaching (COT). The purpose of the Center was to implement The Spectrum of Teaching Styles in a variety of actual school settings. The Center was funded through a grant from the State of New Jersey. The success of our program provided eight years of continuous grant opportunities for implementation of The Spectrum in all grade levels and subjects.

Our perspective – what we were looking for – changed several times during our COT experiences. When first implementing the different teaching styles, our perspective focused on the details of each style and its theoretical accuracy. Was Spectrum theory congruent with classroom action? Many subtle changes in the details of the styles were made and several style names were altered as a result of these classroom experiences. As with any new theory, fact verification must be your first perspective.

Once the factual details of the theory were verified and consistent, we were able to expand our perspectives to see new areas of inquiry. During the training sessions, teachers prepared micro-teaching videotaped episodes of each style. We observed that the preparation and taping practice time took too long, and for some teachers, it was very stressful. There were too many micro-teaching re-tapes before demonstrating a degree of congruence with the style's structure. We realised that teachers needed a tool – a Style Analysis Tool – per style that outlined the specific decisions and order of presentation. There was just too much information in the beginning for teachers to recall. Style Analysis Tools per style decreased micro-teaching re-takes and contributed to teachers' faster acquisition of each style's structure. These tools are still being used.

Implementation of any new idea on any level will follow similar perspectives: first fact verification that supports the theory, then reliable practices, and finally, supportive follow-up procedures. Knowledge of The Spectrum should not be thought of as an imposition or another theory to learn for a college course but, rather, it needs to be viewed as the universal framework that underlies all teaching endeavours. It is a structure that needs to be so automatic that it offers teachers pedagogical freedom to select and design the multiple approaches they need to expand their students' development from Command to Discovery.

Future perspectives

Foundational knowledge saves time. It allows the practitioner to focus on accomplishing the intent of the experience rather than consistently constructing a structure to accomplish the experience. Thinking about how to drive an automobile takes your attention away from the traffic events that surround you. Feeling confident about driving frees you to think about the current happenings that immediately surround you. In pedagogy, this means we need to come together as a profession and universally accept a framework that delineates the most unifying pedagogical structure as the foundation for our basic understanding of teaching. Such a framework is not fixed or closed rather open and inclusive of diverse and even opposing positions. We need consistency and reliability in our thinking about what we do – which is – teaching that results in learning.

This proposition is not suggesting that every teacher implements only the 11 Spectrum Landmark Styles, rather it is proposing that teachers acquire a teaching repertoire of alternative teaching-learning approaches and that they are able to deliberately articulate their learning focus. The Spectrum is a framework that delineates the structure of teaching – all teaching events. It embraces others' works. Every teaching experience is a chain of decisions. Every teaching behaviour has its own Anatomy of decisions. Every teaching experience triggers specific cognitive operations, and every teaching and learning interaction emphasises specific attributes on the different developmental channels. Why can't we agree on that? Shouldn't our goal be to teach our next generation a reliable and solid foundational theory, rather than continuing to promote the ever-changing idiosyncratic approach?

As a profession, we need to collectively decide to accept the notion that a unifying view of teaching is desirable. It's time for a paradigm shift. The 53-year history of The Spectrum has revealed that a unifying and universal framework is possible in pedagogy. The next 50-year history will lead us to new perspectives in development that could only be imagined.

References

Ashworth, S. (2017). The Theory: The Cognitive Clusters [image]. Retrieved from www.spectrumofteachingstyles.org/index.php?id=20

Ashworth, S. (2017). The Theory: The Framework [image]. Retrieved from www.spectrumofteachingstyles.org/index.php?id=20

Learning to learn: the way forward in curriculum development: consultation document. (2000, November). Hong Kong: The Council. Retrieved from: www.edb.gov.hk/attachment/en/curriculum-development/cs-curriculumdoc-report/learn-learn-1/overview-e.pdf

Mosston, M., & Ashworth, S. (2008). *Teaching Physical Education*. San Francisco, Ca: Benjamin Cummings. Retrieved from www.spectrumofteachingstyles.org/e-book-download.php

Chapter 3

The Spectrum: my journey

Mark Byra

My 'compass' as a teacher educator has been The Spectrum. I was first intro-duced to The Spectrum as an undergraduate student at the University of Victoria, British Columbia, Canada, in the mid-1970s (Mosston, 1966), which led me to incorporate the styles in the physical education lessons I taught to my junior high school students during the early and mid-1980s. I also incor-porated some of The Spectrum teaching styles in the extra-curricular school sports I coached, and during the time I served as a graduate student teach-ing assistant when completing my master's degree at Dalhousie University, Halifax, Nova Scotia, Canada. Although this introduction to The Spectrum during my undergraduate program was minimal in nature (i.e. The Spectrum presented as a small part of a larger teaching methods course), it left enough of an impression on me that I was wanting to 'try out' some of the teaching styles in my teaching and coaching. This is how I initially 'got to know' The Spectrum (Mosston, 1981), but clearly, it was just the beginning!

In the late 1980s, I was re-introduced to The Spectrum while completing my doctoral studies at the University of Pittsburgh. This time around, The Spec-trum was presented to me both as an instructional framework and a framework for examining and conducting research on teaching and teacher education, in an effort to better understand the processes of teaching and learning in physical education. A part of my studies included completing a graduate level course devoted to The Spectrum (Mosston & Ashworth, 1986), and, as importantly, completing three different pilot research studies in which several different Spec-trum styles were examined. Dr. Michael Sherman, my academic advisor, taught the Spectrum course and introduced me to Spectrum research.

The Spectrum to me represented an 'encompassing' or 'holistic' view of teaching and learning, a new way to envision the relationships between teach-ing and learning for purposes of instruction and conducting research. The Spectrum embraces the idea of using many different teaching styles to teach students. It emphasises the value of involving students in the learning pro-cess by empowering them through decision making. Student decision making pertains to all of The Spectrum teaching styles, those in the reproduction cluster and those in the production cluster.

To this day I am grateful for the knowledge and enthusiasm that Dr. Sherman brought to his Spectrum class, and his never-ending support in helping me better understand The Spectrum as an "encompassing" framework for instruction and research. Clearly, my lifelong interest in The Spectrum got its true start under the tutorage of Dr. Sherman.

While completing my doctoral studies, I was introduced to two future Spectrum colleagues through the assigned course readings. These two individuals, Drs. Sara Ashworth and Michael Goldberger, have also played an important role in driving my interest in The Spectrum. I met both Sara and Michael for the first time at a national conference in Boston in the late 1990s where we all presented on The Spectrum during a Spectrum symposium. Over the past 25 plus years I have spent time at different meetings with both discussing The Spectrum. Both have been important colleagues to me over the years and have helped and encouraged me to become a more knowledgeable consumer of The Spectrum.

By the time I graduated with my doctoral degree, I had gained an in-depth understanding of The Spectrum as a researcher, teacher and 'teacher educator to be'. I left the University of Pittsburgh for my first position in higher education armed with sufficient knowledge, interest, and enthusiasm to develop a Spectrum-based Physical Education Teacher Education (PETE) program. In the next section of this chapter, I will describe how The Spectrum is embedded in the PETE program at the University of Wyoming. Incorporating The Spectrum as one of several foci of the PETE program has been a fruitful and impactful 30 year journey for me. Over 30 years, it has impacted many students who have completed our PETE bachelor and master degree programs. To frame this undertaking and the journey of students learning The Spectrum I will use Windschitl's (2002) dilemmas for examining constructivism in practice. Windschitl identifies four dilemmas facing teachers in their learning and implementation of instructional methods that are based on the rhetoric of constructivism: a conceptual dilemma, pedagogical dilemma, cultural dilemma and political dilemma. The Spectrum is a theoretical instructional framework that includes elements of constructivism as reflected in student decision making.

A Spectrum-based PETE program

The importance of developing a meaningful undergraduate teacher preparation program was but a thought in my mind when I arrived in my first position in higher education at the University of Wyoming in 1989. This thought turned to reality in a hurry when I was given the task of redesigning the PETE program. In retrospect, an opportunity of this nature, however daunting it was, is not afforded to many new faculty in their first two years in a position. In developing a PETE program that included a foundation of The Spectrum theory and practice, I was able to directly connect my Spectrum research agenda to my teaching.

By this point in my career I viewed The Spectrum as a 'holistic' or 'encompassing' instructional framework; that is, as a continuum of teaching styles from which one could select teacher-centred (Command and Practice), student/teacher-centred (Reciprocal, Self-Check and Inclusion), or student-centred (styles from the production cluster) instructional approaches based on the needs of the students, the instructional outcomes to be met and the curricular models to be used. The Spectrum for me is clearly 'inclusive'. It encompasses or encapsulates the instructional approaches required of different curricular models like Sport Education (Siedentop et al., 2011), Tactical Games (Metzler, 2011), Cooperative Learning (Dyson & Casey, 2012), Teaching Social and Personal Responsibility (Hellison, 2011), and these curricular models serve as the foundation of physical education reform (Kirk, 2013). For example, when implementing the Sport Education curriculum model, teachers must be well versed in the Reciprocal, Inclusion, Guided Discovery, Convergent Discovery and Divergent Discovery Styles because student/teacher-centred and student-centred teaching styles are at the core of this curricular model (Siedentop, Hastie, & van der Mars, 2011).

In the early 1990s, PETE programs had been targeted as significant contributors to the lack of quality physical education programs in K-12 schools (Griffey, 1987; Locke, 1992; Siedentop, 1987; Siedentop & Locke, 1997). Siedentop and Locke (1997) described this as a systemic failure, "one that involves the relationship of physical education in public schools with teacher preparation in higher education" (p. 26). In redesigning PETE programs for systemic success, Siedentop and Locke proposed a set of minimum conditions. First, the program must have a focus, and faculty who accept the focus. Second, enough time or credits must be associated with the program to ensure that participants know the content well enough to experience success as novice teachers. Third, pre-service teachers must be placed at school sites where partnerships have been forged between the university faculty and school teachers through collaborative efforts. These placements must be directly controlled by the faculty and teachers involved in the program. Fourth, the program must allow for "selective admission and retention of students" (p. 13). Fifth, adequate resources (human, materials and space) must be available to program faculty and support staff to ensure a positive learning environment for the students enrolled in the program. Sixth, faculty must be rewarded for the roles they play in the program and the type of scholarship they perform. Seventh, research efforts must be encouraged between faculty within the program unit and faculty across the university. Finally, the program must be accredited.

The PETE program at the University of Wyoming has been purposefully designed to embrace numerous attributes associated with coherent pre-service teacher education programs as described by Siedentop and Locke (1997). In addition, Joyce, Weil and Showers' (1992) strategies for successfully implementing a newly acquired method or strategy of teaching (i.e. theoretical rationale, observing demonstrations and practicing under controlled conditions with feedback) was carefully incorporated in the implementation of this program.

A sequence of educational experiences that combines theory, observation of demonstration, practice and feedback in a peer teaching setting and practice and feedback in a school setting serves to enable the pre-service teachers at the University of Wyoming to experience success in The Spectrum, and, in turn, understand the teaching-learning process. Knowing the underlying principles of The Spectrum and the individual Landmark Styles provides the undergraduates with a foundational knowledge-base from which to then put these styles into practice. Observing demonstration lessons for each Spectrum style as presented by an experienced Spectrum teacher allows the undergraduates to visualise how each style unfolds in action, and how different teaching styles can be arranged in an episodic fashion (Chatoupis, 2016). Peer teaching with specific feedback allows the undergraduate to get a 'feel' of each style. Finally, implementing the different Spectrum styles in the K-12 school setting enables undergraduates to develop their Spectrum 'tool box'.

The Spectrum is woven into the movement core, professional preparation and field experience components of the four-year PETE program at the University of Wyoming. The movement core component of the PETE program is comprised of five courses that are based upon Thorpe and Bunker's (1986) teaching games for understanding approach, the Sport Education model (Siedentop et al., 2011), and Graham, Holt-Hale, Parker, Hall and Patton's (2020) skill themes and movement concepts approach to teaching physical education. The students' first exposure to The Spectrum takes place in the *Net and Target Games* movement core course. In this course the students read a series of applied articles specific to The Spectrum (Garn & Byra, 2002; Hall & McCullick, 2002; Jackson & Dorgo, 2002; Jenkins & Todorovich, 2002; McCullick & Byra, 2002), participate in lessons that are taught using The Spectrum styles, and teach their peers using The Spectrum styles while receiving post-lesson feedback from the instructor. Teaching styles from the reproduction and production clusters are presented to the PETE students in this course. This represents the student's first formal exposure to The Spectrum.

During this movement core course, each student teaches four ten-minute style-specific lessons to groups of six to eight peers in the content areas of volleyball, quick start tennis, badminton and archery. This means that during each lesson taught, the PETE majors formally specify the teaching style to be used, the decisions to be made by the students and what their role is during the episodes delivered. For example, in a Divergent Discovery episode, the PETE teacher would say,

> Hello class. During our first task today, you will play a 10 minute 3 v 3 half-court game of volleyball. After five minutes, I will stop you and ask that

you discuss with your three teammates game-related "things" that you did that led to successes during the game. I call these things game tactics or game cues. At the end of the game, you will write three game cues on your task sheet that you have discovered and why you want to employ these cues in the game. The game cues that one group of three identifies may not be the same as the cues identified by another group. At the end of this episode, I will ask each group to share one of their game cues with the rest of the class. As you are playing, I will be around to ask you questions about what you are thinking. Do you have any questions? Please get into mixed-gender groups of three, choose an opponent, and begin your 3 v 3 game.

After being formally introduced to The Spectrum in the movement core course, the PETE undergraduates complete an assessment and teaching methods course as a part of their professional preparation coursework. In this course, the underlying premises and assumptions of The Spectrum and individual teaching styles are presented to the students via lecture, discussion, observation and demonstration. Opportunity to practice each style with fellow classmates (teaching 12–15 peers) is also provided during the assessment and methods course. After having gained a minimal level of competence and comfort in using The Spectrum styles, the undergraduates take these styles into their field experience in the public schools (teaching third to fifth graders). Styles from both the reproduction and production clusters are implemented, albeit more from the reproduction than the production side of The Spectrum. This field experience takes place concurrently with their enrollment in the assessment and methods course. One or more Spectrum episodes are embedded in the movement lessons that they teach each week for the semester.

By the end of the semester, the PETE undergraduates will have practiced each teaching style, from Command Style to Divergent Discovery Style, three or more times with the school children under the observation of a university supervisor and peer coach. Typically, the students demonstrate more comfort with one or two of the teaching styles by the end of the semester because they have attempted these teaching styles a greater number of times than the others. In some cases, they will have attempted one or two styles a dozen times. This is important to note as Joyce et al. (1992) report that until teachers or pre-service teachers try a new teaching strategy 10 or more times, they will continue to feel some level of discomfort. Teachers tend to only return to a new teaching strategy if they have experienced considerable comfortable with it (Joyce et al., 1992).

It is important to understand that The Spectrum represents a new way of viewing teaching; it is a paradigm shift for the PETE students. The Spectrum is more than simply applying "instructional strategies in which the teacher is the principle actor and the students are objects upon whom action is taken" (Windschitl, p. 132). It involves accepting the fact that learners are not passive recipients of knowledge, but rather active participants in making meaning (Rovegno & Dolly, 2006) of their environment through decision making. Conceptually, this is different from what the PETE majors have experienced for 12 years during school physical education, hence it requires in depth class discussions to reconcile the PETE majors' current beliefs about teaching with those pedagogical orientations espoused by The Spectrum, orientations that support a constructivist learning environment.

A style-related outcome associated with this field experience is that more often than not the PETE undergraduates will have practiced implementing a greater number of episodes from the reproduction cluster of teaching styles than the production cluster. This outcome seems to be a function of their K-12 physical education experiences. It is highly likely that the PETE majors experienced a style of teaching that falls under the umbrella of the Command Style or Practice Style during their K-12 physical education experience as has been reported in many research studies (Cothran et al., 2005; Jaakola & Watt, 2011; Syrmpas, Digelidis, & Watt, 2016; Syrmpas, Digelidis, Watt, & Vicars, 2017). Thus, their reliance on the Command Style and Practice Style during their field experience materialises because of their past experiences (i.e. what they are used to).

Once the PETE undergraduates have completed the assessment and methods course in conjunction with the field experience practicum, they are encouraged to continue incorporating The Spectrum teaching styles while enrolled in their third field experience and subsequent student teaching experience. In both of these teaching experiences, they are provided further opportunity to apply theories and concepts learned during their undergraduate program, including The Spectrum. However, the expectation of continued use of the teaching styles learned is embedded in the reality that these students may not be under the tutorage of a cooperating teacher who is knowledgeable with The Spectrum. We encourage our pre-service teachers to extend their working knowledge of The Spectrum during this final field experience practicum and as they go on to their student teaching experience.

When attempting to further implement The Spectrum styles during their subsequent field experience and student teaching experience, the PETE students will face questions related to the practical application of The Spectrum styles, questions that represent pedagogical dilemmas derived from inviting learners to be decision makers in the instructional process. As stated by Windschitl (2002, p. 133), the PETE majors will be asking questions like, "how do I manage a classroom where students are talking to one another rather than to me", and "what does it mean for me to become a facilitator of learning?" The longevity of implementing a variety of The Spectrum teaching styles into the future is going to be dependent upon availability of additional professional development surrounding The Spectrum.

Given that many of our PETE majors have secured physical education positions in schools within Wyoming and the surrounding states, I have developed a graduate level Spectrum course that is delivered via distance education. This course allows our "now" physical educators to further their understanding of The Spectrum while truly serving in the role of a physical educator. Biennially, I offer this course. In this course the teachers learn about The Spectrum through lecture (pre-developed viewed through YouTube), observation of demonstration episodes (pre-developed viewed through You-Tube), readings of Spectrum research articles, face-to-face discussion (takes place via ZOOM) and the application of the teaching styles with their own students. After lecture, demonstration, reading and discussion, the enrollees plan, implement and assess several episodes of the presented teaching style each week within their own school settings. In the subsequent class session, the enrolled teachers are given time to ask questions and share successes during the class discussion (i.e. via ZOOM). This course serves as a comprehensive professional development for the in-service teachers. Without this continued support the teachers would likely revert back to their K-12 physical education experiences where the dominant Spectrum styles used were the Command Style and Practice Style (Cothran et al., 2005; Jaakola & Watt, 2011; Syrmpas et al., 2016; Syrmpas et al., 2017). Within a constructivist framework (Windschitl, 2002), limiting instruction to the Command Style and Practice Style (teacher-centred) will likely become a cultural dilemma for the new teachers in that the existing culture in many schools does not embrace the idea of using a wide variety of teaching styles, specifically ones that include students as active decision-makers. In addition, school administrators who do not value instructional settings where students are actively engaged in meaning making (i.e. talking with one another, making decisions) and teachers facilitating student learning will serve to deter 'the new teacher on the block' from implementing a wide variety teaching styles from The Spectrum.

Summary

The Spectrum is a focal point of our PETE program at the University of Wyoming. It serves to facilitate student understanding of principles and concepts related to teaching and learning. As Mosston and Ashworth (2008) denote, "teaching-learning behaviours within The Spectrum are tools for accomplishing the various functions of education" (p. 5). I believe The Spectrum has provided the PETE majors a 'common language' for understanding teaching and learning, language that is reflective of constructivism in practice (Windschitl, 2002).

What is unique at the University of Wyoming is the manner in which The Spectrum is delivered to the PETE majors. The Spectrum is purposely infused and sequenced across multiple courses. It is not simply introduced to the students through lecture as part of one course. We offer a comprehensive Spectrum experience to our students that combines first-hand participation in Spectrum episodes, group discussion of Spectrum articles written for practitioners, planning and teaching of Spectrum episodes within a peer teaching environment, additional Spectrum theory discussion revolving around assessment specific to the psychomotor, cognitive and affective learning domains, and the delivery of Spectrum episodes to third through fifth graders in the public school setting. This educational sequence enables the pre-service teachers to experience success in The Spectrum.

Many PETE faculty around the world introduce The Spectrum framework to their students in a single course, but rarely as a purposefully sequenced program. Much research in the area of occupational socialisation suggests that the impact or value of a PETE program (i.e. professional socialisation) on its students is dependent upon the teacher educators reinforcing consistent beliefs and values across multiple courses within the program, providing students with opportunity to first practice teaching in controlled settings (e.g. peer teaching) and then progress to teach in school-based settings (i.e. with 'real' school-aged students), and providing supervisory feedback to the pre-service teachers during their field experiences that is consistent with the "common language" taught in the program (Graber, 1993, 1996; Richards, Templin, & Graber, 2014). Based on conversations at state physical education conventions our students clearly indicate that they incorporate different Spectrum teaching styles in their day-to-day instructional practices in the workplace. These anecdotal notes now need to be validated systematically through research to answer the question, what learned behaviours and perceptions/values do the program graduates transfer from the PETE program to the workplace setting?

In closing, I challenge other PETE educators to develop and implement a comprehensive 'purposefully sequenced' Spectrum PETE program at their institution to embrace an instructional framework that has had a history of more than 50 years. In 2016, the 50th anniversary of The Spectrum was celebrated during the International Association for Physical Education in Higher Education (AIESEP) conference held in Laramie, Wyoming. Few events can match a 50th year celebration of an idea that has contributed globally to teaching, teacher education and research in physical education. Although my time as a teacher educator at the University of Wyoming will soon be coming to an end, I plan to continue to be professionally involved with The Spectrum for many years to come. Too much is still left to be learned – too many questions remain unanswered. I look forward to collaborating with my Spectrum colleagues from around the world for as long as I can. My Spectrum journey will continue.

References

Chatoupis, C. (2016). Planning physical education lessons as teaching episodes. *Strategies, 29*(2), 20–26.

Cothran, D. J., Kulinna, P. H., Banville, D., Choi, E., Amade-Escot, C., MacPhail, A., Macdonald, D., Kirk, D. (2005). A cross-cultural investigation of the use of teaching styles. *Research Quarterly for Exercise and Sport, 76*, 193–201.

Dyson, B., & Casey, A. (Eds.) (2012). *Cooperative learning in physical education: A research-based approach*. London: Routledge.

Garn, A., & Byra, M. (2002). Psychomotor, cognitive, and social development Spectrum style. *Teaching Elementary Physical Education, 13*(2), 10–13.

Graber, K. C. (1993). The emergence of faculty consensus concerning teacher education: The socialization process of creating and sustaining faculty agreement. *Journal of Teaching in Physical Education, 12*, 424–436.

Graber, K. C. (1996). Influencing student beliefs: The design of a "high impact" teacher education program. *Teaching and Teacher Education, 12*, 451–466.

Graham, G., Holt-Hale, S. A., Parker, M., Hall, T., & Patton, K. (2020). *Children moving: A reflective approach to teaching physical education* (10th ed.). New York, NY: McGraw Hill.

Griffey, D. (1987). Trouble for sure: A crisis–perhaps. *Journal of Physical Education, Recreation, and Dance, 58*(2), 20–21.

Hall, T., & McCullick, B. A. (2002). Discover, design, and invent: Divergent production. *Teaching Elementary Physical Education, 13*(2), 22–24.

Hellison, D. (2011). *Teaching personal and social responsibility through physical education* (3rd ed.). Champaign, IL: Human Kinetics.

Jaakola, T., & Watt, A. (2011). Finnish physical education teachers' self-reported use and perceptions of Mosston and Ashworth's teaching styles. *Journal of Teaching in Physical Education, 30*, 248–262.

Jackson, J. A., & Dorgo, S. (2002). Maximizing learning through the reciprocal style of teaching. *Teaching Elementary Physical Education, 13*(2), 14–18.

Jenkins, J. M., & Todorovich, J. R. (2002). Inclusion style of teaching: A powerful relationship with national standards. *Teaching Elementary Physical Education, 13*(2), 19–21.

Joyce, B., Weil, M., & Showers, B. (1992). *Models of teaching* (4th ed.). Boston, MA: Allyn and Bacon.

Kirk, D. (2013). Educational value and models-based practice in physical education. *Educational Philosophy and Theory, 45*, 973–986.

Locke. L. (1992). Changing secondary school physical education. *Quest, 44*, 361–372.

McCullick, B., & Byra, M. (2002). Introduction. *Teaching Elementary Physical Education, 13*(2), 6–7.

Metzler, M. W. (2011). *Instructional models for physical education* (3rd ed.). Scottsdale, AZ: Holcomb Hathaway.

Mosston, M. (1966). *Teaching physical education*. Columbus, OH: Merrill.

Mosston, M. (1981). *Teaching physical education* (2nd ed.). Columbus, OH: Merrill.

Mosston, M., & Ashworth, S. (1986). *Teaching physical education* (3rd ed.). Columbus, OH: Merrill.

Mosston, M., & Ashworth, S. (2008). *Teaching physical education* (First Online Edition; 6th ed.). Spectrum Institute for Teaching and Learning. Retrieved from www.spectrumofteachingstyles.org/e-book-download.php

Richards, K. A., Templin, T. J., & Graber, K. (2014). The socialization of teachers in physical education: Recommendations for future works. *Kinesiology Review, 3*, 113–134.

Rovegno, I., & Dolly, J. P. (2006). Constructivist perspectives on learning. In D. Kirk, M. O'Sullivan, & D. Macdonald (Eds.), *Handbook of research in physical education* (pp. 242–261). Thousand Oaks, CA: Sage.

Siedentop, D. (1987). High school physical education: Still an endangered species. *Journal of Physical Education, Recreation, and Dance, 58*(2), 24–25.

Siedentop, D., Hastie, P., & van der Mars, H. (2011). *Complete guide to sport education* (2nd ed.). Champaign, IL: Human Kinetics.

Siedentop, D., & Locke, L. (1997). Making a difference for physical education: What professors and practitioners must build together. *Journal of Physical Education, Recreation, and Dance, 68*(4), 25–33.

Syrmpas, I., Digelidis, N., & Watt, A. (2016). An examination of Greek physical educators' implementation and perceptions of Spectrum teaching styles. *European Physical Education Review, 22*, 201–214.

Syrmpas, I., Digelidis, N., Watt, A., & Vicars, M. (2017). Physical education teachers' experiences and beliefs of production and reproduction teaching approaches. *Teaching and Teacher Education, 66*, 184–194.

Thorpe, R., & Bunker, D. (1986). The curriculum model. In R. Thorpe, D. Bunker, & L. Almond, (Eds.), *Rethinking games teaching* (pp. 7–10). Loughborough: University of Technology, Loughborough.

Windschitl, M. (2002). Framing constructivism in practice as the negotiation of dilemmas: An analysis of the conceptual, pedagogical, cultural, and political challenges facing teachers. *Review of Educational Research, 72*, 131–175.

Chapter 4

Using The Spectrum to interrogate the Teaching Styles of physical education teachers

Brendan SueSee

The title of this chapter may sound a little aggressive and draconian. Perhaps it draws images that are a little 'Big Brother' like in that someone needs to go around watching what teachers do and interrogating them CIA-style under a bright lamp in a dark room. This certainly is not the intention of this chapter. The intention of this chapter is to outline why teaching styles are so important in achieving curriculum or syllabus aims and goals, and how an understanding of The Spectrum can ensure a lens is provided through which teaching styles can be viewed. Furthermore, it is suggested that The Spectrum's ability to provide a common language allows consensus to be reached between teachers, educators, curriculum and syllabus writers, professional development providers and pre-service teacher educators about what teachers' behaviour would look like using specific styles. This would hopefully lead to an alignment between syllabus aims and goals, and the teaching style/s required to create learning episodes to enable students to meet these goals.

The term teaching style is in itself ambiguous as it brings to mind many different things for different people. For example, if Mosston & Ashworth's (2008) Spectrum of Teaching Styles and Metzler's (2011) Instructional Models are considered, there are over 18 teaching styles or instructional models (Pill, Swabey & Penney, 2017). Many of these are talking about the same thing, some about similar things and some using the same word for different things. For example, Metzler's (2011) Direct Instruction and The Spectrum's Command Style have similar attributes. No wonder pedagogy can be confusing and at times difficult to negotiate! However, when The Spectrum is used as a lens to view teaching behaviour, it allows individuals to position the teaching-learning encounter along the decision-making continuum (The Spectrum) with a worthy degree of accuracy and reliability (Goldberger, Ashworth & Byra, 2012). This positioning occurs with a fair degree of certainty as the observer of the learning episode focuses on the decisions being made by the teacher and learner, and which decisions were not made by anyone. Qualifiers such as "in my view" or "in my opinion" are therefore typically not necessary within a Spectrum discussion.

The Spectrum makes no judgement about any teaching approach but rather the choice of approach is only valued with reference to the learning objective. It is suggested that when pre-service teachers, in-service teachers and teacher educators have knowledge of The Spectrum they are able to identify the most appropriate teaching style/s for achieving objectives, and in the theme of valuing health or physical literacy (SueSee & Barker, 2019), I argue that The Spectrum allows the development of pedagogical literacy for teachers. This chapter will outline the value of a common definition of teaching and language that The Spectrum affords in providing a lens through which to view teaching. It will demonstrate how the use of this language and tools enable educators, syllabus writers, physical education teachers and pre-service educators to make a clear link between learning objectives and the choice of teaching styles to achieve that objective.

The need for a common language

My right or your right? Just as it is difficult to lead someone if you do not know where they are beginning, so too it is difficult to discuss anything, with certainty, if we do not have a common understanding, definitions and words for the topic. The inconsistent use of terminology in physical education is one of the principles that Mosston and Ashworth (2008) identified that not surprisingly, they suggested leads to a lack of conceptual agreement, variability of meaning, contradictory results, unreliable communication, different interpretation of events, and unreliable and inaccurate research conclusions (Mosston & Ashworth, 2008). If there is a lack of understanding between pre-service teachers, in-service teachers, coaches and teacher educators then it is unlikely that the field of physical education can provide a platform for them to reach their potential. This point is perhaps especially relevant to syllabus or curriculum documents as teachers attempt to interpret the aims and goals.

If the mantra of a common language sounds like a 'one size fits all' approach, nothing could be further from the truth. Having a common meaning or understanding of how to define teaching and teaching styles does not limit a teacher's individuality or creativity any more than a common understanding of the word 'dog' does between people. Some have argued this point (Sicilia-Camacho & Brown, 2008), suggesting a potential for teachers to lose their individuality and creativity when utilising The Spectrum. The argument is that attempting to universalise and objectify pedagogy would lead to the separation of personhood from pedagogy, and devalue and neglect the important issue of subjectivity (2008). The Spectrum does not attempt to separate the teacher and the chosen pedagogy, rather it allows for a comparison between a teacher's intent and behaviour during lessons (Goldberger et al., 2012). As SueSee, Hewitt and Pill have outlined in the Introduction with a thorough examination of a critique of The Spectrum, Mosston did not "desire to diminish the creativity or individualization of teachers" (Goldberger et al.,

2012, p. 274) but rather to provide them with an adaptable "tool through which they can express their creativity and individuality" (Goldberger et al., 2012, p. 274). In short, if teachers do not have a common language to define, talk about and do research on teaching progress will be slow, if not impossible. I argue that The Spectrum provides this common language.

Curriculum documents

A common language to define teaching styles and the objectives they can meet is necessary for teachers and syllabus document writers when implementing curriculum or syllabus documents to prevent a lack of alignment between syllabus aims and outcomes. SueSee and Barker (2019) suggest internationally, that in the last 15 years, numerous physical education (PE) syllabus documents use terms such as 'critical thinkers', 'creative thinking', 'self-directed', 'problem solvers', 'independent learners', 'self-monitor' and 'self-directed learners' (ACARA, 2016; Scottish National 3 Physical Education, 2012; SHAPE America – Society of Health and Physical Educators, 2014; Skolverket, 2011). Furthermore, numerous scholars have highlighted the multidimensional goals of curriculum documents and suggested that diverse goals cannot be achieved alone through only one cluster style (Digelidis, Theodorakis, Zetou, & Dimas, 2006; Kulinna & Cothran, 2003; Syrmpas et al., 2017). Yet this is what seems to happen regardless of syllabus aims. Whilst speaking more broadly about curriculum change, MacDonald (2003) has likened the change new syllabus or curriculum documents create as like a flurry of activity in a chook house yet unfortunately the activity soon returns to normal. She suggests that this is due to "the goals and processes of change are narrowly proscribed by existing structures, resources and traditions ... " (MacDonald, 2003, p. 139) and it usually results in schools always falling short.

As an example of the argument I am prosecuting, in the Australian state of Queensland (QLD) a syllabus document was written for Queensland senior physical education to be taught to Year 11 and 12 students (the final years of schooling). Some at the time drew conclusions that in the English-speaking world it was nearly without peer (Penney & Kirk, 1998). Reasons for this inference included the notion of *intelligent performance* as movement that will "involve rational and creative thought at a high level of cognitive functioning" (Queensland Studies Authority, 2004, p. 1), and engaging students as not just performers but also as analysts, planners and critics "in, about and through physical activity" (QSA, 2004, p. 1). The last part of this statement clearly related to an Arnoldian perspective of physical education (Arnold, 1979). Furthermore, the Queensland senior physical education syllabus (from this point referred to as the QSPES) (QSA, 2004) required a wide variety of pedagogical approaches to be used, such as "guided discovery, inquiry, cooperative learning, individualised instruction, games for understanding and sport education" (p. 28). Additionally, the QSPES (QSA, 2004) required that learning experiences "should develop students as self-directed, interdependent and independent learners" (p. 29) and provided criteria for *evaluating* (when awarding an 'A' or 'B' standard) in physical performance where a student must: a) implement physical responses through reflection and decision making; and b) independently solve problems by demonstrating solutions in new or unrehearsed contexts. This concept of a new or unrehearsed context (and stipulating that an 'A' or 'B' standard for evaluating can only be given when solving problems in new or unrehearsed contexts) emphasised the value of creativity as an example of a higher order thinking skill and what would appear the use of styles from the production cluster. Production cluster styles are those from Guided Discovery – Inclusion Style and are grouped as they require the learner to produce knowledge new to themselves. The teaching styles from Command Style – Self-Check Style are known as the reproduction cluster as they require students to reproduce knowledge or movements. Given that six styles identifiable on The Spectrum were identified to be used by the QSPES, and that no one teaching style can encompass all learning objectives (Mosston & Ashworth, 2008), it is reasonable to propose that teachers of senior physical education in Queensland would need to use a range of teaching styles to achieve syllabus goals. A process was needed to identify if a range of styles were being used. To do this, a two-pronged approach was used.

The Spectrum Inventory: The Spectrum provided a lens through which to view the QSPES (QSA, 2004) that included a criteria sheet (matrix) and elaborations on what constituted a new or unrehearsed context. A study was conducted whereby 129 teachers of the QSPES (QSA, 2004) responded to a questionnaire (The Spectrum Inventory) asking them to self-report how often they believed they used each of the 11 Landmark Styles of The Spectrum after they read a scenario briefly describing each style. Results from this study indicated that teachers were predominantly using one teaching style (Practice Style, 94.5 percent) when teaching Senior PE, followed by Command Style (77 per cent) and Divergent Discovery Style (73.6 per cent). These results indicated that a range of styles were not being used. This result is consistent with findings in the extant literature (Goldberger & Howarth, 1993; Hasty 1997; Cothran et al., 2005).

Knowing which teaching styles teachers used to teach Senior PE allows some conclusions to be drawn about the implementation of the QSPES (QSA 2004) document. From the self-reported results, it can be concluded that the document was not being implemented the way it was intended, and outcomes were potentially not being met, such as solving problems in new or unrehearsed contexts, as this would not be possible with reproduction cluster styles. Similarly, being cognisant of teaching styles being used allows organisations responsible for professional development and the implementation of syllabus documents to tailor professional development to support teacher's knowledge of teaching styles to allow them to create learning experiences that support the aims and objectives of the document.

The use of The Spectrum Inventory (SueSee, Ashworth & Edwards, 2006) could be replicated with any syllabus document to analyse aims and objectives translation into pedagogical action. If the production of knowledge new to the learner was required, and terms such as discover, create or inquire were used in the language of the learner achievement statements, then production cluster styles would be required by teachers. While the self-reporting of teaching styles allows self-reflection and inferences to be drawn about syllabus implementation, it is the observation of teaching styles that provides further information to confirm (or not) the teaching styles used, and allow greater accuracy with inferences.

Observing teaching styles: Observations of teaching styles used can also confirm the results of self-reporting and conclusions to be drawn about the implementation of syllabus documents. For example, nine teachers of Queensland senior PE were observed across three 1-hour lessons of a 9-week unit, to determine whether syllabus outcomes were being met. The teachers had all completed 4-year training, with three having 0–4 years of teaching experience, three with 5–10 years, and three with 11 years or more. The nine participants' lessons (n=27 lessons) were coded by two coders using Ashworth's (2004) Identification of Classroom Teaching-learning Styles and descriptors of teaching styles from (Cothran et al., 2005) *Teaching Physical Education* (Mosston & Ashworth 2002). The coding protocol used the Instrument for Identifying Teaching Styles (IFITS) (Hasty, 1997) and involved a 10 second observation followed by 10 seconds during which a code was recorded for the observation. The IFITS was used in a study by Hasty (1997) to ascertain the amount of time teachers spent using different teaching styles. This meant that during an observation of a lesson, the coder made a decision every 20 seconds. These decisions involved determining which teaching style was being used during the previous 10 second period. If during an interval two or more styles were identified, the style closest to the production end of The Spectrum was recorded. For example, if Practice Style and Reciprocal Style were both seen during a 10 second period, the trained coder would record the style as Reciprocal Style. The results from this research showed the dominant style used by the participants was Practice Style. Table 4.1 demonstrates the range of styles observed.

These results have been reported elsewhere. For example, some (SueSee et al., 2018a; SueSee et al., 2018b; SueSee & Barker, 2019) have highlighted that teachers will report using a range of styles yet when observed are usually uniform in their approach using overwhelmingly Practice Style. The research of SueSee and Barker (2019) reported similar findings in Sweden with a slightly smaller sample and a curriculum document with similar constructivist underpinning. This is not only common to physical education teachers but to sport coaches as well with Hewitt et al. (2016) reporting a similar phenomenon occurring with tennis coaches.

Table 4.1 Time participants were observed using styles

Teaching Style	Time Teaching Styles Were Observed from Total Lessons (%)	No of Codings N=4465	Time Recorded Using this Style N=24hr:48min: 20 secs
Command Style	3.65	163	54 min 20 sec
Practice Style	69.87	3,120	17 hrs 20 min
Reciprocal Style	2.55	114	38 min
Self-check Style	0.55	25	8 min 20 sec
Inclusion Style	0	0	0
Guided Discovery	0	0	0
Convergent Discovery	0	0	0
Divergent Discovery	0.78	35	11 min 40 sec
Learner Designed Individual Program	0	0	0
Learner Initiated Program	0	0	0
Self-Teaching	0	0	0
Management	22.57	1,008	5 hrs 36 min

By using The Spectrum to code the teaching styles used by teachers, inferences can be made about numerous factors. Just as with the self-reporting conclusion can be drawn about alignment between syllabus/curriculum goals and the teaching styles being used. In the case of the QSPES (QSA, 2004) it was earlier mentioned that to receive the grade of an A or a B, students would need to solve problems in new or unrehearsed contexts. For this to be achieved (a new or unrehearsed context) it would mean that styles such as Convergent Discovery Style or Divergent Discovery Style would need to be used. From the styles observed in Table 4.1, this was clearly not happening. This would mean that any student awarded a grade of an A or a B was not doing so under the circumstances described by the QSPES (QSA, 2004). Given the dominance of Practice Style during the observations, it is very unlikely that the six styles specifically mentioned by the QSPES (QSA, 2004) were being used and that the aims of self-direction and inter-dependence were also unlikely to have been fulfilled. This example further demonstrates the value of The Spectrum as a tool to assist in concluding whether a syllabus document's aims are aligned with the teaching styles being used. If appropriate teaching styles are not aligned with syllabus aims or goals The Spectrum can assist teachers to make a case for the teaching styles that need to be used.

Without alignment between teaching styles and syllabus documents, it is clear from the discussion so far that many undesirable outcomes are likely to occur. First, the syllabus aims and goals are unlikely to reach their potential.

Second, teachers and students are potentially going to become extremely frustrated as they struggle to negotiate the document. Finally, I suggest that frustration will lead to relevant syllabus writing authorities losing credibility as some teachers may conclude that the aims are unachievable. In a sense, that conclusion may be correct as the aims may be unachievable without support such as professional development or knowledge of the alignment between syllabus outcomes or aims and teaching styles.

While the goals mentioned at the beginning of this chapter from numerous syllabi are desirable, these policy documents (ACARA, 2016; Scottish National 3 Physical Education, 2012; SHAPE America – Society of Health and Physical Educators, 2014; Skolverket, 2011) do not provide explicit commentary on how these goals are to be achieved. It is akin to providing a destination without a road map. It is suggested that The Spectrum can provide the 'map' and the range of pedagogies that might prove useful in transforming policy into practice when teachers and teacher educators are working with such documents. If no such guidance is provided then syllabus writers must be presuming that teachers have the knowledge of which teaching styles to use to achieve the syllabus document aims and the knowledge of how to implement such styles.

This was evidently the case with the QSPES (QSA, 2004) referred to earlier in this chapter where six styles were mentioned but with no guidance on how to use them and a presumption that teachers knew when and how to use them. Similarly, other syllabus documents from around the world (ACARA, 2016; Scottish National 3 Physical Education, 2012; SHAPE America – Society of Health and Physical Educators, 2014; Skolverket, 2011) were identified as having aims and goals that could not be achieved with one teaching style yet suggested pedagogical styles are not provided in detail or by name. With regard to physical education curriculum in Sweden some have suggested that the goals relating more to cognition (creativity, curiosity, problem solving) were unlikely to be achieved if policy makers and higher education facilities do not ensure PE teachers are well supported in their implementation of curricula. If teachers are not well supported (Gusky, 2002; Syrmpas et al., 2017), the value of curriculum documents must be questioned and the prescribed outcomes are unlikely to be achieved (SueSee & Barker, 2019). The Spectrum alone would not address this (or for that matter any pedagogical model) however it would be able to provide knowledge of what to do to achieve a wide variety of curriculum goals.

Sporting problems

The challenges identified in the field of physical education can also been seen in sports coaching. For example, the Tennis Australia accreditation coaching courses recommend that tennis coaches should combine the use of direct and discovery teaching styles, with the latter nominated as the preferred teaching style (Tennis Australia (2010a; 2010b). As is the case with teaching physical education, the predominant use of technique focussed coaching is not necessarily compatible with the suggested teaching processes identified in these publications. The need for coaches to understand and effectively use a range of teaching styles to achieve multi-dimensional learning outcomes is important.

As has been previously mentioned concerning physical education, no one teaching style encompasses all learning goals. Therefore, just as with teaching physical education, an effective coach must possess the capability to change and combine teaching styles during sessions so as to achieve 'mobility ability' (Mosston & Ashworth, 2008). This is further supported by Pill, Hewitt and Edwards (2016) when they argue that "the necessity for coaches to understand and purposefully implement a range of teaching styles to achieve various learning outcomes is paramount" (p. 40). If this does not occur problems will arise for athletes and coaches as they are not catering to all learners, developing holistic players or meeting the needs of the aims of their relevant organisations. Once again it is argued that The Spectrum can provide a framework for coaches to understand what they are doing and a lens through which their behaviour can be viewed thus allowing alignment between their aims and their behaviour required to achieve these aims.

How to interrogate teaching styles

So far, this chapter has justified the need to interrogate by referring to alignment between curriculum and syllabus documents aims and teaching styles. This section will briefly suggest how this could be achieved. First, it is recommended that a sound knowledge of Spectrum theory is required for a common language in any conversation between teacher and teacher educator, syllabus writer etc. The pitfalls of not having a common language have been briefly mentioned earlier. This 'crash course' on The Spectrum would involve reading Chapters 1–5 of *Teaching Physical Education* (Mosston & Ashworth, 2008).

For syllabus writers it is suggested that aims and goals and assessment criteria are examined for cognitive verbs. If students are required to use creativity, discovery, perform in unfamiliar circumstances, unrehearsed circumstances, self-reflection, solve problems (previously unknown) then styles from the production cluster will be required. Similarly, if students were required to self-reflect, self-correct, offer feedback to others, then styles such as the Reciprocal Style or the Self-Check Style would be needed. This would be similar for people whose job may be to provide professional development opportunities for teachers implementing syllabus documents. This could include pre-service teacher educators, teachers in charge of leading professional development or syllabus writers.

A tool that may be helpful for getting teachers to reflect on their own teaching and identify teaching styles they use could be The Spectrum Inventory.

The Spectrum Inventory (SueSee, Ashworth & Edwards, 2006) instrument is considered to be particularly useful in the self-assessment or reflection by teachers of their teaching styles; for researchers seeking a more effective understanding and application of The Spectrum; and, as an instructional and feedback instrument for those who work in Physical Education Teacher Education (PETE) courses. In the future, The Spectrum Inventory could be used to evaluate teaching styles of physical education teachers to find adherence to implied expectations of curriculum documents and their goals and aims. If specific goals and aims were being achieved then it is likely that a similar umbrella of teaching styles across a country or region would be observed.

Another tool that could be helpful for interrogating teaching styles would be Ashworth's (2008; 2010) Spectrum Inventory. It is similar to the aforementioned (SueSee, Ashworth & Edwards, 2006) inventory but does not measure teachers' self-reported beliefs. It also has a brief introduction about how it can be used and things to consider to ensure validity. It could be used to provide a short overview of the behaviours demonstrated by teachers when using specific teaching styles. The Spectrum Inventory could also be used to evaluate physical education teachers' 'toolkit' of teaching styles in comparison to each other in schools – including schools in different states and countries. If syllabus documents (with the same aims and goals) are being implemented in line with goals and aims of those documents then it could be assumed that similar teaching styles would be observed. If this was not the case, professional development could be tailored to assist and support teachers if necessary, by organisations responsible for supporting teachers in their implementation of syllabus documents.

One final tool that may be of assistance in providing a useable condensed version of the behaviours seen in each of the teaching styles is Ashworth's (2004) identification of classroom teaching-learning styles. This tool is designed to determine which teaching style(s) are being used in the classroom. Ashworth (2002) stresses that this "tool does not determine the *fidelity* or the *appropriateness* of the teaching-learning approach, but rather it identifies which of The Spectrum landmark teaching-learning styles the classroom behavior most resembles" (p. 1). It perhaps goes without saying that the more thorough a teacher's knowledge of The Spectrum the more accurate their interrogation of teaching styles and syllabus documents will be, and there is no substitute for reading *Teaching Physical Education* (2008) and using each of the styles.

This chapter has made a case for why interrogating teaching styles is important and justified the points by referring to research, the multidimensional nature of syllabus aims and goals and that one teaching style is unable to achieve all outcomes. It has suggested tools that may assist in the interrogation of teaching styles in physical education and what may occur if such practice is not implemented given the challenging nature of syllabus documents and aims. Knowledge of The Spectrum has also been suggested in assisting teachers, teacher educators, professional development providers and syllabus writers align syllabus goals with teaching styles. As has been earlier suggested in this chapter, knowledge alone of The Spectrum (let alone any model of pedagogy) will unlikely be successful in meeting educational outcomes. Support must be provided for teachers if they are to attempt new teaching styles. The concepts presented in this chapter should be thought provoking and helpful for syllabus writers, policy makers, teacher educators and higher education institutions in what may need to occur to ensure physical education teachers are well supported in their implementation of curriculum documents. If teachers are not supported, the value of curricula must be questioned and the prescribed outcomes are unlikely to be realised.

References

Ashworth, S. (2004). Identification of Classroom Teaching-learning Styles. San Francisco, CA. Retrieved from www.spectrumofteachingstyles.org

Ashworth, S. (2008). Descriptions of landmark teaching styles: A spectrum inventory. (United States) Retrieved from www.spectrumofteachingstyles.org

Ashworth, S. (2010). Descriptions of landmark teaching styles: A spectrum inventory. (United States) Retrieved from www.spectrumofteachingstyles.org

Australian Curriculum, Assessment and Reporting Authority. (2016). *The Health and Physical Education Curriculum.* Version 8.2, Sydney, Australia.

Cothran, D., Kulinna, P., Banville, D., Choi, E., Amade-Escot, C., MacPhail, A., Macdonald, D., Richard, J., Sarmento, P., & Kirk, D. (2005). A cross-cultural investigation of the use of teaching styles. *Research Quarterly for Exercise and Sport,* 76(2), 193–201.

Digelidis, N., Theodorakis, Y., Zetou, H., & Dimas, I. (2006). *Physical education 5th–6th grade of primary school: Teachers' book.* Athens: Greek Ministry of Education.

Goldberger, M., & Howarth, K. (1993). The National Curriculum in National Physical Education and the Spectrum of Teaching Styles. *British Journal of Physical Education,* 24(1), 23–28

Goldberger, M., Ashworth, S., & Byra, M. (2012). Spectrum of Teaching Styles Retrospective 2012, *Quest,* 64(4), 268–282.

Guskey, T. R. (2002). Professional development and teacher change. *Teachers and Teaching: Theory and Practice,* 8, 381–391.

Hasty, D. (1997). *The impact of British National Curriculum Physical Education on teacher's use of teaching styles: a case study in one English town.* Unpublished doctoral dissertation. Tuscaloosa, AL: The University of Alabama.

Hewitt, M., Edwards, K., Ashworth, S., and Pill, S. (2016). Investigating the teaching styles of tennis coaches using The Spectrum. *Sport Science Review, 25* (5–6), 321–344.

Kulinna, P. H., & Cothran, D. J. (2003). Physical education teachers' self-reported use and perceptions of various teaching styles. *Learning and Instruction, 13,* 597–609.

Macdonald, D. (2003). Curriculum change and the post-modern world: Is the school curriculum-reform movement an anachronism? *Journal of Curriculum Studies, 35*(2), 139–149.

Metzler, M. (2011). *Instructional models for physical education.*, Scottsdale, AZ: Holcomb Hathaway.

Mosston, M., & Ashworth, S. (2008). *Teaching physical education:* First online edition. Spectrum Institute for Teaching and Learning. Retrieved from https://spectrum ofteachingstyles.org/

Penney, D., & Kirk, D. (1998). Evaluation of the Trial-Pilot Senior Syllabus in Physical Education in Queensland Secondary Schools. Brisbane, Qld: Board of Senior Secondary School Studies Queensland.

Pill, S., Hewitt, M., & Edwards, K. (2016). Exploring tennis coaches' insights in relation to their teaching styles. *Baltic Journal of Sport and Health Sciences, 3* (102), 30–43.

Pill, S., Swabey, K., & Penney, D. (2017). Investigating Physical Education Teacher Use of Models Based Practice in Australian Secondary PE. *Revue phénEPS/PHEnex Journal, 9*(1), 1–19.

Queensland Studies Authority. (2004). *Senior physical education syllabus.* Brisbane, Qld: Queensland Studies Authority (QSA).

Scottish Qualifications Authority. (2012). *National 3 Physical Education Course Specification* (Scotland). Retrieved from www.sqa.org.uk

SHAPE America – Society of Health and Physical Educators. (2014). *National standards and grade-level outcomes for K–12 physical education.* Champaign, IL: Human Kinetics.

Sicilia-Camacho, A., & Brown, D. (2008). Revisiting the paradigm shift from the versus to the non-versus notion of Mosston's Spectrum of teaching styles in physical education pedagogy: a critical pedagogical perspective. *Physical Education & Sport Pedagogy, 13*(1), 85–108.

Skolverket. (2011). Curriculum for the compulsory school, preschool class and the leisure-time centre 2011. Retrieved from www.skolverket.se/publikationer

SueSee, B., & Barker, D. (2019). Self-reported and observed teaching styles of Swedish physical education teachers. *Curriculum Studies in Health and Physical Education, 10*(1), 34–50.

SueSee, B., Ashworth, S., & Edwards, K. (2006). *Instrument for collecting teachers' beliefs about their teaching styles used in physical education: Adaptation of description inventory of landmark teaching styles: A spectrum approach.* Queensland University of Technology, Brisbane, (Australia).

SueSee, B., Edwards, K., Pill, S., & Cuddihy, T. (2018a). Observed teaching styles of senior physical education teachers in Australia. *Curriculum Perspectives, 39*(1), 47–57.

SueSee, B., Edwards, K., Pill, S., & Cuddihy, T. (2018b). Self-reported teaching styles of Australian senior physical education teachers. *Curriculum Perspectives, 38*(1), 41–54.

Syrmpas, I., Digelidis, N., Watt, A., & Vicars, M. (2017). Physical education teachers' experiences and beliefs of production and reproduction teaching approaches. *Teaching and Teacher Education, 66,* 184–194.

Tennis Australia. (2010a). *Junior development coaching course learner guide.* Melbourne, Vic: Tennis Australia.

Tennis Australia. (2010b). *Club professional coaching course learner guide.* Melbourne, Vic: Tennis Australia.

Chapter 5

Using The Spectrum to ground PETE students' pedagogical footings

Shane Pill and Joss Rankin

This chapter describes the use of The Spectrum (Mosston & Ashworth, 2008) for pedagogical accountability in a foundational physical education teacher education (PETE) program. Pedagogical accountability refers to the preparation of teachers who can teach effectively (Ashworth, 1992). Furthermore, we use the concept of foregrounding the learner through transformative tertiary studies in physical education (PE) (Pill & Brown, 2007) to anchor the pedagogical use of The Spectrum in PETE as a deliberate mechanism to disrupt the common technocratic and sport-as-sport techniques (Kirk, 2010) PE student experience constructed as demonstrate-explain-practice (Tinning, 2010). We suggest that foregrounding the learner in the context of PETE requires the intentional construction of learning experiences that assist the PETE students' transition from PE student to "pre-service teacher". The later requiring a framework through which to be able to think about and through their role as "teacher" and by virtue of knowledge, skills and attitudes is qualified to make judgements about what ought to be done with regard to the educative use of physical activity (Paddick, 1976) for education in, through and about movement (Arnold, 1979).

Education in, through and about movement

In the later part of the twentieth century, and into the first decade of the twenty-first century, Arnold's (1979) philosophical conceptualisation of PE as education in, through and about movement became the standard reference for theorising and framing the form and content of school PE. Arnold's (1979) philosophical conceptualisation explained how PE was distinctive from forms of physical training that can be considered for inclusion in curriculum time (Australian Council for Health, Physical Education and Recreation [ACHPER], 2008; Kirk, 1988; Pill, 2012).

Summarising Arnold's three conceptual dimensions of PE:

1. Education about movement (movement as a field of study): Movement can be studied as a body of knowledge in its own right;

2. Education through movement (movement as an instrument of value): PE can be a means of education of the "total person" (Arnold, 1979, p. 172) – cognitively, morally, socially and physically; and

3. Education in movement (movement as a source of personal meaning): PE provides a means for one to learn about the self and the world in which the self resides which "permit(s) the person to actualize the physical dimensions of his being in the form of developed capacities, skilled accomplishments and objective achievements that are in themselves worthwhile" (Arnold, 1979, p. 178). Learning in movement is therefore "knowledge that can only be gained through active participation" (Kirk, 1988, p. 71).

Arnold's conceptualisation of education in, through and about movement continues to influence the shape of PE curricula in Australia through the Australian Curriculum for Health and Physical Education (AC:HPE) (Australian Curriculum and Assessment Authority [ACARA], 2018; Pill & Stolz, 2017).

Although curriculum frameworks have been influenced by Arnold's conceptualisation, learning *in* movement has been the common area of focus for Australian PE, however, many teachers assume that influence occurs in the other two areas (Tinning, Macdonald, Wright & Hickey, 2001). Kirk (2010) described the content of this education focus of learning *in* movement in PE as mainly taking the form of sport-as-sport techniques, emphasising that frequently school PE gave preference to sport experiences rather than lifetime physical activity, including informal and recreational sport. In the Australian context, Clennett and Brooker (2006) noted that Australian PE teachers' historically narrow interpretations of curricula result in a focus on teaching in PE that has frequently concentrated on students developing technical expertise for sport. With respect to instructional style, Metzler (2011) described a common pedagogical emphasis on directive instruction in PE as the 'physical education method', which Tinning (2010) elaborated on as demonstrate-explain-practice (DEP). Both Metzler and Tinning therefore highlight that often PE has been about reproductive behaviour by students rather than PE teaching being for productive thinking by students.

As a consequence of their lived experience of PE in their school years people enter PETE following an apprenticeship of observation (McCormack, 1997) of the form and function of PE, and thus with a narrow conceptualisation of PE content and pedagogy. This apprenticeship of observation is therefore a substantial influence on the beginning PETE student understanding of what PE is, and is not. Some have argued the apprenticeship of observation is more influential on the eventual practice of the teacher than PETE (Ashworth, 1992; Brennan 2006; Hopper 1999; McCormack 1997; Mills, 2006; Oslin, Collier & Mitchell, 2001; Pill, Penney & Swabey, 2012). In this respect, Schempp (1989) stated, "the apprenticeship of observation is an ally of continuity rather than of change" (p. 36).

With respect to the challenge of disrupting the apprenticeship of observation of commencing PETE students, within the context of their work as PE teacher education practitioners at Flinders University, Pill and Brown (2007) asked:

> How then, might Physical Education teacher educators work towards pedagogies that are transformative, rather than reproductive, when beliefs from the past develop expectations of what PETE will offer?

They suggested distinct features of PETE that would be transformative rather than reproductive of a continuing hegemony of the common physical education method (Metzler, 2011). Pill and Brown (2007) place the early exposure to pedagogical knowledge as well as to disciplinary knowledge centrally in the process of forming the beginning PETE student's professional identity and shift from being a student of PE. The influence of the founder of PETE at Flinders University, Robert Paddick, is evident in Pill and Brown's proposition. Paddick's vision of a physical educator was that of a "a person who, by virtue of knowledge, skills and attitudes, is qualified to make judgements about what ought to be done with regard to physical activity" (1976, p. 9). Therefore, a "critical rather than reverential attitude to [their] subject matter" (Paddick 1976, p. 11) is required of the physical educator. To achieve the proposition of PETE at Flinders University as deliberately transformative, The Spectrum is the foundation for pedagogical accountability (Ashworth, 1992).

Transformative pedagogy and pedagogical accountability

The potential for transformative PETE is not just in the education of the PETE student. It is through the agency of pre-service PETE teachers that PETE has the potential to initiate and then progress curriculum reform in school PE (Butler, 2005; Macdonald et al., 2002; Pill et al., 2012; Tinning et al., 2001). Pill (2007) argued that it is PETE graduates who can "carry PE forward" (p. 25) if courses actively promote curriculum innovation and change in an environment that supports the adoption of new ideas. The potential for PETE to act as the stimulus for transformation in curriculum and pedagogy exists where the injection of ideas accompanies the provision of applied implementation experiences and reflective opportunities (Pill & Brown, 2007). Pill and Brown (2007) therefore proposed transformative PETE as an activist pedagogy (Ukpokodu, 2009) that engages beginning PETE students in critical examination of their apprenticeship of observation with the goal of developing a reflective knowledge base, and a sense of critical consciousness and agency (Ukpokodu, 2009).

Student teachers have a role to play in the process of curriculum change or reform. It is no secret that it is during their undergraduate training that most teachers experience the most intensive training phase of their professional lives. It stands to reason that the pre-service phase presents itself as an ideal forum through which new curriculum models can be efficiently and effectively introduced.

(Tinning et al., 2001, p. 230)

The Spectrum provides the footings for pedagogical accountability at Flinders University as transformative PETE. In adopting this footing we are also mindful of avoiding what has been suggested as an evolution of PETE in some institutions whereby educational matters and issues are neglected within degrees favouring scientific functionalism (Fitzclarence & Tinning, 1990; Kirk, 1988) or that have scientised the occupation of teaching and the construction of knowledge in PETE (Gore, 1990). It has been suggested that what has occurred in these instances is degrees that have little effect on graduate teacher effectiveness, as the sub-disciplinary knowledge is often irrelevant to the work of the PE teacher in school settings (Weigand, Bolger & Mohr, 2004).

Pedagogical accountability: Ashworth (1992) described pedagogical accountability as a major theme upon which many of the instructional problems of PE hinge, as teacher pedagogical decision making is central to the quality learning environments. Ashworth's (1992) description of pedagogical accountability comes with a notion of pedagogical autonomy allowing physical education teachers a range of teaching styles, but within an understanding of how each individual teaching style aligns with particular kinds of learner achievement and development (Mosston & Ashworth, 2008).

Ashworth (1992) described the potential for The Spectrum to meet the search for PETE that will positively affect PE reform. She proposed that this can be achieved as The Spectrum provides a "unifying structure" identifying "a possible range and specific structures for a variety of teaching behaviors" that give an understanding of the teaching patterns required to accomplish particular objectives (Ashworth, 1989, p. 9). Pedagogical accountability can also be synonymous with pedagogical effectiveness – that is, what it is that "good" teachers do to raise student learning attainment (Husbands & Pearce, 2012). In both contexts, structure for understanding how teaching behaviours align with teaching objectives and understanding pedagogical effectiveness, pedagogical accountability hinges on what PE teachers do, what they know and the beliefs that inform what they do.

Using The Spectrum as transformative PETE at Flinders University

At Flinders University, The Spectrum is introduced to PETE students in a Foundations of Physical Education topic undertaken during the first

Table 5.1 Lessons aligned to their key content and relationship with The Spectrum in the Foundations of Physical Education topic

Lesson	Overview	Purpose of Lesson and Connection with Spectrum of Teaching Styles
Lecture Series (1 × 1 hour / week)	An introduction to the shape, role and responsibility of physical education as an area of learning. Students explore and consider: • Theoretical frameworks for the teaching of physical education • How these frameworks and other factors shape physical education in curriculum • A range of cultural perspectives of physical education	No direct reference is made to The Spectrum through the lecture series. Lectures provide PETE students with a grounding in historical, epistemological, pedagogical and curriculum perspectives of what Physical Education is, how it has evolved and what its responsibility is as an area of learning. Content foregrounds the learner (Pill & Brown, 2007) and acts as a provocation to critically examine PETE students' apprenticeships of observation (McCormack, 1997).
Workshops (1 × 2 hours / week)	Engagement with the development of fundamental movement skills as foundations of movement Learning within a thematic approach related to game categories Learning in and through games based approaches Exploration of the components of playing games and sports A range of teacher capabilities built upon the P's of pedagogy (Launder, 2001; Launder & Piltz, 2013)	In the first six weeks of semester the workshop tutor provides examples of lessons associated with teaching fundamental movement skills and thematic game categories of sports and games. The workshop tutor applies a range of teaching styles and prompts evaluation and reflection regarding pedagogical approaches, drawing upon understanding that is being developed through the seminar lessons. During this time students are also provided with opportunities for micro teaching that asks them to apply an understanding of the conscious and deliberate act required for effective teaching and learning.

Lesson	Overview	Purpose of Lesson and Connection with Spectrum of Teaching Styles
		This becomes part of the application of a critical examination of an apprenticeship of observation to take a transformative approach to achieve pedagogical accountability (Ashworth, 1992; McCormack, 1997; Pill & Brown, 2007). The subsequent eight weeks that follows the mid-semester break requires students to prepare for and deliver a lesson to peers related to either rhythmic and expressive movement patterns (early childhood and primary specialisation) or invasion games (middle and secondary specialisation). Within this lesson they must also identify and correctly utilise relevant teaching styles as part of a pedagogical toolkit for applying a games-based approach to teaching.
Seminars (1 × 1 hour / week)	Learning specifically associated with The Spectrum to build upon understandings of own practices and application of games-based approaches	Over the first four weeks students engage with tutor lead sessions that introduce them to The Spectrum. Activities centre on what The Spectrum is, its key premise, breadth of application and consideration for own teaching practices. These lessons act as preparation for students to then be able to plan and facilitate a lesson to the rest of the class that identifies, explains and demonstrates an allocated teaching style.

semester of first year of a four-year bachelor of education degree. At the end of 2016, the PE academic team at Flinders University reflected on the current delivery of the PE program and utilised this as an opportunity to refine student learning outcomes and the pedagogical approaches used to achieve these. As a result, Foundations of Physical Education underwent a reshaping of the content and delivery applied. Table 5.1 outlines the lesson structure within the topic to identify how students engage throughout the semester, specifically in relation to The Spectrum. The topic is taught over a 14-week period in which students undertake a one hour lecture, two hour practical workshop and one hour seminar per week.

By taking the approach of focusing attention on the use of The Spectrum within the seminars, discussing broader pedagogical considerations of PE within the lectures, and then applying the concepts throughout the workshop series, students engage with procedures identified by Ashworth (1992) as leading to strong relationships between theory and practice. Such relationships are seen as students design and implement lessons that thoughtfully progress learning by drawing upon a range of teaching styles to teach to purposefully designed and sequenced learning episodes. PETE students consider their role as the teacher during learning and apply a variety of strategies including demonstrations, direct instruction, questioning and student exploration based upon their intended learning outcomes outlined for their students. In doing so, they begin to adopt new ideas and as such, the PETE be considered as transformative (Pill, 2007). The described "micro-teaching" experiences build on an initial overview of The Spectrum and related theory that are supported by observations of the tutor in class. Micro-teaching is a method of teacher education that places PETE students in teaching activities under controlled and simulated circumstances that replicate the complexity of the natural setting of PE teaching in school. The micro-teaching in the context we discuss here engages PETE students in planning and delivery of teaching episodes using multiple procedures for teacher development that empower them with greater abilities to make informed decisions in relation to their own pedagogical approaches (Ashworth, 1992; Byra, 2000).

Foregrounding the learner

PETE students are introduced to The Spectrum as a participant, both practically and theoretically. The first three weeks of seminars are utilised to teach underpinning concepts of The Spectrum, as well as provide examples of a range of styles being applied in practice. Activities are integrated into lessons that require PETE students to engage with styles from both the production and reproduction clusters to generate conversation attaining to outcome-based learning episodes and a range of pedagogical strategies that can be applied to achieve these. Emphasis is then placed on the key premise of The Spectrum by identifying the potential for decision making that is undertaken by either the student or the teacher. Further exploration identifies that no one style is 'better' than another, rather, that each style may be used for a range of reasons (Mosston & Ashworth, 2008).

These initial experiences are intended to foreground the learner (Pill & Brown, 2007) to consider The Spectrum as a pedagogical toolkit to promote learning for their students that addresses the breadth of outcomes identified within the AC:HPE (SueSee & Pill, 2018). PETE students are positioned to consider how learning design impacts the achievement of outcomes for others rather than simply accept the 'truths' of their apprenticeship of observation (McCormack, 1997; Pill & Brown, 2007). The Spectrum therefore acts as a means of foregrounding PETE students' understanding of their apprenticeship of observation of school PE by repositioning the PETE student from reproduction of prior understanding of the role of the PE teacher to a critical consciousness that informs their actions, empowering them as agents for change (Ukpokodu, 2009).

Whilst the first three weeks of seminars are used to engage with The Spectrum theory, during this time the PETE students also engage in workshops through a games-based approach to teaching fundamental movement skills. Various teaching styles are applied by the workshop tutor to demonstrate game-based teaching as a cluster of teaching styles (SueSee & Pill, 2017). Questions are posed to the PETE students about how and why these styles may have been used. In this way, disruption of the common 'physical education method' (Metzler, 2011) as a technocratic approach (Kirk, 2010) occurs to demonstrate the scope of possibility for teaching to multiple ways of knowing and the development of multiple domains of learning (physical, cognitive, personal, social and affective). The PETE students are therefore further moved to begin to consider their role in learning design and facilitation of the learning process. For example, Week 4 of the topic is used to demonstrate how the Reciprocal Style (Style C) can be applied to the context of technical development, as an alternative to a traditional demonstrate-explain-practice approach (Tinning, 2010). The demonstration also acts as an example for their assessable component of the seminar series; to plan, teach and evaluate a lesson that applies a specific style of teaching from The Spectrum.

Critical examination of apprenticeship

Earlier, we outlined that the contexts PETE students have experienced of PE as school students play a pivotal role in the development of PETE students' understanding of the shape, role and responsibility of the subject area and its teachers. The PETE students' apprenticeship of observation creates an initial philosophical understanding of PE teaching (McCormack, 1997). The potential pedagogical limiter on PETE students future teaching behaviour is, however, that the PETE student may choose to do what they see as always having being done in their 'apprenticeship', accepting this as the 'norm' of what is considered learning rather than considering its pedagogical value. We believe it is therefore imperative to expose the PETE students' apprenticeship of observation to critical examination. Individual professional identities then have the opportunity to evolve as students examine their apprenticeship with a critical consciousness. Engaging with The Spectrum is used deliberately as a tool to promote a shift from being a student of PE to pre-service teacher by identifying the deliberate relationship between intent, action and outcome within lessons (Mueller & Mueller, 1992).

The Spectrum is used to engage PETE students with activities that build capabilities within the teaching, planning and reflective process from the perspective of applying a range of teaching styles. In this way, PETE students begin to remove themselves from teaching as an intuitive action based on their apprenticeship of observation to a "conscious and deliberate act in planning, activating and evaluating teaching" (Mueller & Mueller, 1992, p. 48). Building on the experience of the content as a participant, students engage in a lesson that demonstrates the deliberate use of the reciprocal style of teaching. This experience allows them to observe how one particular style might be applied, as well as providing them some experience and responsibility in the role of the 'teacher'. From week five onwards, PETE students then conduct micro-teaching using small group peer teaching. They are required to conduct a 40 minute practical lesson that demonstrates the use of an allocated style. Across a period of eight weeks, the PETE students engage in peer delivered lessons that apply the use of different styles from The Spectrum, one of which they have been responsible for. This scaffolding of content knowledge, exposure as a participant, one-on-one teaching and small group teaching, all accompanied by intentional reflection and deliberate analysis on the question, 'What are the implications for what I teach and the way I teach?' (Tinning et al., 2001), acts as a transformative process. Through this process students build a conscious awareness of applying teaching styles to promote the achievement of student learning outcomes (Byra, 2000). We position this reflective action involving conscious consideration of the assumptions underpinning the beliefs they bring from their apprenticeship of observation and the consequences for students arising from those beliefs with the assumptions of The Spectrum and the implications for how one teaches deliberately to orientate the PETE students to be reflective of their work. In this way we address with PETE students the important question for their transformation from PE students to beginning teachers, 'What sort of PE teacher do you want to be?' (Tinning et al., 2001).

Conclusion

In providing students with content knowledge and enabling them to engage in a range of practical experiences to apply and evaluate pedagogical approaches via The Spectrum, the Foundations of Physical Education topic seeks pedagogical accountability. By presenting teaching as a deliberate and proactive act, the use of The Spectrum challenges PETE students to examine teaching behaviours as purposeful and evolving (Mueller & Mueller, 1992). Through this examination, PETE students are provided with a pedagogical language and toolkit that guides observation and action in refining approaches to teaching PE for educational purposes – one of the key ideas of the AC:HPE (ACARA, 2018). It seems reasonable then to suggest that this deliberate use of The Spectrum as a provocation for the PETE students' apprenticeship of observation acts as a way of preparing them to teach effectively, thereby enacting a pedagogical accountability in PETE (Ashworth, 1992; Pill & Brown, 2007). As such, an intentional shift from PE student to pre-service teacher begins.

References

Australian Council for Health, Physical Education and Recreation (ACHPER). (2008). *Draft Statement on a national curriculum and physical education – Information and feedback*. Retrieved July 2011 from www.achper.org.au/new.php

Australian Curriculum and Assessment Authority. (2018). *Key ideas- Health and physical education propositions*. Retrieved October 2018 from www.australiancurriculum.edu.au/f-10-curriculum/health-and-physical-education/key-ideas/

Arnold, P. (1979). *Meaning in movement, sport and physical education*. Portsmouth, NH: Heinemann Educational Publishers.

Ashworth, S. (1989). Problems of teaching and teacher training. The Spectrum of Teaching Styles pre-student teaching program: A first year study. In L. Telama (Ed.), *Physical Education and Life-Long Physical Activity. Proceedings of the Jyvaskyla Sport Congress: Movement and Sport, AIESEP World Convention* (pp 248–259). Jyvaskyla, Finland.

Ashworth, S. (1992). The Spectrum and teacher education. *Journal of Physical Education, Recreation, and Dance, 63*(1), 32–35, 53.

Brennan, P. (2006). From Rhetoric to Reality: A case study of partnerships for improvement. *The Bulletin of Physical Education, 42*(1), 16–33.

Butler, J. (2005). TGfU pet-agogy: Old dogs, new tricks and puppy school. *Physical Education and Sport Pedagogy, 10*(3), 225–240.

Byra, M. (2000). A coherent PETE program: Spectrum style. *Journal of Physical Education, Recreation & Dance, 71*(9), 40–43.

Clennett, A., & Brooker, R. (2006). *Teaching health & physical education in contemporary Australian school education: Rethinking teachers' curriculum and pedagogical work*. Paper presented at the AARE Conference, Adelaide, 2006. Retrieved from https://pdfs.semanticscholar.org/0fd6/3d8d13a336219cdaeb4ef1430eb78ecbdade.pdf

Fitzclarence, L., & Tinning, R. (1990). Challenging hegemonic physical education. In D. Kirk & R. Tinning (Eds.), *Physical education, curriculum and culture: Critical issues in the contemporary crisis* (pp. 79–108). London: Falmer Press.

Gore, J. (1990). Pedagogy as text in physical education teacher education. In D. Kirk & R. Tinning (Eds.), *Physical education, curriculum and culture: Critical issues in the contemporary crisis* (pp. 131–148). London: Falmer Press.

Hopper, T. (1999). The grid: Reflecting from preservice teachers experiences of being taught. *Journal of Physical Education, Recreation and Dance, 70*(7), 53–59.

Husbands, C., & Pearce, J. (2012). What makes great pedagogy? Nine claims from research. *National College for School Leadership*. Retrieved from https://assets. publishing.service.gov.uk/government/uploads/system/uploads/attachment_data/ file/329746/what-makes-great-pedagogy-nine-claims-from-research.pdf

Kirk, D. (1988). *Physical education and curriculum study: A critical introduction*. London: Croom Helm.

Kirk, D. (2010). *Physical education futures*. New York, NY: Routledge.

Launder, A. (2001). *Play practice: The games approach to teaching and coaching Sports*. Champaign, IL, Human Kinetics.

Launder, A., & Piltz, W. (2013). *Play Practice: Engaging and developing skilled players from beginner to elite* (2nd ed.). Champaign, IL, Human Kinetics.

McCormack, A. (1997). *Impacting on the socialisation of beginning teachers of physical education and health through collaboration*. Paper presented at AARE. Brisbane, November, 1997. Retrieved from www.aare.edu.au/data/publications/1997/mccoa021.pdf

Macdonald, D., Hunter, L., Carlson, T., & Penney, D. (2002). Teacher knowledge and the disjunction between school curricula and teacher education. *Asia-Pacific Journal of Teacher Education, 30*(3), 259–275.

Metzler, M. (2011). *Instructional models for physical education* (3rd ed.). Scottsdale, AZ: Holcomb Hathaway.

Mills, C. (2006). *Pre-service teacher education and the development of socially just dispositions: A review of the literature*. Paper presented at the AARE Conference, Adelaide, 2006. Retrieved from www.aare.edu.au/data/publications/2006/mil06221.pdf

Mosston, M., & Ashworth, S. (2008). *Teaching physical education, first online edition*. Retrieved from www.spectrumofteachingstyles.org/pdfs/ebook/Teaching_Physical_ Edu_1st_Online_old.pdf

Mueller, R., & Mueller, S. (1992). The spectrum of teaching styles and its role in conscious deliberate teaching. *Journal of Physical Education, Recreation & Dance, 63*(1), 48–53.

Paddick, R. (1976). *Physical education at Flinders – Professional training?* Unpublished seminar paper, Flinders University, Australia.

Oslin, J. Collier, C., & Mitchell, S. (2001). Living the curriculum. *Journal of Physical Education, Recreation and Dance, 72*(5), 47–51.

Pill, S. (2007). Junior Primary/Primary pre-service teachers' perceptions of their work as effective teachers of physical education. *Healthy Lifestyles Journal, 4*(3/4), 25–31.

Pill, S. (2012). *Rethinking sport teaching in physical education*. Unpublished Doctor of Philosophy thesis. Launceston, Tas: University of Tasmania.

Pill, S., & Brown, R. (2007). *Tertiary studies in physical education: Transformative Pedagogy – foregrounding the learner*. PACE Yourself ACHPER Australia International Biennial Conference. Fremantle, 3–6 October.

Pill, S., Penney, D., & Swabey, K. (2012). Rethinking sport teaching in physical education: A case study of research based innovation in teacher education. *Australian Journal of Teacher Education, 37*(8), 118–138.

Pill, S., & Stolz, S. (2017). Exploring Australian secondary PE teachers' understanding of PE in the context of new curriculum familarisation. *Asia Pacific Journal of Health, Sport and Physical Education*, Published online: 8 January 2017. DOI: http:// dx.doi.org/10.1080/18377122.2016.1272425

SueSee, B., & Pill, S. (2018). Game-based teaching and coaching as a toolkit of teaching styles. *Strategies, 31*(5), 21–28.

SueSee, B., Pill, S., & Edwards, K. (2016). Reconciling approaches – a game centred approach to sport teaching and Mosston's spectrum of teaching styles. *European Journal of Physical Education and Sport Science, 2*(4), 69–86.

Tinning, R. (2010). *Pedagogy and human movement: Theory, practice, research.* New York, NY: Routledge.

Tinning, R., Macdonald, D., Wright, J., & Hickey, C. (2001) *becoming a physical education teacher: Contemporary and enduring issues.* Frenchs Forest, NSW: Pearson Education.

Ukpokodu, O. (2009). The practice of transformative pedagogy. *Journal on Excellence in College Teaching, 20*(2), 43–67.

Weigand, R. Bulger, S., & Mohr, D. (2004). Curricular issues in physical education teacher education. *Journal of Physical Education, Recreation and Dance, 75*(8), 47–56.

Chapter 6

Considering the application of a range of teaching styles from The Spectrum that promotes the holistic development of tennis players in a variety of learning domains

Mitch Hewitt

Research has suggested that Landmark Practice Style is the dominant instructional behaviour of tennis coaches in Australia (Hewitt, 2015). The application of this style located in the reproduction cluster of The Spectrum promotes development of motor skills and techniques which are representative of the physical development channel. The learning aims and objectives in relation to learning tennis, however, equally demands development in the cognitive channel which refers to thinking capacity (e.g. knowledge of tactics, strategies and decision making during game-play); the emotional channel which highlights motivation, self-reliance, tolerance and self-regulation among other attributes and also the social development channel. This domain incorporates human attributes including, communication, teamwork, negotiation and patience. As no one teaching style encompasses all learning eventualities, an effective coach must have the capacity to select, change, combine and transition between various teaching styles during sessions. This chapter will explore a range of teaching styles from The Spectrum and provide a series of practical tennis games and play practices that appeal to the holistic development of tennis players in a variety of learning domains. Finally, this chapter is framed from the perspective of the sports coach as educator (Jones, 2006). This narrative positions the coach as a professional with a primary role as an educator and an expert guide in the learning process. From this viewpoint, the sports coach and PE teacher share a common ambition that encapsulates sport teaching pedagogy.

It is suggested that "the coach occupies a position of centrality and considerable influence in efforts to improve sporting performance" (Lyle & Cushion, 2010, p. 43). A coach's actions affects players' "behavior, cognitions and affective responses, and coaches can influence whether athletes learn and achieve at a high level, enjoy their experience, demonstrate effort and persistence, and develop a sense of confidence and self-determined motivational orientation" (Amorose, 2007, p. 33). If coaching is not provided in a correct or appropriate manner the outcomes may result in poor performance, low self-esteem, and high levels of competitive anxiety or burnout (Amorose, 2007). Consequently, it has been acknowledged that the words and actions of coaches impact not only on performance but also on the social and emotional well-being and perceptions of the players they are coaching (Miller, 1992; Jones, Housner & Kornspan, 1995; Horn, 2002). Coaching has physical, affective, cognitive, behavioural and social features that ultimately impact on the practices of coaches (Lyle & Cushion, 2010). Provided that the coach's professional intervention is multidimensional and achieved in diverse contexts of practice, it necessitates widespread knowledge and capabilities, adjusted to the specific conditions of the practice environment (Abraham & Collins, 1998; Pill, 2016). Learning tennis is a measured procedure that involves realising the most appropriate movement patterns related to game situations. The challenges that tennis players encounter are comprehensive. They are required to learn a variety of physical movements and techniques in addition to attending to which environmental cues are significant and which are redundant in order to selectively concentrate on the most pertinent information. Players need to choose techniques and tactics that will provide them with the optimal opportunity to win a point in addition to accurately coordinate movement patterns that will effectively accomplish these selected tactics (Hewitt, Pill & McDonald, 2018; Pill, 2017).

Much has been written about the various instructional practices and behaviours available for coaches to employ during coaching sessions (Lyle & Cushion, 2010). Traditionally, the educational association between coach and player has been "largely autocratic and prescriptive in nature" (Jones, 2006, p. 43). Under these instructional conditions, the coach has been considered as the "sole source of knowledge and has been responsible for the unidirectional transmission of this information to athletes who have adopted a largely passive role in the teaching and learning process" (Jones, 2006, p. 43). However, as diverse learning conditions and experiences are often created by employing different teaching styles, the necessity for coaches to understand and implement purposefully a variety of teaching styles to achieve learning outcomes would seem paramount. Coaches must be prepared to cater for the diversity of players' learning needs, interests, preferences and developmental readiness or stage of learning. Additionally, tennis involves learning aims and objectives from the psychomotor (physical/motor skill), cognitive (decision making) and affective (emotions and feelings) domains. This might indicate the application of specific teaching styles to develop each learning area comprehensively. Regrettably, research suggests that these considerations often do not occur (Hewitt, Edwards & Pill, 2016; Hewitt, Edwards, Ashworth & Pill, 2016). This chapter will now explore and illustrate a range of teaching styles from The Spectrum and provide a series of practical tennis games and play practices that appeal to the holistic development of tennis players in a variety of learning domains.

Practice style – in practice

Coaches have been encouraged to select teaching styles that harmonise with a number of considerations and the intent of their instruction. For instance, there may be occasions when coaches want players to achieve consistency with regard to the execution of motor responses. In these instances, the coach might be more concerned with repetition of practice activities, developing the capacity to produce a motor response and individual learning than they are with more complex cognitive constructed learning or socialisation outcomes. In this case, implementing Practice Style located in the reproduction cluster might be considered most appropriate. Goldberger and others (2012) have suggested that Landmark Practice Style and its many associated canopy designs on The Spectrum (Mosston & Ashworth, 2008), presents a highly effective teaching style in achieving basic motor acquisition (Goldberger et al., 2012). The guiding features of Practice Style include the development of independent and private practice of a memory/reproduction task with an emphasis on repetition of practice while receiving private feedback from the teacher (Mosston & Ashworth, 2008). Figure 6.1 outlines the anatomy of decisions relating to Practice Style.

A practical example of Practice Style, is described and illustrated in Figure 6.2 with the game 'Crosscourt Chargers'. In this game, players are provided with task instructions from the coach in the pre-impact or planning phase of the session. The task is for players to practice hitting forehand groundstrokes in a crosscourt direction. Players are then requested to practice this task(s) during the impact or implementation phase, while the teacher provides private feedback in relation to the performance of these movements in the post-impact or feedback and assessment phase.

- **Pre-impact (planning)**: The coach makes all subject matter and logistical decisions about the task;
- **Impact (implementation)**: The player privately practices the memory/reproduction task. The player practices hitting a forehand groundstroke in a crosscourt direction. Players determine the starting time for the task, the pace and rhythm and the initiation of questions to the coach for clarification; and
- **Post-impact (feedback and assessment)**: During the implementation phase, the coach circulates and provides private feedback to each player in regard to how they are performing the task i.e., observing their performance and ability to hit a forehand groundstroke in a crosscourt direction, and assisting players to achieve this outcome.

Figure 6.1 The anatomy of decisions of Practice Style

'Crosscourt Chargers'

Organisational layout: Players form pairs and are positioned at opposite ends of the court

Practice task: To hit the ball using a forehand groundstroke in a crosscourt direction

1. Players form pairs and are positioned at opposite ends of the court;
2. Player 1 commences the rally with a drop hit or overarm serve in a crosscourt (diagonal) direction;
3. Each player practices hitting a forehand groundstroke in a crosscourt direction to a partner in a cooperative rally;
4. Player's keep an individual and private tally of how many times they are able to successfully perform the practice task; and
5. The coach provides individual and private feedback to each player.

During this activity, the coach is making all the decisions in relation to the performed task in addition to the feedback and assessment. However, players are afforded some level of decision making during the impact or implementation phase. These include:

1. Determining the starting time for each task;
2. The pace and rhythm for each task; and
3. Initiating questions to the coach for the clarification of each task.

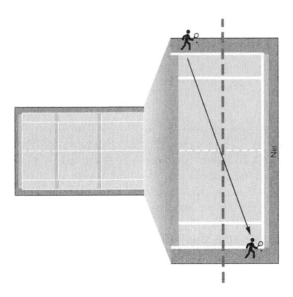

Figure 6.2 Practice Style and 'Crosscourt Chargers'

While the application of Practice Style caters primarily to the physical development channel, the game of tennis – as previously indicated – also requires players to think, make decisions and solve tactical and strategical problems. Therefore, if coaches wish to enhance and develop the independent decision-making ability of players to discover new and novel responses, the implementation of teaching styles located in the production cluster of The Spectrum might serve as an appropriate pedagogical practice. In this instance, activating learning in the cognitive development channel becomes the priority. This notion is supported by Goldberger and others (2012) in highlighting the requirement for coaches to adopt appropriate teaching styles to cater for the requirements of a particular learning domain or development channel. An illustration of how coaches may activate learning in this development channel will now be explored.

Divergent Discovery – in practice

The central features of Divergent Discovery Style develops the player's cognitive capacity to produce multiple solutions to the same question or series of unknown and new situations (Mosston & Ashworth, 2008). Figure 6.3 illustrates the anatomy of decisions associated with Divergent Discovery Style.

A practical application of Divergent Discovery Style is described and illustrated in Figure 6.4 with the game 'Triple Treat'. In this game, players are provided with a question or problem from the coach – "How can you set up an attack and win the point from the net?" in the pre-impact or planning phase of the session. Players are then requested to produce multiple discovered solutions to the problem in the impact or implementation phase, and then engage in self-assessment of these solutions under observation of the coach in the post-impact or feedback and assessment phase.

'Triple Treat'

Organisational layout: Players form pairs and are positioned at opposite ends of the court

- **Pre-impact (planning):** The coach makes the decision about the specific subject matter and divergent question to be posed to the players;
- **Impact (implementation):** The player produces multiple solutions to the problem/question. Players attempt to solve the divergent question posed by the coach and produce multiple solutions to the problem/question stated above; and
- **Post-impact (feedback and assessment):** The player engages in self-assessment of the multiple solutions to the problem/question, while the coach offers neutral feedback about the player's responses.

Figure 6.3 The anatomy of decisions of Divergent Discovery Style

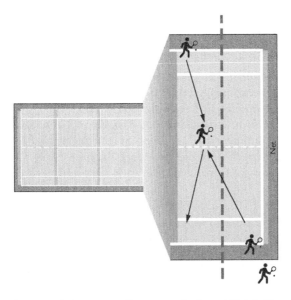

Figure 6.4 Divergent Discovery Style and 'Triple Treat'

Divergent question: "How do you set up an attack to win the point at the net?"

1. Players form pairs and are positioned at opposite ends of the court;
2. Player 1 commences the rally with a drop hit or overarm serve;
3. Players rally the ball until an error is made;
4. Players are awarded 3 points if they successfully win the point as a result of the volley;
5. Players alternate commencing the point; and
6. Play first to 12 points or until teacher calls "time".

Inclusion Style – in practice

Effective coaches have the ability to "tailor their content and instruction to the specific learning readiness and interests of their students, by integrating concepts and implementing teaching strategies that are responsive to the students' diverse needs" (Lyle & Cushion, 2010, p. 52). Arguably, the most vital coach behaviour "corresponds with the athlete's developmental needs and individual particularities" (Lyle & Cushion, 2010, p. 52). One concept that advocates the development of coaching content, practices and behaviours specifically designed to cater to player needs is the notion of differentiation (Graham, 1995; Tomlinson, 1995; Tomlinson, 1999). According to the differentiated instructional model (Tomlinson, 1999), coaches "respond to the needs of all learners, with consideration being given to the student's

> - **Pre-impact (planning):** The coach makes all the subject matter decisions, including the different levels of difficulty and entry points for the player;
> - **Impact (implementation):** The player selects the appropriate entry point or level of challenge provided by the coach. These choices are outlined above in the pre-impact (planning) phase; and
> - **Post-impact (feedback and assessment):** The coach circulates to observe, clarify and confirm the accuracy of the player's choices and assessment. The coach does not necessarily suggest entry point changes but rather engages in conversation with the player regarding their choices.

Figure 6.5 The anatomy of decisions of Inclusion Style

readiness, interest, and capabilities" (Whipp, Taggart, & Jackson, 2012, p. 2). Similarly, Vygotsky (1997) stated that "the fundamental prerequisite of pedagogics inevitably demands an element of individualization, that is, conscious and rigorous determination of individualized goals" (Vygotsky, 1997, p. 324). Lyle and Cushion (2010) argued that this notion of "responsiveness to diversity rather than imposition of sameness in coaching" (p. 52) has yet to pervade entirely the practices of coaches, with many adopting a *one size fits all* approach to coaching players (Lyle & Cushion, 2010). This viewpoint translates to a reduced collaboration between the coach and the player. However, the players' circumstances and contexts are not necessarily all the same, therefore a *one size fits all* approach may not suffice as an effective instructional guideline (Amorose, 2007). The provision of activities, games and tasks with equivalent entry points and challenges designed for all students may only serve to accentuate what players of limited ability cannot 'do'. Similarly, it may simultaneously disengage players that possess abilities beyond this particular challenge point. Inclusion Style is specifically designed to promote the innumerable capabilities and differences of all players.

The defining characteristics of this style are inclusion and participation of students in the same task. Tasks are designed with multiple levels of challenge whereby players examine the levels of difficulty then select an entry point to practice – making adjustments of their respective choices where appropriate. In this style, no one is excluded and every player is afforded the opportunity for continued participation (Mosston & Ashworth, 2008). The anatomy of decisions applied to Inclusion Style are outlined in Figure 6.5.

Inclusion Style and game modification – in practice

An example of Inclusion Style can be applied to the game 'Triple Treat' outlined in Figure 6.4. As indicated in this game, players have been provided with the divergent question of "How do you set up an attack to win the point from the net?". Applying the principles of Inclusion Style, the coach provides a series of prescribed levels of difficulty for players to engage in. The pedagogical feature called game modification that occurs by exaggeration or reduction of certain game elements provides a platform to manipulate the various levels of difficulty to enhance players' participation. The CHANGE IT formula associated with the Game Sense teaching approach (Schembri, 2005) presents as an appropriate tool that complements the features of Inclusion Style. This formula describes the different task, performer and environmental constraints that can be modified by "eliminating, refining, or adding to game rules and playing conditions to focus attention on specific technical or tactical game understanding" (Pill, 2013, p. 9). The words – CHANGE IT – represent an acronym of which each letter describes how an aspect of a game or activity may be altered. For instance, the letter 'E' in the CHANGE IT formula (Schembri, 2005) denotes equipment, and how this element of the learning environment might be changed. Similarly, the letter 'A' represents the size and shape of the playing area for games and activities. These considerations, among others, also provide a platform for coaches to increase and decrease the level of complexity that formulate a range of entry points and levels of challenge for players to choose from. In this way, coaches can apply the principles of Inclusion Style and the notion of providing player choice of challenge points by formulating these differentiated game constraints as options for players to choose their entry point. In the game 'Triple Treat' (Figure 6.4), for instance, whereas in the common form of tennis the ball is only permitted to bounce once in the court, players may be offered the choice of one or two bounces to play the ball based on where they determine their entry point lies during the game. Alternatively, players may have the option of first tapping the ball with the racquet to first control the ball, with or without letting the tapped ball bounce after being hit to gain control, before returning the ball to their opponent. Similarly, players may choose a lower compression ball – which travels through the air slower – in order to increase time to obtain a balanced body position prior to returning the ball over the net. Eliminating racquets in favour of throwing and catching the ball during the game presents as another entry level choice for players who may not have the physical or technical abilities to fulfil the tactical objectives of the game.

Shifting decisions to create new learning and teaching episodes

The three examples of Practice Style, Divergent Discovery Style and Inclusion Style described and illustrated in this chapter so far have been presented as isolated styles during two games with the outcome to appeal to the respective and specific learning outcomes and relevant development channel to be promoted. However, each example has the capacity to adjust its objective and decision distribution and apply an alternative style in an attempt to cater for a new learning and teaching episode. Individual teaching styles may be implemented for an entire session, or alternatively, a range of styles represented by smaller teaching episodes, might be deemed appropriate to apply during a coaching session – all conditional to the session objectives. This point is apparent in the game 'Triple Treat' (Figure 6.4). Players can be provided with a divergent question designed to promote problem-solving and solutions to new and unknown knowledge, however, the features of Inclusion Style were infused into this episode to allow for all students to participate in the task – regardless of their individual physical capabilities. Goldberger and colleagues refer to this shifting of styles as 'mobility ability', or "the skill of easily moving from one teaching style to another as circumstances suggest" (Goldberger et al., 2012, p. 274).

A teaching style in which the learner makes all the decisions and the teacher or coach "serves as more of a resource" (Goldberger et al., 2012, p. 270) is the teaching style, Self Teaching Style. A practical example of this teaching style might be a tennis student who decides to participate in a self-developed practice routine based on knowledge acquired in a formal tennis coaching session. For instance, practicing the tennis serve against a wall at the local park. According to Goldberger and others, these two end styles (where teacher makes all decisions (Command Style) and learner makes all decisions (Self Teaching Style) are definitive and universal. Between these bookend styles, Mosston thoughtfully and deliberately shifted the sets of decisions between teacher and learner to form different teaching styles (Mosston, 1966; Goldberger et al., 2012, p. 271).

A different and new teaching style is therefore distinguished when a profoundly different teacher-learner relationship emerges. For instance, Practice Style was "revealed to Mosston when a particular set of decisions was shifted to the learner" (Mosston & Ashworth, 2008, p. 271). This specific construction of decisions that shifts to the learner does not alter the episode's objective. The learner continues in their endeavour to copy the routine as provided by the teacher or coach. It does, however, "provide each learner with some personalised 'wiggle' room or options about how this is accomplished (e.g. making the decision about pace/rhythm, starting time, posture)" (Mosston & Ashworth, 2008, p. 271). The example provided in the following paragraph contrasts a Practice Style teaching episode with a Reciprocal Style teaching episode and the shift in decisions from coach to player resulting in altered outcomes in development channels. In the case of tennis, the coach may wish to shift from Practice Style to Reciprocal Style to promote, enhance and develop a player's emotional and social skills. These outcomes are distinguished by the objectives of Practice Style which has a particular emphasis on the physical development channel.

- **Pre-impact (planning):** The coach makes all the subject matter, criteria and logistical decisions prior to commencement of the session;
- **Impact (implementation):** The players work in a partnership relationship with one as the 'doer' who performs the task while the other player is the 'observer' who is providing immediate and on-going feedback to the 'doer' in regard to the accuracy of the task's criteria checklist provided by the coach; and
- **Post-impact (feedback and assessment):** The coach circulates and provides players with private feedback and assessment statements to the observer in relation to their role.

Figure 6.6 The anatomy of decisions of Reciprocal Style

Practice Style to Reciprocal Style – in practice

The next teaching style located on The Spectrum (Mosston & Ashworth, 2008) following Practice Style is Reciprocal Style. The guiding features of Reciprocal Style positions a priority on the social and emotional development channels. In contrast to the principle learning objectives of Practice Style, the development of physical skills is not identified as the key learning objective. Some of the specific human attributes being developed when shifting decisions from Practice Style to Reciprocal Style entail:

1. Players expand their socialisation and interaction skills;
2. Players learn to give and receive feedback from peers;
3. Players develop patience, tolerance and acceptance of others' differences in performance;
4. Players develop empathy and social manners; and
5. Players practice the task without the coach.

The defining characteristic of Reciprocal Style consists of social interaction while learning to provide and receive feedback. In this case, a player assesses another player's performance (i.e. a partner). This is achieved through a performance criteria checklist provided by the coach (Mosston & Ashworth, 2008). Figure 6.6 outlines the anatomy of decisions relating to Reciprocal Style.

In the shifting of decisions between Practice Style and Reciprocal Style, the "decision transfer occurs in the post-impact set of decisions" (Mosston & Ashworth, 2008, p. 271), or the feedback and assessment phase of the episode. An example will now be provided to illustrate the shifting of decisions between Practice Style and Reciprocal Style. In this example we will use game 'Triple Treat' (Figure 6.4). In this game, players are now provided with a performance criteria checklist (Table 6.1).

Table 6.1 Performance criteria checklist of the forehand volley

Order	Skill Criteria	Always	Sometimes	Rarely
a	• Assume a basic ready position • Non-hitting hand supporting the throat of the racquet			
b	• Compact backswing with initial turn of the shoulders • Racquet face in line with the path of the ball • Non-hitting arm used for balance			
c	• Racquet face behind the ball to meet the ball • Step toward the contact point with opposite leg			
d	• Racquet face is vertical through the contact zone • Contact occurs in front of the body while the body moves forward • Head remains stable and eyes focused on the contact point			
e	• Wrist and forearm remain stable • Racquet follows a path towards the target			
f	• Achieve a balanced recovery and ready position			

During the game – whereby players are attempting to set up an attack by winning the point from the net as a result of a volley – one player is observing the performance of the other player (the 'doer') to perform the technical movements associated with the forehand volley. The performance criteria checklist, seen in Table 6.1 provides the 'observer' with both a visual representation pertaining to the key biomechanical movements associated with each stage of the forehand volley in addition to a written description of the actions. After each point or series of points, the 'observer' offers assessment based on the criteria checklist provided by the coach. Players then alternate roles. Reciprocal Style is not limited to providing an avenue for offering feedback, as it also presents opportunities for "social development as the partners systematically 'help' each other within a constructive relationship to learn the task at hand. Giving and accepting feedback are important social skills that can be learned and practiced" (Mosston & Ashworth, 2008, p. 271). While there might exist numerous references to behaviour that implies Reciprocal Style, the vast majority represent Practice Style with a partner relationship (Mosston & Ashworth, 2008). Many of these teaching episodes do not comprise teacher or coach criteria that serves to guide observation, feedback or communication skills in a reciprocal relationship (Mosston & Ashworth, 2008). This is also illustrated in SueSee, Edwards and Pill (2016) examination of the Game Sense approach through the lens of The Spectrum.

This chapter has presented a variety of tennis games and play practices adhering to the guiding principles of a range of teaching styles on The Spectrum. Each of these styles serve to promote players in a variety of development channels. As tennis involves learning aims and objectives from the physical, cognitive, emotional and social development channels, it would seem highly applicable to foreground the implementation of a range of teaching styles to promote a comprehensive and holistic understanding of the game to players during coaching sessions. It is advocated that the behaviour of coaches act as an avenue to link player understanding to the content presented in the session (Hall & Smith, 2006). Consequently, it is crucial that coaches "consider the objectives of the session, so that he or she can determine whether given behaviours are relevant to the task" (Lyle & Cushion, 2010, p. 52). The Spectrum provides a continuum of teaching styles for coaches to enact these objectives and to maximise progress in the various learning domains. While this chapter has focused on tennis as the vehicle to explore the pedagogical descriptions of The Spectrum, the theoretical sentiments described can be applied to a range of other sports and PE endeavours.

References

Abraham, A., & Collins, D. (1998). Examining and extending research in coach development. *Quest, 50,* 59–79.

Amorose, A. J. (2007). Coaching effectiveness: exploring the relationship between coaching behaviour and self-determined motivation. In M. S. Hagger & N. L. D. Chatzisarantis (Eds.), *Intrinsic motivation and self-determination in exercise and sport* (pp. 209–227). Champaign, IL: Human Kinetics.

Cushion, C. J. (2010). Coach Behaviour. In J. Lyle & C. Cushion (Eds.), *Sports coaching: Professionalism and practice.* London: Churchill Livingstone, Elsevier.

Goldberger, M., Ashworth, S., & Byra, M. (2012). Spectrum of teaching styles retrospective 2012. *Quest* (64), 268–282.

Graham, G. (1995). Physical education through students' eyes and in students' voices. *Journal of Teaching in Physical Education,* 14(4), 364–371.

Hall, T. J., & Smith, M. A. (2006). Teacher planning and reflection: What we know about teacher cognitive processes. *Quest, 58,* pp. 424–442.

Hewitt, M. (2015). *Teaching styles of Australian tennis coaches: An exploration of practices and insights using Mosston and Ashworth's Spectrum of Teaching Styles.* Unpublished doctoral thesis dissertation. University of Southern Queensland.

Hewitt, M., Edwards, K., Ashworth, S., & Pill, S. (2016). Investigating the teaching styles of tennis coaches using the Spectrum. *Sport Science Review,* 25(5/6), 321–344.

Hewitt, M., Edwards, K., & Pill, S. (2016). Exploring tennis coaches' insights in relation to their teaching styles. *Baltic Journal of Sport and Health Science,* 102(3), 30–43.

Hewitt, M., Pill, S., & McDonald, R. (2018). Informing Game Sense Pedagogy with a Constraints-Led Perspective for Teaching Tennis in Schools. *Ágora para la Educación Física y el Deporte, 20*(1), 46–67.

Horn, T. S. (2002). Coaching effectiveness in the sport domain. In T. S. Horn (Ed.), *Advances in sport psychology* (pp. 309–354). Champaign, IL: Human Kinetics.

Jones, R. L. (2006). *The sports coach as educator: Re-conceptualising sports coaching.* London: Routledge.

Jones, D. F., Housner, L. D., & Kornspan, A.S. (1995). A comparative analysis of expert and novice basketball coaches' practice planning. *Applied Research in Coaching and Athletics Annual, 10,* 201–226.

Lyle, J., & Cushion, C. (Eds.). (2010). *Sports coaching: Professionalisation and practice.* Edinburgh: Churchill Livingston Elsevier.

Miller, A. W. (1992). Systematic observation behaviour similarities of various youth sport soccer coaches. *Physical Education 49*(3), 136–143.

Mosston, M. (1966). *Teaching physical education.* Columbus, OH: Merrill.

Mosston, M., & Ashworth, S. (2008). *Teaching physical education* (1st ed.). Online: Spectrum Institute for Teaching and Learning. Retrieved from: www.spectrum ofteachingstyles.org/e-book-download.php

Pill, S. (2013). *Play with Purpose – Game sense to sport literacy, Edition 3.* Hindmarsh, SA. ACHPER publications.

Pill, S. (2017). Taking theory into coaching practice: Teaching tennis using a game sense approach. *International Journal of Physical Education: A Review Publication, 54*(2), 13–25.

Pill, S. (2016). Implementing game sense coaching approach in Australian football through action research. *Agora for Physical Education and Sport, 18*(1), 1–19.

Rieber, R. W. (Ed.) (1997). *The collected works of L.S Vygotsky, vol 4: The history of the development of higher mental functions.* New York, NY: Plenum Press.

Schembri, G. (2005). *Playing for life: Coach's guide.* Canberra, ACT: Australian Sports Commission.

SueSee, B., Pill, S., Edwards, K. (2016). Reconciling approaches – a game centred approach to sport teaching and Mosston's spectrum of teaching styles. *European Journal of Physical Education and Sport Science, 2*(4), 69–86.

Tomlinson, C. A. (1995). Deciding to differentiate instruction in middle school: One school's journey. *Gifted Child Journal, 39*(2), 77–87.

Tomlinson, C. A. (1999). *The differentiated classroom: Responding to the needs of all learners.* Alexandria, VA: Association for Supervision and Curriculum Development.

Whipp, P., Taggart, A., & Jackson, B. (2012). Differentiation in outcome – physical education: pedagogical rhetoric and reality. *Physical Education and Sport Pedagogy, 7*(12), 1–11.

Chapter 7

Reconciling approaches

Mosston and Ashworth's Spectrum of Teaching Styles as a tool to examine the complexity of any teaching (or coaching) approach

Brendan SueSee, Shane Pill and Mitch Hewitt

In recent years, constraints-led theory has gained popularity within the field of sports coaching, motor learning and physical education. Briefly, it contends that skill acquisition occurs as a result of the interaction between constraints morphology, emotions, cognition, intentions, environment, task and rules. It is then the teacher or coach's job to manipulate the constraints to facilitate the emergence of movement patterns and decision making (Chow et al., 2006). Within a constraints-led approach (CLA) there is also an expectation that physical educators need to implement a variety of constraints to help learners search for successful movement solutions, along with an assumption that discovery learning takes place to overcome or adapt to the constraint (Renshaw et al., 2010). Constraints-led theory has been a useful addition to explanations of practice design. Our purpose is to examine two CLA learning episodes and to identify the decisions being made between the teacher and student/s. This will then allow these two constraints-led learning episodes to be placed on The Spectrum. By doing this it will detail important pedagogical concepts and pedagogical decision making. The chapter adopts a similar structure to SueSee, Pill and Edwards (2016) examination of a Game Sense approach teaching episode using The Spectrum.

This chapter aims to reveal some of the complexities of a CLA using The Spectrum. It does not pit The Spectrum against a CLA. Rather, it demonstrates the value of The Spectrum as a lens through which teachers, mentors and teacher educators may view the complexity of any teaching (or coaching) approach. In viewing two examples (or learning experiences) of a CLA through The Spectrum, we hypothetically examine the decision making taking place in the episodes between the teacher and the learner/s, the intent of these decisions and the language used during the episode. In line with The Spectrum ideology, it will be done from a non-versus perspective in that no judgement will be made about the value of the learning experiences in comparison to other teaching styles or approaches.

The Spectrum

The structure of The Spectrum (Mosston & Ashworth, 2008) is underpinned by the central premise that every deliberate act of teaching is a result of a previous decision. Mosston organised these many possible decisions into three main sets that comprise the *Anatomy of any Style*. These sets are identified as: 1) *pre-impact set*; 2) *impact set*; and 3) *post-impact set*. The *pre-impact set* involves making decisions in relation to the planning of the teacher-learner interaction. The *impact set* relates to implementation of the decisions that occur during the teacher-learner face-to-face interaction. The *post- impact set* refers to assessment decisions that can occur at any point during the face-to-face interaction by either the teacher or the learner (Mosston & Ashworth, 2008). By identifying who (i.e. the teacher or learner) makes which decisions, the 11 teaching styles emerge (Figure 7.1).

One of the key aspects relating to the use of various teaching styles is matching the appropriate style to the intended learning outcome(s) of the lesson. Each teaching style has strengths and limitations that can render it more or less beneficial to pupil learning. As Mosston (1992) summarised: "the fundamental issue in teaching is not which style is better or best, but rather which style is appropriate for reaching the objectives of a given episode. Every style has a place in the multiple realities of teaching and learning" (Mosston, 1992, p. 28).

Furthermore, The Spectrum suggests the capacity for *production* and *reproduction* should be viewed as complementary rather than mutually exclusive. For instance, after a learner has discovered how to apply spin to a forehand

---

Teaching Styles

Command (A)
Practice (B)
Reciprocal (C)
Self-Check (D)
Inclusion (E)
Guided Discovery (F)
Convergent Discovery (G)
Divergent Discovery (H)
Learner-Designed Individual Program (I)
Learner-Initiated (J)
Self-Teaching (K)

Figure 7.1 The 11 teaching styles on The Spectrum

Source: Reprint from Teaching Physical Education First Online Edition, 2008 are used with permission from Dr. Sara Ashworth, Director of the Spectrum Institute. Free Digital Download Available at: https://spectrumofteachingstyles.org/index.php?id=16

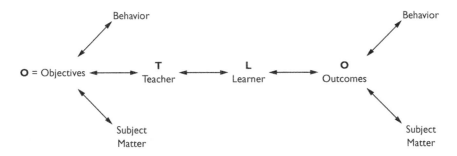

Figure 7.2 The Pedagogical Unit: O-T-L-O

Source: Reprint from Teaching Physical Education First Online Edition, 2008 are used with permission from Dr. Sara Ashworth, Director of the Spectrum Institute. Free Digital Download Available at: https://spectrumofteachingstyles.org/index.php?id=16

groundstroke in tennis (Convergent Discovery) a sufficient volume of repetition will be required to master the skill (Practice Style). The Spectrum theory suggests that the interface that exists between the teacher (or coach) and the learner always reflects a specific teaching behaviour, learning behaviour as well as particular sets of objectives that are achieved (Mosston & Ashworth, 2008). Each teaching style episode comprises its own "objectives, teaching and learning behaviour, and outcomes" (Goldberger, Ashworth & Byra, 2012, p. 277). This relationship is shown in Figure 7.2.

Objectives (O) represent the intent of the episode with regards to content. The Teaching-Learning behaviour (T-L) outlines the interaction between the teacher and learner during the mastery of the content. The Outcome (O) relates to the extent the objectives were accomplished. These components are referred to as a "pedagogical unit" (Mosston & Ashworth, 2008, p. 15).

The Spectrum therefore rests on the NON-VERSUS notion. That is, each style has its place in reaching a specific set of objectives; hence, no style, by itself, is better or best" (Mosston, 1981, p. viii). Therefore, while it is acknowledged that The Spectrum does not identify a teaching style called Game Centred, Game Based, or CLA, The Spectrum does have the capacity to recognise and identify any teaching, coaching and learning behaviour. This notion is based on The Spectrum's premise that all teaching behaviour is about decision making.

A constraints-led approach

The study of movement behaviour has often been explained by a 'motor program' metaphor. This suggests that an abstract representation of movement stored in the performers' brain organises and directs the motor behaviour of a performer. The conceptual viewpoint of a motor program metaphor can be considered in terms of what directs motor development: that is, information processing. Input from the performance environment is processed using the stored information (the motor program) in the performer's brain to determine a motor response. Feedback from perception of the results of the motor behaviour provide information that can be contrasted and/or integrated with the existing stored information to refine or alter the stored motor program (Gallahue, Ozman & Goodway, 2012). The motor program metaphor suggests one can only perform on the basis of the motor program that the individual has developed.

An alternative to the 'motor program' metaphor is the 'constraints' metaphor. The constraints metaphor suggests information transactions between a performer and their environment direct the motor behaviour of a performer. Motor behaviour is emergent and dynamic, shaped by the interaction between three categories of constraints – performer (the organism), environment and task. The dynamic interaction between the three categories of constraints 'tune' a functional relationship between movement and information in the specific situated momentary dynamics of the environment. This is called information-movement coupling (Anson, Elliott & Davids, 2005). Motor behaviour in a CLA is therefore considered to emerge from the interaction of the constraints.

Constraints are, therefore, like the boundaries which shape the emergence of motor behaviour. The interaction of constraints 'forces' the performer, through a self-organising process, to stable and effective motor behaviour. A key underpinning of a CLA perspective is the mutuality of the performer and the environment (Davids, Araujo, Shuttleworth & Button, 2003; Renshaw, Chow, Davids & Hammond, 2009). The pedagogical emphasis in a CLA in physical education (PE) is therefore the linking of information in the environment to game behaviour in a representative manner (Rankin, Pill & Magias, 2018). PE teachers must then be able to identify key information sources that students can use in specific performance contexts, and structure practice so that this information is available so performers can attune their movements to the information sources – creating effective information-movement couplings to guide performers' motor behaviour. Some CLA advocates indicate that the purpose of implementing relevant constraints in a practice environment in PE is to help students effectively 'search' for successful movement solutions – a 'discovery approach' (Renshaw et al., 2009).

The concept of a 'representative task' is central in a CLA. Representative tasks are those which allow the player to be able to use the same information sources (visual cues) in practice tasks as are present in the game to contextualise decisions and motor behaviour in practice situations. This contextualisation of practice means movement behaviour in practice tasks replicates the demands of movement enactment in the performance contexts, which is known as action fidelity (Krause et al., 2018). With this perspective, movement skill is seen as an emergence of an adaptive functional relationship between the performer and the practice environment (Araujo & Davids, 2011; Chow & Atencio, 2014).

The CLA perspective has been linked to the concept of purposeful game modification and the pedagogy of deliberate use of astute questions by teachers to create a 'guided discovery' style of teaching in sport coaching and PE settings where game-based approaches, such as Teaching Games for Understanding (TGfU) and the Game Sense approach, are used. Specifically, in game-based approaches, game modification occurs by exaggeration, elimination or simplification of conditions of the game, which can be explained by a CLA perspective (Breed & Spittle, 2011; Chow et al., 2007; Gill et al., 2014; Pill, 2013; 2014; Rankin et al., 2018; Tan, Chow & Davids, 2012). However, it has been suggested that the effective manipulation of task constraints to encourage the emergence of desirable movement solutions requires physical educators with mastery of knowledge of games, sport and physical activity (Renshaw, Chow, Davids & Hammond, 2010), which may make use of the CLA beyond the pedagogical capability of the 'average' PE teacher. A claim also made for game-based approaches such as TGfU (Launder, 2001).

Discussion

Two examples of a CLA will now be examined using The Spectrum to identify the decision making that is occurring. In particular, who is making the decisions, when the decisions are being made and the intent of these

Table 7.1 A 3 v 1 CLA learning experience for an invasion game (Adapted from Chow & Atencio, 2014, p. 1048)

Emphasis	Activity	Features of complex and non-linear pedagogical approach
Modified game with an emphasis on invasion	X1 Y1 Direction of attack X2 X3	Territorial gains and invasion into opponents' territory. Key aspects of territorial game present. Situated in a game setting. Task manipulation (overload condition of greater number of attackers to defenders; five passes before the ball can be played across the end line) to encourage passing behaviours but non-prescriptive. Lots of variability in a situated setting. Many possible states of behaviours can emerge in this game setting. *Non-proportional changes* to be expected. (e.g. slight movement off the ball can create huge opportunities for a pass or none at all depending on positions of players involved in the game). Students asked to reflect and consider how offensive and defensive roles differed, as well as specific movements, techniques and understandings that emerged. Possible prompting could involve how the complex learning system changes when the physical space is modified.

decisions will be considered. In line with Spectrum theory, we will do this from a 'non- versus' perspective in that evaluative suggestions about the episodes being 'good' or 'bad' will not be made. Evidence will be presented to support the claims based on the places where decisions are being made (*pre-impact, impact and post-impact*) and by who (teacher or student/s) and about what. We are not suggesting that the two examples we are providing are the best or the worst that a CLA can offer. We have chosen the examples more as a representation of a typical CLA in the extant literature.

Episode 1. In the previous learning episode (Table 7.1), the teacher has decided that the student/players need to develop the skill of invasion in a 3 v 1 scenario. The teacher may explain that the players will play in the rectangle (environment constraint). A team of 3 will pass the ball and move the ball from one end of the grid to the opposite end (task constraint). Presuming the activity is football the team of 1 (the defender) will attempt to stop the ball from moving into and across their end line. Student X2 stands between two markers which are approximately five meters wide and student X3 does the same (task constraint). The teacher applies conditions such as no handling the ball (as opposed to pushing it), or the stick head cannot leave the ball before it is pushed (all task constraints). Students then attempt to solve the problem of how to score a goal while playing the game.

When this episode is viewed through The Spectrum lens, the decisions which are being made are represented in Figure 7.3.

In this learning experience (Figure 7.3), the teacher chooses the subject matter in the pre-impact set. During the impact set the players are most likely

---

- Pre-impact: – Teacher chooses subject matter (move the ball from one end to the other – attacking 3. Attempt to stop the ball moving into and across their end line-defender).
- Impact set: – Students practice passing or dribbling a ball the way they have before. They were not instructed by the teacher to 'discover' or 'create' a way to propel the ball which they have not done before. They were most likely told: "The aim of this game is to pass the ball over your opponent's line/goal."
- The subject matter is passing the ball over the opponent's line or defending the line.
- Students may be stopped during the impact set and asked questions using a Guided Discovery approach as the text says to 'reflect and consider' and 'possible prompting' (Chow & Atencio, 2014, p. 1048) to help students identify problems experienced.
- Post impact: – Teacher may give feedback about answers to questions, or may ask questions related to the task manipulation.

Figure 7.3 The Spectrum analysis of a CLA

using a technique or method to pass or dribble the ball that they have used before. Whether that technique or method is with their toes, the instep of their foot or the outside of their foot, it will likely be a technique they have used before. This is assumed as the teacher did not ask or direct the students to "create a way to pass or dribble the ball which you have not used before". If the teacher did ask the students to create, it could be suggested that they were directing the student to use creativity as the dominant cognitive operation. However, in the situation described, the teacher does not instruct the student to use creativity. If the student has used a method which they have not used before, it could be claimed that creativity was used. However, as the teacher has not directed the student to use creativity or discovery then the teacher cannot claim to have instructed the student/s to use these cognitive operations. Therefore, if the student has used one of these cognitive operations it is due to their free will and not due to the teacher decision.

Viewed through The Spectrum lens, it may be argued that the terminology or instructions being used is broad or non-specific about the cognitive direction they wish the player/s to take and the subject matter in the form of the motor pattern required to perform the task. For example, the teacher has not asked the player/s to reproduce any subject matter (i.e. "Pass or dribble the ball like this") but to "Pass the ball and move the ball from one end of grid to opposite end", suggesting that this is the subject matter and any method is acceptable as long as it is within the constraints established. Similarly with the defender whose instructions were, "attempt to stop ball from moving into and across their end line". These instructions do not suggest using any technique specifically (the foot is presumed) so it is unlikely they would attempt to discover or create a new way. We believe that it is reasonable to suggest that the player/s will be practicing a method of passing or moving the ball which they knew before the lesson. The player/s are still making the decision, that is to reproduce subject matter deciding on pace, rhythm, amount of passes, as they would in Practice Style. After the students have passed the ball the scenario indicates that the teacher is likely to offer feedback about how the task was performed. This is also in line with the characteristics of Practice Style, where "the teacher moves from learner to learner, observing both the performance of the task and the decision making process, then offers feedback and moves on to the next learner" (Mosston & Ashworth, 2008, p. 99).

After the 3 versus 1 game, the example provided suggested the students will be "asked to reflect and consider how offensive and defensive roles differed, as well as specific movements, techniques and understandings that emerged" (Chow & Antencio, 2014, p. 1048). This would occur in the *pre-impact* set and the teacher could use Guided Discovery Style to help players find answers to the problems experienced during play. However, the terms 'reflect' and 'consider' are ambiguous, as they do not guarantee that all students are reflecting or that all students are considering. Similarly, 'reflection' and 'considering' do not denote a specific conscious thought process of memory, discovery or creativity. Reflection can only be done after the event and, therefore, is heavily reliant on memory, especially if the teacher is asking the player/s to reflect on what has been successful or unsuccessful.

Mosston and Ashworth suggested that Guided Discovery Style episodes "require more than one question" (2008, p. 214). Through a Spectrum lens, it is questionable that the teacher is using Guided Discovery Style in the scenario to find the answers to the questions. The Spectrum defines Guided Discovery as, "the logical and sequential design of questions that lead a person to discover a predetermined response" (Mosston & Ashworth, 2008, p. 212). This means that when the teacher asks a specific sequence of questions in a structured process, the player correspondingly responds until that player has discovered the only correct answer for each of the questions asked by the teacher. Therefore, considering the scenario through The Spectrum, there are two aspects to consider. The first is that in a class of 25 students, all learners are not starting from the same/exact challenge point or point of knowledge with regards to passing/dribbling. The second aspect is the processing speed of the 25 students when thinking and responding to the questions from the teacher. The students' processing speeds would all need to be identical (an unrealistic assumption) so that when the teacher asked the questions associated with using a Guided Discovery Style all 25 students would be able to discover the exact same predetermined response and discover it at the same time. When this episode is viewed through The Spectrum lens it could be considered that the one student who is engaged in answering the question/s is the one producing, or discovering, new knowledge (Mosston & Ashworth, 2008). However, the other player(s) (who are maybe listening to the teacher's questions and students' responses) may learn by reproducing the new knowledge that was produced by the player responding, and the overall teaching style for these students' remains then Practice Style. Alfieri, Brooks, Aldrich and Tenenbaum (2011) suggested that "unassisted discovery-learning tasks involving hands-on activities, even with large group discussions do not guarantee that learners will understand the task or that they will come into contact with the to-be-learned material" (p. 2).

Episode 2. The second example of a CLA involves player/s learning "to spin the ball (with disguise), requiring them to identify the type of spin on the ball and couple their response to this action by catching it" (Renshaw, Chow, Davids & Hammond, 2010, p. 133). Table 7.2 outlines how to play 'Spin it to win it'. This game has been designed to "provide practice task constraints to facilitate progression in the skill of bowling spin and perceiving spin for batting" (Renshaw, Chow, Davids & Hammond, 2010, p. 131).

For this second activity, it will be presumed that the teacher provides no other instructions except those included in Table 7.2, as Renshaw, Chow, Davids and Hammond point out that "developing this ability does not require verbal coaching instruction, but can be learned via exposure to bowling deliveries" (2010, p. 133). The first rule is explicit in stating where the

Table 7.2 Example of cricket activities (Adapted from Renshaw, Chow, Davids & Hammond, 2010, p. 131)

	Task	Organisation	Questions
0–10 mins	Game 1: spin it to win it. 1. To develop perceptual skills of 'picking' spin bowlers 2. To develop the skill of catching 3. To develop disguise in bowling Rules: 1. Standing on the edge of one side of the square, the ball must be delivered underarm to land on your opponent's side of the court 2. Your opponent must catch the ball before it bounces twice or you score a point 3. Alternate 'serves' 4. Play a five-point game (win 5–0, 4–1, 3–2) Extensions: 1. Catch with one hand 2. Increase length of pitch (you can now stand where you want but you have to let the ball bounce)	2 × 2 m square with a line across halfway (one ball and four cones)	How can you make it more difficult for your opponent? How can you work out what spin is on the ball? Where is the best place to stand in the 'long court' game?

players stand and that the ball must be delivered underarm. The remainder of the rules in the task column are organisational, scoring and extension activities. For The Spectrum analysis, we will presume questions are asked either/or before the activity or during the activity.

In the *pre-impact* set, the teacher has again chosen the subject matter. During the *impact* set it will be presumed that the teacher gives no instructions except for those in Table 7.2 as Renshaw, Chow, Davids and Hammond (2010) highlight that developing the ability to identify spin by a bowlers' action does not require verbal coaching. This does make it difficult to place this learning experience on The Spectrum due to the defining characteristic of teaching being decision making. If no instructions are given with regards to conscious decision making and the cognitive operations of memory, creativity or discovery that students are to use, then The Spectrum theory suggests that it is likely that memory will be chosen.

When this episode is placed on The Spectrum, it could be considered more than one teaching style. First, it may be considered as Practice Style, as the students will play a game and use known movement or movements to spin the ball. If they do decide to create ways to spin the ball then it could be considered Divergent Discovery, as multiple ways of spinning the ball are created. With regard to reading spin, spinning the ball to the left will cause it to bounce and travel to the left. Students playing this game either know this or they don't before they start to play. If they know it then they will be practicing reading the cues. Renshaw et al. (2010) have suggested it is important for batters to become attuned to perceptual information from the bowler's arm. Improving perceptual attunement is achieved through practice and seeing the stimulus over and over. For example, Renshaw and Fairweather (2000) found that expert batters in cricket show greater perceptual discrimination when facing bowling and that this ability was linked to previous exposure. In this situation, The Spectrum theory would suggest that this is Practice Style as the batter is basing their knowledge or discrimination on previous exposure. Previous exposure denotes memory and the recalling of known facts. However, if players do not know this information then it may be that this learning episode will provide them with the opportunity to discover the relationship and cues. This then is Convergent Discovery Style. Convergent Discovery Style's defining characteristic is to, "discover the correct (predetermined) response using the convergent process" (Mosston & Ashworth, 2008, p. 237). Furthermore, the learner's role is to "engage in reasoning, questioning, and logic to sequentially make connections about the content to discover the answers" (2008, p. 237).

With regards to the three questions asked, they potentially represent three different teaching styles. The first question asks, "How can you make it more difficult for your opponent"? If you are the person throwing the ball you have multiple ways to do this: spin the ball right, spin the ball left, backspin and topspin. Your hand positioning can have the fingers cocked on top of the ball, or pronating so they slide down the inside of the ball. These multiple ways to deceive your opponent would mean that it is potentially Divergent Discovery Style if these options were unknown to the player before the learning experience began. However, if the player knew these options before the learning experience began, it would be Practice Style in operation.

The second question, "How can you work out what spin is on the ball?", could be suggested to be potentially typical of two styles. If the player knows to look at the two coloured tennis balls, the highlighted seam or the bowlers hand position to identify the spin, then it will be Practice Style as the player will be recalling the cues. However, this game is to allow player/s to practice identifying "the type of spin on the ball and couple their response ... " (Renshaw et al., 2010, p. 133). If player/s do not know how to identify the cues then they will be discovering and it will be Divergent Discovery Style as the player/s will be discovering multiple options (ball spin, hand position).

The third question, "Where is the best place to stand in a long court game?", could again be potentially one of two teaching styles depending on the player/s knowledge. For example, if they know that standing deep and in the middle of the court gives them more time to read and react and cover the spin angles, then it is Practice Style. If they do not know this (and they need to discover the answer), then it is Convergent Discovery Style as there is one answer/principle to discover. We highlight in this discussion that "the prior knowledge which the student brings to the learning experience plays a big part in assessing which style is being used in meeting the objectives of the teaching episode" (SueSee et al., 2016, p. 86).

Conclusion

This chapter examined two CLA episodes from the extant literature through the lens of The Spectrum, and identified the decisions being made between the teacher and player/s. Based on the decisions being made, and the learners' prior knowledge, these episodes were placed on The Spectrum. In doing so, we have highlighted important pedagogical concepts, such as the effect that instructions, questioning and terminology can have on directing player/s to use specific cognitive operations. We have also shown how The Spectrum provides a unifying pedagogical lens by defining teaching as decision making and allows the viewer to see the decisions that take place. Furthermore, The Spectrum enables the viewer to see that taking learners across the 'discovery threshold' and into an intentionally designed space to develop 'thinking players' is not a straightforward task.

References

Anson, G., Elliott, D., & Davids, K. (2005). Information processing and constraints-based views of skill acquisition: Divergent or complementary? *Motor Control, 9,* 217–241.

Araujo, D., & Davids, K. (2011). What exactly is acquired during skill acquisition? *Journal of Consciousness Studies, 18*(3–4), 7–23.

Breed, R., & Spittle, M. (2011). *Developing game sense through tactical learning: A resource for teachers and coaches.* Port Melbourne, Vic: Cambridge University Press.

Chow, J. Y., & Atencio, M. (2014). Complex and nonlinear pedagogy and the implications for physical education. *Sport, Education and Society, 19*(8), 1034–1054.

Chow, J. Y., Davids, K., Button, C., Shuttleworth, R., Renshaw, I., & Araujo, D. (2006). Nonlinear pedagogy: A constraints-led framework to understand emergence of game play and skills. *Nonlinear Dynamics, Psychology and Life Sciences, 10*(1), 71–104.

Chow, J. Y., Davids, K., Button, C., Shuttleworth, R., Renshaw, I., & Araujo, D. (2007). The role of nonlinear pedagogy in physical education. *Review of Educational Research, 77*(3), 251–278.

Davids, K., Araujo, D., Shuttleworth, R., & Button, C. (2003). Acquiring skill in sport: A constraints-led perspective. *International Journal of Computer Science in Sport, 2*(2), 31–39.

Gallahue, D. L., Ozmun, J. C., & Goodway, J. D. (2012). *Understanding motor development: Infants, Children, Adolescents, Adults.* New York, NY: McGraw Hill.

Gill, A., Araujo, D., Garcia-Gonzalez, L., Moreno, M. P., & del Villar, F. (2014). Implications of instructional strategies in sport teaching: A nonlinear pedagogy-based approach. *European Journal of Human Movement, 32,* 104–124.

Goldberger, M., Ashworth, S., & Byra, M. (2012). Spectrum of teaching styles retrospective 2012. *Quest, 64*(4), 268–282.

Krause, L., Farrow, D., Reid, M., Buszard T., & Pinder, R. (2018). Helping coaches apply the principles of representative learning design: validation of a tennis specific practice assessment tool. *Journal of Sports Sciences, 36*(11), 1277–1286.

Launder, A. (2001). *Play practice: The games approach to teaching and coaching sports.* Champaign, IL: Human Kinetics.

Mosston, M., & Ashworth, S. (2008). *Teaching physical education.* (1st ed.). Online: Spectrum Institute for Teaching and Learning. Retrieved 10 March 2009, from: www.spectrumofteachingstyles.org/e-book-download.php

Mosston, M. (1992). Tug-o-war, no more: Meeting teaching-learning objectives using the Spectrum of Teaching Styles. *Journal of Physical Education, Recreation, and Dance, 63*(1), 27–31, 56.

Pill, S. (2013). *Play with purpose: Game sense to sport literacy.* Hindmarsh, SA: ACHPER Publications.

Pill, S. (2014). Informing game sense pedagogy with constraints led theory for coaching Australian football. *Sport Coaching Review, 3*(1), 46–62.

Rankin, J., Pill, S., & Magias, T. (2018). Informing the coaching pedagogy of game modification in a game sense approach with affordance theory. *Ágora para la Educación Física y el Deporte, 20*(1), 68–89.

Renshaw, I., Chow, J-Y., Davids, K., & Hammond. (2010). A constraints-led perspective to understanding skill acquisition and game play: a basis for integration of motor learning theory and physical education praxis? *Physical Education and Sport Pedagogy, 15*(2), 117–137.

Renshaw, I., & Fairweather, M. (2000). Cricket bowling deliveries and the discrimination ability of professional and amateur batters. *Journal of Sports Sciences, 18*(12), 951–957.

SueSee, B., Pill, S., & Edwards, K. (2016). Reconciling approaches – a game centred approach to sport teaching and Mosston's spectrum of teaching styles. *European Journal of Physical Education and Sport Science, 2*(4), pp. 69–96

Tan, C. W. K., Chow, J. Y., & Davids, K. (2012). 'How does TGfU work?': examining the relationship between learning design in TGfU and a nonlinear pedagogy. *Physical Education and Sport Pedagogy, 17*(4), 331–348.

Chapter 8

An analysis of Spectrum research on teaching

Study 2

Constantine Chatoupis

This chapter provides ten years of follow-up to Chatoupis' (2010a) content analysis of Spectrum Research on Teaching (SRT). Chatoupis' (2010a) analysis referred to SRT conducted between 1970 and 2008. He found that SRT has increased in number over the years and focused mainly on the psychomotor domain. Also, he found that SRT used teaching styles from the reproduction cluster most frequently and was conducted mainly in elementary school settings. Almost half of the analysed studies did not use any form of systematic observation. The purpose in the present study was to identify, categorise, and analyse relevant research since 2009. Thirty-three Spectrum studies conducted between 2009 and 2019 were included in this study. All studies focused on the effects of one or more teaching styles on learning outcomes. Given that the "Spectrum can help identify areas of omission in the body of research on teaching in physical education literature" (Goldberger, 1991, p. 372), this chapter complements Chatoupis' (2010a) content analysis.

The research

According to Silverman and Skonie (1997), one way to understand the prosperity and growth of research in an area is to analyse its research. Content analysis is a research tool used to determine the presence of certain words or concepts within a text. Researchers quantify and analyse the presence, meanings and relationships of such words and concepts, then make inferences about the messages within the text (Rife, Lacy, & Fico, 2005). To conduct a content analysis, the text is coded or broken down into manageable categories on a variety of factors (e.g. research focus, design, population, method and variables used). This type of analysis allows for gathering information and drawing conclusions about those factors (Silverman & Skonie, 1997). Moreover, content analysis can provide directions for future studies and for planning research. It goes without saying that analysis of research is different from literature review in that content analysis categorises research while literature review synthesises the results.

The author selected that area of teacher effectiveness to analyse because (a) SRT addresses practical issues in education settings and focuses on factors that are related to effective teaching; (b) analysis of SRT can provide anyone, who is interested in conducting such research, with insights into research trends and directions for planning Spectrum research; and (c) analysis of SRT can show the progress of the field and can serve as a resource for those conducting research in the field.

Identifying research

The author undertook an exhaustive literature search utilising electronic databases (i.e. ERIC, ISI Web of Science, Google scholar). The search used specific keywords (e.g. The Spectrum, teaching styles, Mosston) to identify all data-based SRT completed from January 2009 to July 2019, inclusive. Dissertation abstracts and research papers in books, journals, or conference proceedings were investigated. First, paper titles or abstracts were reviewed to decide which studies met the criteria of focusing on SRT (process-product research on The Spectrum of Teaching Styles, English language, 2009–2019). Then, those studies which met the criteria were examined in greater depth. In cases where the original article was not available, the investigation was based on the abstract. The investigation resulted in 33 studies that met the criteria of SRT.

To determine reliability of article inclusion, the author and an expert on the field re-reviewed them. To calculate inter-coder reliability, *Scott's Pi coefficient of reliability* was used (van der Mars, 1989). Inter-coder agreement for the two sets of decisions was estimated to be 89 per cent. The formula for determining reliability is as follows:

$$\%R = n \text{ agreements}/(n \text{ agreements} + n \text{ disagreements}) \times 100$$

The Spectrum research related to teacher education and curriculum was not included in the analysis. Furthermore, The Spectrum research where the focus was on teachers' use of or attitudes towards teaching styles was excluded. The review was delimited in order to provide an in-depth analysis of SRT over a number of years.

Categorising research

Specific categories were determined based on Chatoupis' (2010a) content analysis. The draft with the initial categories was piloted coded on 10 randomly selected papers to make sure that the instrument was usable. Three categories from Chatoupis' (2010a) analysis were not included due to time restraints imposed when I was invited to conduct this project (i.e. general methodology employed, type of class, aptitude treatments interaction effects). A fourth category (decade the study was published) was not used because it was not applicable in the present analysis.

The final draft included the following categories: (a) publication outlet/dissertation research, (b) country of origin, (c) teaching styles used, (d) population, (e) focus and (f) whether systematic observation was used. Each study was categorised on each of the six dimensions. Prior to actual coding, coding reliability was determined by randomly selecting 15 papers and recoding them. The percentage of agreement for each category and for all categories combined was around 85 and 88 per cent, respectively.

Data analysis

All studies were analysed for each category to provide summary information. In particular, statistical analysis provided frequencies and percentages for each category. The SPSS (version 20.0) was used for all calculations. Each paper was coded for; (a) publication outlet/dissertation research; (b) country of origin; (c) teaching styles used; (d) population, (e) focus and; (f) observation used. All categories and subcategories are listed in Figure 8.1.

Results

Trends by decade of publication outlet/dissertation research

The number of SRT studies has grown over the years. As noted in Table 8.1, the majority of research was published in journals (n= 27), while little research could be found in proceedings (n=5) and no research in books. Also, only one dissertation completed in Finland was traced. A complete breakdown of publication trends/dissertation research is provided on Table 8.1.

Publication Outlet	Observation Used
Journal	Systematic observation
Proceeding	None
Book	Teaching Style Used
Dissertation	Reproduction
Country of Origin	A, B, C, D, E
America	Production
Europe	F, G, H, I, J, K
Asia	Population
Focus (more than one, if appropriate)	School-aged
Psychomotor domain	Preschool
Affective domain	Elementary
Cognitive domain	Secondary (Middle and High)
Social domain	College/University
Moral domain	

Figure 8.1 Coding categories for SRT studies

Table 8.1 Trends of publication outlet/dissertation research

Decade	Journal	Dissertation	Proceeding	Book
2009-2019a	27 (81.81)	1 (3.03)	5 (15.15)	0 (0.00)

Note. Values enclosed in parentheses represent percentages.
a 2009 data is included for the whole year while 2019 data up to July.

Country of origin

SRT that has been located has been primarily conducted in Greece ($n=15$). Then, followed by Indonesia ($n=5$), USA ($n=4$), Turkey ($n=4$), Spain ($n=2$), Finland ($n=1$), Belgium ($n=1$) and Hong Kong ($n=1$). Therefore, during the current decade most SRT has been conducted in Europe, followed by Asia and North America.

Teaching Styles used

Teaching Styles from the reproduction cluster have been used in most studies. The least investigated style from that cluster is Inclusion Style ($n=8$). Reciprocal Style has been researched in 20 studies followed by Practice Style ($n=10$) and Command Style ($n=10$). On the contrary, teaching styles from the production cluster have not been researched to a great extent. For example, Convergent Discovery Style and Guided Discovery Style have been studied in five and two studies, respectively. No research has been conducted for Self-Teaching Style and Learner-Initiated Style. Table 8.2 presents the teaching styles used in full detail.

Population

The vast majority of SRT has been conducted in school settings ($n=24$). Sixteen studies were conducted with elementary school-aged children. No research occurred in preschool education settings. College/university students were included in nine studies. The population is presented in Table 8.3.

Focus

Eleven studies exclusively focused on the psychomotor domain with another eight studies focusing exclusively on the affective domain. Studies that exclusively focused on the cognitive and social domains represent a small proportion of SRT ($n=2$ and $n=1$, respectively). The moral domain has not been investigated at all. Research focusing on multiple domains is well represented ($n=11$) (see Table 8.4).

Table 8.2 Teaching styles used

Teaching style	Number of studies	Percentage of total
Reproduction cluster		
Command Style	10	30.30
Practice Style	10	30.30
Reciprocal Style	20	60.60
Self-check Style	9	27.27
Inclusion Style	8	24.24
Production cluster		
Guided Discovery Style	2	6.06
Convergent Discovery Style	5	15.15
Divergent Production Style	1	3.03
Individual Program	1	3.03
Learner-Initiated Style	0	0.00
Self-Teaching Style	0	0.00

Note Each of the 33 studies investigated more than one teaching style. Therefore, they were tallied more than once on the table.

Table 8.3 Population of study participants

Level	Number of studies	Percentage of total
School-aged children	24	72.72
Preschool	0	0.00
Elementary	16	48.48
Secondary	8	24.24
College/university	9	27.27
Total	33	100

Observation used

Systematic observation to verify teaching style implementation was used in only 10 studies. In the remaining, it was not used at all or at least it could not be ascertained whether observation techniques were used or not because this information was not given.

Discussion

Considering the results of a previous content analysis (Chatoupis, 2010a) as well as the results of the present analysis, it can be argued that the number of The Spectrum studies has gradually increased since 1970s, with the last decade (2009–2019) being most productive in terms of The Spectrum research

Table 8.4 Focus

Domains	Number of studies	Percentage of total
Psychomotor	11	33.33
Affective	8	24.24
Cognitive	2	6.06
Social	1	3.03
Moral	0	0.00
Multiple	11	33.33
Total	33	100

conducted (*n*=33). The growing number of SRT reveals that the influence and benefit of Spectrum theory continues to contribute considerably and largely to the understanding of the classroom learning process. This is in line with the scholarship's contention that The Spectrum is a concrete model for conducting research in PE (Chatoupis, 2009; Goldberger, Ashworth, & Byra, 2012; Sicilia-Camacho & Brown, 2008).

Tracing authorship from all over the world is important in reaching conclusions about the spread of The Spectrum knowledge globally. The present analysis revealed that a few countries have conducted SRT over the last ten years (i.e. Greece, Indonesia, USA, Turkey, Spain, Finland, Belgium and Hong Kong). Of these countries Indonesia, Turkey, Spain, Finland, Belgium and Hong Kong had not conducted any SRT during the period from 1970 to 2008, while Greece and USA have been steadily involved in SRT since 1970 (see Chatoupis, 2010a). Although SRT started in the USA (Chatoupis, 2010a), new countries have been added to the list of researchers who have incorporated The Spectrum framework in their research. The premise that The Spectrum is a universal theory is reinforced by the fact that so many countries have adopted and investigated this framework. This worldwide adaptability is encouraging and promising for the future of The Spectrum theory.

In a personal communication with Sara Ashworth, I was told that The Spectrum colleagues from other countries such as Portugal, Czech Republic, Israel, South Korea, Japan have also conducted SRT. This research has been published but is perhaps not easily accessible or conveniently retrievable. If researchers want to make their work more available to others, they need to publish their work in internationally renowned journals and make the published work available on the official Spectrum web site (www.spectrum ofteachingstyles.org).

Research investigating different aspects of the various reproduction styles has been and continues to be the primary focus of most SRT (see Table 8.2 and Chatoupis, 2010a). The predominant research focus on the reproduction styles is probably due to two reasons: (a) It is possibly less complex and requires less time to design research examining issues related to the reproduction rather than the production teaching styles; and (b) the reproduction teaching styles are more familiar to and more frequently used by PE teachers globally (Chatoupis, 2018).

Although teaching styles were examined with learners of different age groups (see Table 8.3), in 24 out of 33 studies the participants were elementary or secondary school students. In the remaining nine studies the participants were university/college students. Analyses of research on teaching in PE yielded similar results of a research focus on school PE (Chatoupis, 2010a; Silverman, 1987; Silverman & Skonie, 1997; Silverman & Manson, 2003). Given that SRT conducted with school-aged children addresses issues relating to teaching style effectiveness, it can be argued this research can help PE teachers in resolving issues related to PE teaching practices (Silverman & Skonie, 1997).

Like other similar analyses (Chatoupis, 2010a; Silverman, 1987; Silverman & Skonie, 1997; Silverman & Manson, 2003), the overwhelming majority of SRT focused on the psychomotor domain (motor skill acquisition or fitness). This is probably because the first priority of an effective school PE program is to provide children with the motor skills needed to be enthusiastic participants in physical activities and be inclined to lead later on, as adults, a physically active lifestyle (Rink & Hall, 2008; Solmon, 2003). Also, development of motor skills and refinement of sport-specific skills are aims of PE curricula worldwide (Dudley, Okely, Pearson, & Cotton, 2011; Hardman, 2008; United Nations Educational, Scientific, and Cultural Organization [UNESCO], 2014).

Research focusing on multiple domains represented a good proportion of the sample ($n=11$). The focus of these studies indicates that The Spectrum researchers are interested in investigating students' feelings and cognition while also investigating the developmental effects of motor skills. This research has enhanced our understanding about the comprehensive, complex and integrative nature of human development – the whole child. In other words, SRT has addressed diverse and varied questions concerning multiple human dimensions and domains of learner's development. Unfortunately, few SRT studies have examined the cognitive, social and moral domains, which is in line with previous research (Chatoupis, 2010a). Considering that in the last 20 years the national curriculum of many countries have reflected educational objectives associated with domains other than the psychomotor domain (ACARA – Australian Curriculum: Health and Physical Education, 2016; Scottish National 3 Physical Education, 2012; SHAPE America – Society of Health and Physical Educators, 2014), it is necessary to answer questions regarding these domains.

Unlike Chatoupis' (2010a) and Silverman and Skonie's (1997) analyses, the present study revealed that in most studies the treatment was not verified by means of systematic observation. The studies which did not use observation tools suffer from a weak treatment effect which biases the results of the research. Silverman (1985) holds that a major drawback of studies, which do not use some kind of systematic observation, is that the treatment is not verified. Thus, there is no way of knowing whether or not it was implemented accurately. The employment of systematic observation necessitates the development of valid and reliable observation tools that comply with The Spectrum theory. Three such observation systems have been identified in the literature (i.e. Ashworth, 2010; Goldberger, 1989; Sherman, 1982). Researchers are encouraged to use them when they conduct SRT.

Conclusion

It is apparent that the field of SRT has increasingly expanded since the 1970s. SRT has addressed many different questions concerning multiple domains of learner's development. Additionally, teaching styles are examined with learners of different age groups. Furthermore, researchers still cross the discovery threshold and investigate teaching styles from the production cluster. However, such production cluster research efforts need to be intensified due to the very small number of studies in that area. Unfortunately, current SRT is still being conducted that has methodological deficiencies (i.e. no use of systematic observation), despite a word of caution voiced in the past (Chatoupis, 2010a; Chatoupis, 2010b; Chatoupis & Vagenas, 2011).

The present content analysis focused on certain categories. Future content analysis on SRT research should include other categories such as sample size, methods of data collection (quantitative or qualitative), the sampling method, the effect size, the statistics used and the statistical assumptions. Moreover, it would be interesting to investigate the number of authors as well as the gender of the first author (see Ward & Ko, 2006). Finally, apart from using descriptive statistics such as means and frequencies to report results in content analysis, it is advisable to employ more advanced statistics (e.g. linear regression) (see Zhang & deLisle, 2006) to fully explore trends in SRT.

Despite the considerable number of publications on SRT, research on the effects and influence of The Spectrum to teaching and learning is far from being exhausted (Chatoupis, 2009). The results of this study represent some critical considerations in the design of SRT as well as showing areas of omission of SRT on which The Spectrum colleagues should concentrate when they design future research.

References

Ashworth, S. (2010). *Description inventory of landmark teaching styles: A Spectrum approach*. Retrieved 20 July 2019 from www.spectrumofteachingstyles.org/pdfs/literature/Ashworth2004_Description_Inventory_OfLandmark.pdf

Australian Curriculum, Assessment and Reporting Authority (ACARA). (2016). *The Health and Physical Education Curriculum*. Version 8.2, Sydney, Australia.

Chatoupis, C. (2009). Contributions of The Spectrum of Teaching Styles to research on teaching. *Studies in Physical Culture and Tourism, 16*, 193–205.

Chatoupis, C. (2010a). An analysis of spectrum research on teaching. *The Physical Educator, 67*(4), 188–197.

Chatoupis, C. (2010b). Spectrum research reconsidered. *International Journal of Applied Sports Sciences, 22*(1), 80–96.

Chatoupis, C. (2018). Physical education teachers' use of Mosston and Ashworth's teaching styles: A literature review. *The Physical Educator, 75*(5), 878–898.

Chatoupis, C., & Vagenas, G. (2011). An analysis of published process-product research on physical education teaching methods. *International Journal of Applied Sports Sciences 23*(1), 271–289.

Dudley, D., Okely, A., Pearson, P., & Cotton, W. A. (2011). A systematic review of the effectiveness of physical education and school sport interventions targeting physical activity, movement skills, and enjoyment of physical activity. *European Physical Education Review, 17*, 353–378.

Goldberger, M. (1991). Research on teaching physical education: A commentary on Silverman's review. *Research Quarterly for Exercise and Sport, 52*(4), 369–3 73.

Goldberger, M., Ashworth, A., & Byra, M. (2012). Spectrum of Teaching Styles retrospective 2012. *Quest, 64*, 268–282.

Hardman, K. (2008). Physical education in schools: A global perspective. *Kinesiology, 40*(1), 5–28.

Rife, D., Lacy, S., & Fico, F. G. (2005). *Analyzing media messages: Using quantitative content analysis in research* (2nd ed.). Mahwah, NJ: Lawrence Erlbaum.

Rink, J., & Hall, T. J. (2008). Research on effective teaching in elementary school physical education. *Elementary School Journal, 108*, 207–218.

Scottish Qualifications Authority. (2012). *National 3 Physical Education Course Specification*. Retrieved 20 July 2019 from www.sqa.org.uk

SHAPE America – Society of Health and Physical Educators. (2014). *National standards & grade-level outcomes for K–12 physical education*. Champaign, IL: Human Kinetics.

Sherman, M. A. (1982). *Style analysis checklists for Mosston's Spectrum of Teaching Styles*. Unpublished manuscript, University of Pittsburgh, PA.

Sicilia-Camacho, A., & Brown, D. (2008). Revisiting the paradigm shift from the versus to the non versus notion of Mosston's Spectrum of teaching styles in physical education pedagogy: A critical pedagogical perspective. *Physical Education and Sport Pedagogy, 13*(1), 85–108.

Silverman, S. (1985). Critical considerations in the design and analysis of teacher effectiveness research in physical education. *International Journal of Physical Education, 22*(4), 17–24.

Silverman, S. (1987). Trends and analysis of research on teaching in doctoral programs. *Journal of Teaching in Physical Education, 7*, 61–70.

Silverman, S., & Manson, M. (2003). Research teaching in physical education doctoral dissertation: A detailed investigation of focus, method, and analysis. *Journal of Teaching in Physical Education, 22*, 280–297.

Silverman, S., & Skonie, R. (1997). Research on teaching in physical education: An analysis of published research. *Journal of Teaching in Physical Education, 16*, 300–311.

Solmon, M. A. (2003). Student issues in physical education classes: Attitudes, cognition, and motivation. In S. J. Silverman & C. D. Ennis (Eds.), *Student learning in physical education: Applying research to enhance instruction* (pp. 147–164). Champaign, IL: Human Kinetics.

United Nations Educational, Scientific, and Cultural Organization. (2014). *World wide survey of school physical education*. Retrieved 20 July 2019 from http://unesdoc.unesco.org/images/0022/002293/229335e.pdf

Van der Mars, H. (1989). Observer reliability: Issues and procedures. In P. W. Darst, D. B. Sakrajsek, & V. H. Mancini (Eds), *Analyzing physical education and sport instruction* (pp. 53–80). Champaign IL: Human Kinetics.

Ward, P., & Bomna, K. (2006). Publication trends in the Journal of Teaching in Physical Education from 1981 to 2005. *Journal of Teaching in Physical Education*, 25, 266–280.

Zhang, J., & deLisle, L. (2006). Analysis of AAHPERD research abstracts published under special populations from 1968 to 2004. *Adapted Physical Activity Quarterly*, 23, 203–217.

Chapter 9

Featuring The Spectrum in an eclectic PETE program

Matthew D. Curtner-Smith

The primary purpose of this chapter is to describe how The Spectrum (Mosston, 1981; Mosston & Ashworth, 2008) has been featured in an eclectic physical education teacher education (PETE) program at the University of Alabama (UA) in the 28 years I have worked at that institution. To this end, I will include descriptions of: (a) PETE at UA; (b) how The Spectrum has been incorporated within the core PETE program at UA; and (c) graduate student involvement with The Spectrum.

My goal in providing this description is to promote thought among, and give some concrete ideas to, other PETE faculties who may be interested in integrating The Spectrum in their own programs, but are not yet ready to do so, or wish to include other theoretical and practical elements in their programs as well as The Spectrum. I should stress that I am certainly not claiming that what we have done with The Spectrum at UA is best practice in general, rather, that it has worked for myself and colleagues in terms of our efforts at preparing, training, and working with undergraduate pre-service teachers (PTs) and graduate students either interested in improving their own practice or becoming teacher education faculty.

PETE at UA

In my time working in PETE at UA, we have had somewhere between 50 and 100 undergraduate PTs at any one time, and between 5 and 15 doctoral students. We also have a small master's degree program for certified teachers either attempting to improve their practice or move on to the doctoral degree for which master's work is a prerequisite. All three of our degree programs are taught traditionally on campus, and, to-date, we have resisted the pressure to include online coursework.

Having completed the university's broad core requirements (i.e. coursework in the arts, humanities, and sciences), courses in educational theory (i.e. educational sociology and philosophy; educational psychology, computer applications, special education) and courses in the kinesiological subdisciplines (e.g. exercise physiology, biomechanics, motor development, ecological aspects of health), our PTs are admitted to and take courses in what we refer to as the "core PETE program" which has been designed, taught and administrated by between two and four faculty members with specialist qualifications in sport pedagogy. The spine of this core program is comprised of three methods courses (secondary, elementary and advanced), with related early field experiences in local schools, and the culminating internship which involves PTs teaching full-time for half a semester (i.e. seven weeks) in an elementary school and half a semester in a secondary school. In addition, the core includes five content courses (net/wall games, track and field, striking/fielding games, invasion games, target games, dance and gymnastics, swimming and health-related fitness), which involve PTs completing some work on campus but are largely field-based in the local schools, a course on evaluation and an adapted physical education course in which PTs work with individual or small groups of children and youth with various physical and mental disabilities who are bussed to the university campus.

The degree program in which our doctoral students are enrolled has two objectives. First, to prepare them to become PETE faculty members. Second, to prepare them to conduct research in sport pedagogy (e.g. research on physical education teaching, teachers, teacher education, teacher educators and curriculum; or research on sport coaching, coaches, coach education and coach educators). To realise the first objective, we attempt to get our doctoral students engaged in the core PETE program as much as possible and form a community of practice (MacPhail, Patton, Parker, & Tannehill, 2014) with the faculty. Specifically, we ask them to team-teach courses with us, teach courses by themselves, and supervise PTs during early field experiences and their internships. Wherever possible, we also attempt to give our doctoral students' voice in terms of expressing their opinions about core PETE program coursework, evaluation and PTs' progress.

In congruence with most PETE programs, some elements of our undergraduate and graduate degrees have changed over the last 28 years in response to both internal factors (e.g. changes in faculty and departmental organisation) and external factors (e.g. changes in state education department requirements, and national and international trends in education and physical education). Other components of the program have remained constant and fairly stable or ebbed and flowed in terms of the degree to which they are relatively central or peripheral. Our use of The Spectrum, for example, while always featured, was central to our program in the early 1990s, became relatively peripheral in the late 1990s, and has returned to a central position in the last 15 years.

The Spectrum within the core PETE program at UA

The conceptual framework which has guided more recent practice within our undergraduate core PETE program at UA is presented in Figure 9.1. The figure indicates that the elements driving our program have been eclectic and included permeating theories and perspectives, foundational pedagogies and instructional models.

Permeating theories and perspectives

The eight permeating theories and perspectives listed in Figure 9.1 inform and drive our work across the courses in the core PETE program. One of these is theory of The Spectrum which is introduced to PTs very early in their training. *Occupational socialisation theory* (Richards, Templin, & Graber, 2014) is important in our efforts to deconstruct the faculty beliefs and values about physical education with which many of our PTs enter the core PETE program, and to break the cycle of non-teaching physical education teachers that exist in our state (Curtner-Smith, 2009). We attempt to achieve this outcome by asking PTs to examine their own acculturation and orientations to

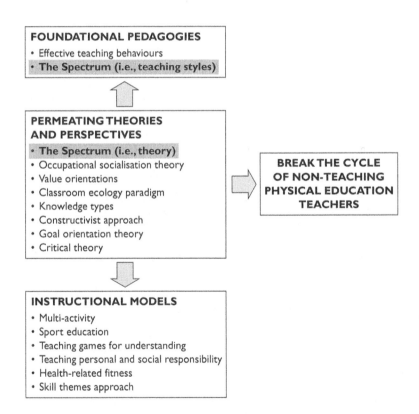

Figure 9.1 Conceptual Framework for the Core PETE Program at the University of Alabama

the subject (Curtner-Smith, 2017). The work on *value orientations* (Curtner-Smith, Baxter, & May, 2018) is included because we want our PTs to consider realising different and broad educational objectives (i.e. disciplinary mastery, learning process, self-actualisation, social reconstruction, social responsibility and ecological integration) and to link them to narrower objectives in physical education (e.g. motor skill acquisition, leisure education, cognitive development, health and fitness and personal and social development). We also employ a number of concepts and constructs from the *classroom ecology paradigm* (Doyle, 1977; Hastie & Siedentop, 1999; McEntyre & Curtner-Smith, 2020). These include the concepts that teaching consists of a series of tasks which are often negotiated (Wahl-Alexander, Curtner-Smith, & Sinelnikov, 2018), and that the degree to which and how these tasks are completed by students depends on the extent to which they are held accountable through informal and formal evaluation. In addition, we ask PTs to examine the instructional, managerial and transitional systems they build and how they deal with or accommodate the student social system.

The work on *knowledge types* that teachers should master (Shulman, 1986; Ward & Ayvazo, 2016), particularly pedagogical knowledge, content knowledge, pedagogical content knowledge, curricular knowledge and knowledge of students, is also key to our core program. Moreover, we attempt to model and advocate a *constructivist approach* (MacPhail, Tannehill, & Goc Karp, 2013) to teaching by asking our PTs to draw from and build on their current knowledge and past experiences in order to construct new knowledge as teachers, and requiring them to do the same thing with their students in a physical education context. In addition, we have drawn from *goal orientation theory* (Ames, 1992; Todorovich & Curtner-Smith, 2002, 2003) by asking PTs to comprehend task (i.e. focused on self-improvement) and ego (i.e. focused on comparing performances with others) orientations to achievement and the practices that they might employ to create climates that promote either of these orientations (Todorovich & Curtner-Smith, 2002, 2003). Finally, we have attempted to include a *critical element* in our program when attempting to deliver critically oriented methods classes, based on Kirk's (1986) inward focus on the analysis of teaching and outward focus on curriculum studies, in an attempt to examine political, moral and social issues and the themes of elitism, racism, classism and sexism (Curtner-Smith & Sofo, 2004a).

We introduce these theories and perspectives to PTs in as practical and straightforward manner as possible. Once they appear to have an understanding, we also ask PTs to consider the relationships between these theories and perspectives and how they complement or contradict each other. For example, in terms of The Spectrum, we ask PTs which teaching styles could be used to promote each value orientation, or employed when taking a constructivist or critical approach, and creating an ego-involving or task-involving motivational climate. Similarly, we ask which content might be best taught with the reproduction cluster of teaching styles and which with the production cluster of styles. Finally, we might ask PTs which teaching styles their own teachers employed, why they think they used these styles and what they think their value orientations and objectives were.

Foundational pedagogies

The two sets of foundational pedagogies we wish our PTs to acquire are also shown in Figure 9.1. These are *effective teaching behaviours* and the actual teaching styles within The Spectrum.

Effective teaching behaviours. The first set of foundational pedagogies, effective teaching behaviours, comes from the positivistic process-product teacher effectiveness research (Dunkin & Biddle, 1974; Graham & Heimerer, 1981; Silverman, 1991) and features direct instruction – the collection of behaviours teachers can use to ensure that the time in which students engage with content is substantial and high quality. We consider the relatively skilled use of and comfort with effective teaching behaviours in general, and direct instruction in particular, as a prerequisite for being introduced to and learning the teaching styles within The Spectrum.

Initially, we introduce the concept of direct instruction by requiring PTs to code multiple films of physical education teaching with the Physical Education Assessment Instrument (PETAI; Phillips, Carlisle, Steffen and Stroot, 1986). This is a computerised systematic observation instrument which records the time spent by teachers and students in various instructional and managerial behaviours. The PETAI can be used to assess the extent to which teachers are able to decrease the amount of time they spend managing and increase the time they spend instructing (specifically actively monitoring, giving group or individual performance feedback and providing motivational feedback) during lessons. Similarly, the instrument reveals the extent to which teachers are able to decrease the amount of time their students spend in managerial tasks, transitioning from one instructional task to another, waiting to engage in instructional tasks, or listening to the teacher describe or explain instructional tasks; and the degree to which teachers can increase the amount of time students spend successfully engaged in instructional tasks. Once familiar with the concept of direct instruction, PTs are filmed teaching during early field experiences and their internships, asked to code their own teaching with the PETAI, and to reflect on their use of effective teaching behaviours.

Teaching styles within The Spectrum. The second set of foundational pedagogies in our core PETE program – the teaching styles within The Spectrum – is layered on top of the effective teaching behaviours with which PTs are already familiar. Initially, PTs are introduced to the theory of The Spectrum and the five teaching styles in the reproduction cluster (i.e. Command Style, Practice Style, Reciprocal Style, Self-Check Style and Inclusion Style), and the three original teaching styles in the production cluster (i.e. Guided Discovery Style, Divergent Style and Going Beyond Style) (Mosston, 1981) in a classroom setting through lecture, discussion and watching film of teachers in action. We made the decision to include only the original three production styles because we found that PTs found it very difficult to distinguish between the six production styles in the most recent versions of The Spectrum (Mosston & Ashworth, 2002; 2008). Having gained an understanding of the theory of The Spectrum and the eight teaching styles, PTs are taught the same content (e.g. dribbling in soccer) by a faculty member through each of the eight styles before being asked to instruct their peers in different content of their choice using each of the styles and while receiving feedback from a faculty member. In all subsequent teaching episodes during methods classes, early field experiences and the internship, The Spectrum becomes a key lens through which PTs' teaching is planned, discussed, critiqued and evaluated. Moreover, once they are familiar with The Spectrum, PTs are asked about its compatibility with direct instruction. A good number of them come to the realisation that direct instruction is, essentially, high class Command and Practice Style teaching, but is not compatible with the higher order reproduction styles or any of the production styles of teaching further along The Spectrum continuum.

Instrument for identifying Teaching Styles. At various points in time, we have also asked PTs to code film of their teaching for teaching style use with another systematic observation instrument developed specifically for the purpose known as the Instrument for Identifying Teaching styles (IFITS; Curtner-Smith, Hasty, & Kerr, 2001). IFITS is an interval recording instrument that estimates how much time teachers employ each of the eight teaching styles described by Mosston (1981). When viewing a lesson (either filmed or live), the coder makes a decision about which teaching style is being used by the teacher every 20 seconds (10 seconds observe/10 seconds record). If the teacher is not employing one of the eight teaching styles during an interval, he/she is engaged in some form of management and is so coded. During intervals in which a teaching style is employed, but within which management also occurs, the teaching style is given preference and recorded. During intervals in which the coder observes two or more teaching styles, the most indirect style (i.e. the style which is furthest along The Spectrum continuum from Command Style) is given preference and recorded. Thus, PTs coding their own teaching with IFITS can build an objective description of their use of teaching styles in one lesson or across a series of lessons. Moreover, they can use IFITS to compare the range of teaching styles they use when teaching different classes and children and youth of different ages, when employing different instructional models, or when emphasising different objectives within the same model.

Instructional models

Figure 9.1 indicates that once PTs are familiar with and have used foundational pedagogies while peer teaching, we introduce them to and require they employ a number of different instructional models. Specifically, PTs have been asked to employ the traditional Multi-Activity (Curtner-Smith & Sofo, 2004b) and Sport Education models (Siedentop, Hastie, & van der Mars, 2019) during the secondary early field experience. During the elementary early field experience, they have been required to teach through the Skill Themes approach (Graham, Holt/Hale, & Parker, 2013), and Sport Education, Teaching Games for Understanding (TGfU) (Bunker & Thorpe, 1982; Thorpe, Bunker, & Almond, 1984), and Teaching Personal and Social Responsibility (TPSR) (Hellison, 2011) models. During the health-related fitness content course, PTs are required to employ the Health-Related Fitness model (Harris & Cale, 2019). Additional Skill Themes, Multi-Activity, TGfU and TPSR units, and further Sport Education seasons, are taught within the advanced methods course and other content courses in a variety of local elementary and secondary schools. Finally, prior to the commencement of their internships, PTs meet with their university supervisors and cooperating teachers to discuss which instructional models and which content they will employ in the coming semester.

Once PTs have been introduced to and are at least somewhat familiar with the various instructional models, they are invited to discuss which models are compatible and align with each value orientation. Moreover, they are asked which teaching styles they believe are primarily employed within each model or what patterns of teaching style use they would expect from a teacher using each model. For example, we guide PTs towards the understanding that well-taught Multi-Activity units are likely to involve teachers primarily employing the Practice Style, but that more experienced and expert teachers are more likely to slip into other styles further along The Spectrum continuum, especially if they are trying to realise affective and cognitive objectives as well as those in the psychomotor domain. By contrast, we help the students realise that when teaching Sport Education seasons, the goal is to shift gradually from employing direct (reproduction) styles, in which the teacher makes most of the decisions, to indirect (production) styles, in which the students make most of the decisions as a season progresses and so are given more control over their own learning. In addition, we stress the importance of teachers using the Guided Discovery and Divergent Discovery Styles during Skill Themes and TGFU units and using the production cluster of styles when attempting any form of critical pedagogy such as purposefully negotiating the curriculum with their students (Enright & O'Sullivan, 2010; Guadalupe & Curtner-Smith, 2019).

Graduate students' involvement with The Spectrum

While some of our doctoral and master's degree students begin their programs with a good understanding of The Spectrum, many arrive at UA unfamiliar with it. These graduate students learn about The Spectrum alongside the undergraduates when they team-teach the secondary methods course with a faculty member. This learning may be reinforced during a graduate course on systematic observation when they are trained to use IFITS. In addition, graduate students are also encouraged to consciously experiment with different teaching styles during their own teaching before being asked to provide undergraduate PTs with feedback on their teaching style use when supervising them during early field experiences and the internship. Sometimes the focus of this supervision is exclusively on describing or changing PTs' teaching style use and data are gathered with IFITS. At other times, when graduate students collect data from several perspectives (e.g. motivational climate, managerial systems constructed, amount of feedback provided, amount of time in which students are engaged successfully in instructional tasks) including PTs' teaching style use, they simply record the number of times each teaching style is observed.

Finally, as well as using The Spectrum as a framework through which to supervise PTs, a number of our graduate students have conducted research with a faculty member in which teaching styles have been the main focus (Curtner-Smith, Hasty, & Kerr, 2001, Curtner-Smith, Todorovich, McCaughtry, & Lacon, 2001, Parker & Curtner-Smith, 2012), or in which The Spectrum has been employed as a lens through which to examine other pedagogical topics (e.g. occupational socialisation: Prior & Curtner-Smith , 2020); negotiations between teachers and students: Wahl-Alexander & Curtner-Smith, 2015), or to confirm treatment fidelity in experimental work (see Bryant & Curtner-Smith, 2009; Pennington, Curtner-Smith, & Wind, 2019). For example, two studies (Curtner-Smith, Hasty, & Kerr, 2001, Curtner-Smith, Todorovich, McCaughtry, & Lacon, 2001) in which data were generated with IFITS indicated that the introduction of a national curriculum for physical education in England and Wales had little impact on the teaching styles teachers employed by teachers in rural and urban schools, despite the claims of policy makers. In another study, and also using IFITS, Parker and Curtner-Smith (2012) found that PTs' patterns of teaching styles were not congruent with those thought to be optimal for Multi-Activity teaching and within Sport Education units.

Conclusion

Our use of The Spectrum within an eclectic PETE program has been somewhat unique. Nevertheless, we have found it to be an incredibly useful framework through which to develop our PTs' pedagogical skills and our graduate students' understanding of teaching, supervisory prowess and research. Moreover, both PTs and graduate students appear to complete their respective degrees with a good understanding of The Spectrum and confident in their ability to employ it. We see The Spectrum as being central to our program for the foreseeable future, and look forward to discovering new ways in which it can be employed, applied and adapted.

References

Ames, C. (1992). Classrooms: Goals, structures, and student motivation. *Journal of Educational Psychology, 84*, 261–271.

Bryant, L. G., & Curtner-Smith, M. D. (2009). Effect of a physical education teacher's disability on high school pupils' learning and perceptions of teacher competence. *Physical Education and Sport Pedagogy, 14*(3), 311–322.

Bunker, D., & Thorpe, R. (1982). A model for the teaching of games in secondary schools. *Bulletin of Physical Education, 18*(1), 5–8.

Curtner-Smith, M. D. (2009). Breaking the cycle of non-teaching physical education teachers: Lessons to be learned from the occupational socialization literature. In L. D. Housner, M. Metzler, P. G. Schempp, & T. J. Templin (Eds.). *Historical traditions and future directions of research on teaching and teacher education in physical education* (pp. 221–225). Morgantown, WV: Fitness Information Technology.

Curtner-Smith, M. D. (2017). Acculturation, recruitment, and the development of orientations. In K. Lux Gaudreault & K. A. Richards (Eds.), *New perspectives on teacher socialization in physical education*, (pp. 33–46). Abingdon: Taylor & Francis.

Curtner-Smith, M. D., Baxter, D. S., & May, L. K. (2018). The legacy and influence of Catherine D. Ennis's value orientations research. *Kinesiology Review, 7*(3), 211–217.

Curtner-Smith, M. D., Hasty, D. L., & Kerr, I. G. (2001). Teachers' use of productive and reproductive teaching styles prior to and following the introduction of National Curriculum Physical Education. *Educational Research, 43*(3), 333–340.

Curtner-Smith, M. D., Todorovich, J. R., McCaughtry, N. A., & Lacon, S. A. (2001). Urban teachers' use of productive and reproductive teaching styles within the confines of the National Curriculum for Physical Education. *European Physical Education Review, 7*(2), 177–190.

Curtner-Smith, M. D., & Sofo, S. (2004a). Influence of a critically oriented methods course and early field experience on preservice teachers' conceptions of teaching. *Sport, Education and Society, 9*(1), 115–142.

Curtner-Smith, M. D., & Sofo, S. (2004b). Preservice teachers' conceptions of teaching within sport education and multi-activity units. *Sport, Education and Society, 9*(3), 347–377.

Doyle, W. (1977). Paradigms for research on teacher effectiveness. In L.S. Shulman (Ed.), *Review of research in education*, (pp. 163–198). Itasca, IL: Peacock.

Dunkin, M., & Biddle, B. (1974). *The study of teaching*. New York, NY: Holt, Rinehart, & Winston.

Enright, E., & O'Sullivan, M. (2010). "Can I do it in my pyjamas?" Negotiating a physical education curriculum with teenage girls. *European Physical Education Review, 16*(3), 203–222.

Graham, G., & Heimerer, E. (1981). Research on teacher effectiveness: A summary with implications for teaching. *Quest, 33*, 14–25.

Graham, G., Holt/Hale, S. A., & Parker, M. (2013). *Children moving: A reflective approach to teaching physical education*. (9th ed.). McGraw-Hill.

Guadalupe, T., & Curtner-Smith, M. D. (2019). "She was really good at letting us make decisions:" Influence of purposefully negotiating the physical education curriculum on one teacher and a boys middle school minority class. *Curriculum Studies in Health and Physical Education*.

Harris, J., & Cale, L. (2019). *Promoting active lifestyles in schools*. Champaign, IL: Human Kinetics.

Hastie, P. A., & Siedentop, D. (1999). An ecological perspective on physical education. *European Physical Education Review, 5*, 9–29.

Hellison, D. (2011). *Teaching personal and social responsibility through physical education* (3rd ed.). Champaign, IL: Human Kinetics.

Kirk, D. (1986). A critical pedagogy for teacher education: Toward an inquiry-oriented approach. *Journal of Teaching in Physical Education, 5*(4), 230–246.

MacPhail, A., Patton, K., Parker, M., & Tannehill, D. (2014). Leading by Example: Teacher Educators' Professional Learning through Communities of Practice. *Quest, 66*(1), 39–56.

MacPhail, A., Tannehill, D. & Goc Karp, G. (2013). Preparing pre-service teachers to design instructionally aligned lessons, *Teaching and Teacher Education, 33*, 100–112.

McEntyre, K., Curtner-Smith, M. D., & Wind, S. (2020). Negotiation Patterns of a preservice physical education teacher and his students during sport education. *European Physical Education Review*.

Mosston, M. (1981). *Teaching physical education* (2nd ed.). Columbus, OH: Merrill.

Mosston, M., & Ashworth. (2002). *Teaching physical education* (5th ed.). Boston: Benjamin Cummings.

Mosston, M., & Ashworth. (2008). *Teaching physical education* (1st online ed.). Retrieved from www.spectrumofteachingstyles.org/

Parker, M., & Curtner-Smith, M. D. (2012). Preservice teachers' use of production and reproduction teaching styles within multi-activity and sport education units. *European Physical Education Review, 18*(1), 127–143.

Pennington, C., Curtner-Smith, M. D., & Wind, S. (2019). Impact of a physical education teacher's age on elementary school students' perceptions of effectiveness and learning. *Journal of Teaching in Physical Education, 38*(4), 279–285.

Phillips, D, A., Carlisle, C., Steffen, J., & Stroot, S. (1986). *The computerised version of the physical education assessment instrument*. Unpublished manuscript, University of Northern Colorado, Greeley, CO.

Prior, L. F., & Curtner-Smith, M. D. (2020). Influence of Occupational Socialization on Elementary Physical Education Teachers' Beliefs and Curricula. *Journal of Teaching in Physical Education, 39*(1), 9–17.

Richards, K. A, Templin, T. J., & Graber, K. (2014). The socialization of teachers in physical education: Review and recommendations for future works. *Kinesiology Review, 3*, 113–134.

Shulman, L. S. (1986). Those who understand: Knowledge growth in teaching. *Educational Researcher, 15*, 4–14.

Siedentop, D., Hastie, P. A., & van der Mars, H. (2019). *Complete Guide to Sport Education* (2nd ed). Champaign, IL: Human Kinetics.

Silverman, S. (1991). Research on teaching in physical education. *Research Quarterly for Exercise and Sport, 62*(4), 352–364.

Thorpe, R., Bunker, D., & Almond, L. (1984). Four fundamentals for planning a games curriculum. *Bulletin of Physical Education, 20*(1), 24–29.

Todorovich, J. R., & Curtner-Smith, M. D. (2002). Influence of the motivational climate in physical education on sixth grade pupils' goal orientations. *European Physical Education Review, 8*(2), 119–138.

Todorovich, J. R., & Curtner-Smith, M. D. (2003). Influence of the motivational climate in physical education on third grade students' goal orientations. *Journal of Classroom Interaction*, 38(1), 36–46.

Wahl-Alexander, Z., & Curtner-Smith, M. D. (2015). Influence of negotiations on preservice teachers' instruction within multi-activity and sport education units. *Sport, Education and Society*, 20(7), 834–854.

Wahl-Alexander, Z., & Curtner-Smith, M. D., Sinelnikov, O. A. (2018). Influence of a training program on preservice teachers' ability to negotiate with students. *Journal of Teaching in Physical Education*, 37(2), 144–153.

Ward, P., & Ayvazo, S. (2016). Pedagogical content knowledge in physical education. *Journal of Teaching in Physical Education*, 35, 194–207.

Chapter 10

Inclusion Style of teaching

Student autonomy and responsibility

Mark Byra

In this chapter, I provide an in-depth description of The Spectrum's Inclusion Style, including a scenario which depicts how an Inclusion Style lesson may unfold in the real world of teaching physical education. I then describe how Inclusion Style relates to the physical, cognitive and affective educational learning domains, and follow-up with some suggestions for implementation. But let me begin with the question, why the focus on The Spectrum's Inclusion Style?

In addition to students making the same decisions in Inclusion Style as they do in Practice Style about pace, location and start and stop time, they also make decisions about performing a task at a self-selected level of difficulty and assessing their own performance of the task with the help of a task sheet (Mosston & Ashworth, 2008). In an Inclusion Style episode, the teacher creates a plan to challenge and motivate learners of varying skill ability so that each can engage in optimal practice (Byra & Jenkins, 1998; Chatoupis & Emmanuel, 2003). Students are empowered in Inclusion Style through the decisions they are invited to make. It is a powerful teaching style that reflects current educational reforms regarding teachers employing instructional approaches that provide students greater responsibility and autonomy over their learning.

The impact of being favourably motivated in school physical education lessons has received considerable attention over the past few decades as a result of the research findings that tie motivation to level of student engagement in learning tasks (Perlman, 2010, 2011; Perlman & Goc Karp, 2010; Spittle & Byrne, 2009; Wallhead & Ntoumanis, 2004). The literature on self-determination theory indicates that students are influenced by the way teachers interact and communicate with students (Reeve, 2006; Reeve & Jang, 2006). In the physical education setting, Perlman (2013) found that students taught in an autonomy supportive learning context were more physically active (i.e. moderate-to-vigorous) than students taught within a non-autonomy supportive learning context. Lonsdale, Sabiston, Raedeke, Ha and Sun (2009) found that self-determined motivation and opportunity to make choices were associated with higher levels of physical activity in secondary level students. Mandigo, Holt, Anderson and Sheppard (2008) found that using autonomous supportive instructional strategies like giving students time to practice on their own, praising quality of performance, and listening to students in game lessons fostered feelings of intrinsic motivation in upper elementary-aged school children. Kirby, Byra, Readdy and Wallhead (2015) found students who were taught under the conditions of Inclusion Style fostered more internalised forms of behavioural regulation. Clearly the literature suggests that when teachers use instructional practices that provide students greater responsibility and autonomy over their learning, as in Inclusion Style, it enhances their self-determined motivation.

Description of Inclusion Style

The Inclusion Style emanates from The Spectrum's reproduction cluster (Mosston & Ashworth, 2008). The general pattern of interaction between the teacher and learners from Command Style to Inclusion Style involves students practicing a demonstrated task (teacher driven) while using feedback (teacher or student driven) to reduce the number of movement errors in the demonstrated task. As is the case in Practice Style, Reciprocal Style and Self-Check Style, students in Inclusion Style are invited to make decisions about where they locate in the movement setting, when they start, stop and move on to new tasks, and the pace at which they practice a task, all within parameters established by the teacher. What sets Inclusion Style apart from the other reproduction teaching styles are the decisions that students make in regard to self-selecting level of difficulty at which to practice a task, and self-assessing task performance. In Command Style through Self-Check Style, all students practice a task at one teacher-prescribed level of difficulty; no planned attempt to accommodate for individual differences in students' skill ability is made within these teaching styles. In Inclusion Style, students are provided legitimate options for practicing a task, options based on factors or variables that make the task more and less difficult. In addition, students assess their own task performance with the help of a task sheet and guidance provided by the teacher (see Figure 10.1). The primary goal of Inclusion Style is to challenge and motivate students to engage in tasks at an appropriate skill level (Byra & Jenkins, 1998; Chatoupis & Emmanuel, 2003). Individualising instruction to permit greater student success is the underlying premise of Inclusion Style (Mosston & Ashworth, 2008). Given the degree of autonomy offered the students through decision making, Inclusion Style is reflective of a student-centred instructional approach.

Let me further describe, in the format of a *scenario*, the essence of a lesson that includes two Inclusion Style episodes. The episodes presented are designed to be used with third or fourth grader learners.

> At the end of their 8-minute beginning-of-class muscular endurance exercise routine (a series of ten tasks presented within the conditions of Inclusion Style), Ms. Berry gathers her third grade students to review the major

---

NAME _____   Inclusion Style Task Sheet
DATE _____   CLASS TEACHER _____

STRIKING WITH A LONG-HANDLED IMPLEMENT – BATTING

TASK		SIZE OF BALL	
Level	Task Description	Level	Size
1	Bat a ball from a tee.	1	Large
2	Bat an underhand tossed ball from the side.	2	Medium
3	Bat an underhand tossed ball from in front.	3	Small

DIRECTIONS TO THE STUDENT

1. Select a task and ball size for your first set of 5 trials.
2. Write the level of the task and ball size chosen in the appropriate box below.
3. Write the number of successful hits you think you will make out of 5 trials (prediction).
4. Now complete 5 trials. Record the number of successful attempts out of 5 (actual).
5. After completing the first set of 5 trials, decide the task and ball size you wish to use to complete a second set of 5 trials. Follow DIRECTIONS 2, 3, and 4 above.
6. After completing the second set of 5 trials, decide the task and ball size you wish to use to complete a third set of 5 trials. Follow DIRECTIONS 2, 3, and 4 above.

Set	Task (level)	Ball (level)	Prediction	Actual	Prediction	Actual
1			/5	/5	/5	/5
2			/5	/5	/5	/5
3			/5	/5	/5	/5

PERFORMANCE CUES (Graham, Holt/Hale, Parker, Hall, & Patton, 2020)

1. Bat back (bring the bat way back over your shoulder so it sticks up like a toothpick)
2. Watch ball (keep your eyes on the ball all the time)
3. Side to target (turn your side to the target or field)
4. Level swing (extend your arms to swing flat as a pancake)
5. Rotate and shift (roll over the shoelaces of your back foot)

Figure 10.1 Task sheet for striking with a bat

concepts and skills taught in the previous lesson (part of a throwing, catching and striking unit). She then re-demonstrates the critical skill cues associated with throwing a ball underhanded. During the demonstration, she explains that the students must decide upon the size of foam ball to use (tennis ball, softball, or handball) and the distance from which to throw the ball at a target located against the wall (10, 15 or 20 feet). She also lets them know that after each set of five trials, they must self-check their performance against the critical cues posted on the wall charts and decide whether to increase, retain, or decrease the difficulty level of the task in the subsequent sets of trials they complete. After checking their understanding of the task, she announces to the students that she calls this style of teaching "being included". After allowing the students to select the size of ball to use, the distance from which to throw, and the wall target to throw at, the students begin to practice throwing the ball underhand at their own pace while self-checking performance. While her students are engaged in the activity, Ms. Berry observes their performance and provides individual feedback by asking specific questions about level of difficulty chosen and the critical skill cues they are and are not performing to determine whether they are self-checking performance accurately. After the students have completed 3 to 5 sets of trials, she gathers them and provides some general positive feedback about the choices they made regarding level of task difficulty and accuracy of self-checking performance.

In the second episode, Ms. Berry introduces striking with a bat in the "being included" teaching style. First, she highlights through demonstration and explanation the five critical skill cues of focus for striking with a bat. Then Ms. Berry demonstrates three different versions of the task (different levels of performance), striking a ball off a batting tee, striking a ball that is underhand tossed by a partner from the side (5 feet away), and striking a ball that is underhand tossed by a partner from in front (15 feet away) while using one of three different sized foam balls (tennis, softball, or handball). As was the case with the throwing task, she lets the students know that after each set of five trials they must self-check their performance against the critical cues posted on the wall charts and decide whether to increase, retain, or decrease the difficulty level of the task in the subsequent sets of trials performed (see Figure 10.2). After checking their understanding of the task, she once again announces to the students that she calls this style of teaching "being included". She then instructs the students to choose a partner, who serves in a supporting role (i.e. retrieves hit ball from a batting tee or tosses the ball underhand to the batter and then retrieves the ball), and to begin striking at the initial level of task difficulty they have chosen. As in the first episode, while her students are engaged in practice, Ms. Berry observes their performance and provides individual feedback by asking specific questions about level of difficulty chosen and the critical skill cues they are and are not performing to determine whether they are self-checking performance

PERFORMANCE CUES FOR BATTING

1. Bat Back (over shoulder, sticks up like a toothpick)

2. Watch Ball (eyes on the ball all the time)

3. Side to Target (turn your side to the target)

4. Level Swing (swing flat as a pancake)

5. Rotate and Shift (roll over shoelaces of back foot)

Figure 10.2 Wall chart posted on a gymnasium wall for striking with a bat (performance cues)

accurately. After the students have completed 3 to 5 sets of trials, she gathers them in and provides some general positive feedback about the choices they made in regard to level of task difficulty and accuracy of self-checking performance. During the last two minutes of the lesson, she asks the students to tell her about this teaching style named "being included" to examine their perceptions of Inclusion Style.

Inclusion Style – a holistic instructional approach: psychomotor, cognitive and affective educational learning domains

The psychomotor educational learning domain is highly emphasised in Inclusion Style. Motor engagement at an appropriate level is at a maximum when given the opportunity to select the level of task difficulty that best matches one's initial ability level. In Inclusion Style, the teacher accepts individual ability differences among learners and provides individualised instruction by giving students options to make a task more or less difficult. Individualised instruction as provided through Inclusion Style enhances student opportunity to succeed (i.e. learn). Standards 1 and 3, "demonstrates competency in a variety of motor skills and movement patterns" and "demonstrates the knowledge and skills to achieve and maintain a health-enhancing level of physical activity and fitness" (p. 12), respectively, from the U.S. national standards for K-12 physical education are highly aligned with Inclusion Style (Society for Health and Physical Education America [SHAPE America], 2014). Elements from both the physical and psychological learning domains align well with the Australian definition of physical literacy (Keegan et al., 2019) and sub-strands from two of the *Strands* embedded within the Australian Curriculum for Health and Physical Education, "movement and physical activity", and "personal, social, and community health" (Australian Curriculum, Assessment, and Reporting Authority [ACARA] 2015, pp. 1–5).

The level of student decision making is significant in Inclusion Style, and this decision making is closely associated with students developing responsible personal and social behaviour (Standard 4, SHAPE America, 2014; Strand: Personal, social, and community health, ACARA, 2015). In addition, Inclusion Style emphasises that leaners are different (i.e. ability level, prior experience, etc.) and that these differences are welcomed and are to be respected (Standard 5, SHAPE America, 2014; Strand: Personal, social, and community health, ACARA, 2015). Elements from the social domain that develop physical literacy (Keegan et al., 2019), specifically relationships, society and culture and connectedness, seem closely aligned with the affective educational domain of learning.

The development of higher order cognitive operations like applying, analysing, problem solving and evaluating (Krathwohl, 2002) is deliberate in Inclusion Style. These cognitive operations are fundamental to self-assessing task performance, and self-selecting level of task difficulty. Standard 2 from the U.S. national standards for K-12 physical education, "applies knowledge of concepts, principles, strategies, and tactics related to movement" (SHAPE America, 2014, p. 12) is clearly aligned with Inclusion Style, as is the cognitive domain as described by Keegan et al. (2019), specifically for the elements of content knowledge, and purpose and reasoning. The sub-strand "developing movement and concept strategies" (p. 4) from the "movement and physical activity" (pp. 3–5) Strand also aligns well the cognitive educational learning domain (ACARA, 2015).

Implementing Inclusion Style

When first introducing Inclusion Style, limit student decision making to selecting level of difficulty at which to practice a task. After the students have had some experience at selecting level of difficulty, then introduce them to the process (decision making) of self-assessing performance. Inclusion Style is complex; break it down for your students. Make it palatable. Presenting an Inclusion Style episode in phases will also serve to help you (teacher) because offering skill feedback to students after assessing their performance is second nature to physical educators; asking students to assess their own skill performance is contrary to what many of us think is our role as a physical education teacher (i.e. that teachers should be the providers of skill feedback).

The task sheet is a guide that students use during activity time. It should inform the students about levels of task difficulty, sets of tasks/trials to be completed and critical performance cues for the task. Simple pictures that represent the performance cues are desirable. A place where students can record skill scores may also be included when wanting to formally collect

information about student performance. This information can be presented
to the students in the form of individual task sheets (see Figure 10.1) or in the
form of large wall charts (see Figures 10.2 and 10.3), which can be fastened
to the gymnasium walls. Referring your students to a task sheet or wall chart
when asked questions about task clarification will allow you more time to
observe and offer performance feedback.

When implementing an Inclusion Style episode for the first few times,
remember the phrase, *repetition, repetition, repetition.* Your level of success
with the Inclusion Style episode will likely be marginal during the first few

LEVELS OF TASK DIFFICULTY FOR BATTING

TASK (Variable 1)

Level	Task Description	Right Handed	Left Handed
1	Bat ball from batting tee.	▲ Tee	▲ Tee
2	Bat underhand tossed ball from side. (tosser kneeling 5 feet from batter)	Tosser	Tosser
3	Bat underhand tossed ball from front. (tosser standing 15 feet from batter)	◼ ⟵ Tosser	◼ ⟵ Tosser

SIZE OF BALL (Variable 2)

Level	Size		
1	Large	⬤	8 inch foam ball (handball size)
2	Medium	⬤	5 inch foam ball (softball size)
3	Small	●	3 inch foam ball (tennis ball size)

Figure 10.3 Wall chart to be posted on a gymnasium wall of different performance variables (levels of difficulty)

attempts because it is new to you and likely new to your students; however, with additional practice the rate of you successfully implementing the new teaching style and your students making appropriate decisions related to selecting level of task difficulty and self-assessing performance will increase dramatically. Joyce, Weil and Showers (1992) report that teachers continue to feel a certain level of discomfort with a new teaching strategy until attempted 10 or more times. Just as it takes a third grader many repetitions to execute the overhand throw at the utilisation level of skill proficiency, it will take you repeated Inclusion Style episodes to reach that level of success that you want. Keep this caveat in mind!

Conclusion

According to Keegan et al. (2019), physical literacy is comprised of four learning domains, physical, psychological, social and cognitive. The four defining statements that embody this Australian definition of physical literacy are:

> *Core* – Physical literacy is lifelong holistic learning acquired and applied in movement and physical activity contexts; *Constitution* – Physical literacy reflects on going changes integrating physical, psychological, cognitive, and social capabilities; *Importance* – Physical literacy is vital in helping us lead healthy and fulfilling lives through movement and physical activity; *Aspiration* – A physically literate person is able to draw on their integrated physical, psychological, cognitive, and social capabilities to support health promoting and fulfilling movement and physical activity relative to their situation and context, throughout the lifespan. (pp. 111–112)

These four learning domains are embedded within The Spectrum. The Inclusion Style clearly meets the goals associated with all four of these learning domains. A teaching style that favourably motivates students in physical education and provides some level of autonomy over learning, as is the case in the Inclusion Style, seems destined to influence an individual's journey to becoming physically literate. Past research confirms that teachers' perceptions of the learning process are typically more transmissive than constructive (Widodo & Duit, 2002). In a transmissive learning environment, students passively reproduce knowledge as presented by the teacher, while in a constructivist learning environment, students are encouraged to think critically with the result of knowledge *construction* by the learner (Windschitl, 2002). Student-centred instructional approaches, like Inclusion Style, are at the crux of the constructivist learning process. Rovegno (1998) and others in the field of physical education (Chen & Rovegno, 2000; Ennis, 1999; Kirk & MacPhail, 2002) support the notion that a constructivist approach to learning should be at the core of a pedagogical framework. In Inclusion Style learners construct knowledge about movement as a result of selecting level of task difficulty and self-checking performance. Inclusion Style empowers students through decision making.

References

Australian Curriculum, Assessment, and Reporting Authority (ACARA). (2015). *Health and physical education: Sequence of content F-10*. Retrieved from www. australiancurriculum.edu.au/f-10-curriculum/health-and-physical-education/pdf-documents/

Byra, M., & Jenkins, J. (1998). The thoughts and behaviors of learners in the inclusion style of teaching. *Journal of Teaching in Physical Education, 18*, 26–42.

Chatoupis, C., & Emmanuel, C. (2003). Teaching physical education with the inclusion style: The case of a Greek elementary school. *Journal of Physical Education, Recreation, and Dance, 74*(8), 33–38, 53.

Chen, W., & Rovegno, I. (2000). Examination of expert and novice teachers' constructivist-oriented teaching practices using a movement approach to elementary physical education. *Research Quarterly for Exercise and Sport, 71*, 169–185.

Ennis, C. D. (1999). Creating a culturally relevant curriculum for disengaged girls. *Sport, Education and Society, 4*, 31–49.

Graham, G., Holt-Hale, S. A., Parker, M., Hall, T., & Patton, K. (2020). *Children moving: A reflective approach to teaching physical education* (10th ed.). New York, NY: McGraw Hill.

Joyce, B., Weil, M., & Showers, B. (1992). *Models of teaching* (4th ed.). Boston, MA: Allyn and Bacon.

Keegan, R., Dudley, D., Bryant, A., Evans, J., Farrow, D., Lubans, D., ... Barnett, L. (2019). Defining physical literacy for application in Australia: A modified Delphi method. *Journal of Teaching in Physical Education, 38*, 105–118.

Kirby, S., Byra, M., Readdy, T., & Wallhead, T. (2015). The effect of the practice and inclusion styles of teaching on basic psychological needs satisfaction and self-determined motivation. *European Physical Education Review, 21*, 521–540.

Kirk, D., & MacPhail, A. (2002). Teaching games for understanding and situated learning: Rethinking the Bunker-Thorpe model. *Journal of Teaching in Physical Education, 21*, 177–192.

Krathwohl, D. R. (2002). A revision of Bloom's taxonomy: An overview. *Theory into Practice, 41*, 212–218.

Lonsdale, C., Sabiston, C. M., Raedeke, T. D., Ha, A. S. C., & Sum, R. K. W. (2009). Self-determined motivation and students' physical activity during structured physical education lessons and free choice periods. *Preventative Medicine, 48*, 69–73.

Mandigo, J., Holt, N., Anderson, A., & Sheppard, J. (2008). Children's motivational experiences following autonomy-supportive games lessons. *European Physical Education Review, 14*, 407–425.

Mosston, M., & Ashworth, S. (2008). *Teaching physical education* (First Online Edition; 6th ed.). Spectrum Institute for Teaching and Learning. Retrieved from www. spectrumofteachingstyles.org/e-book-download.php

Perlman, D. (2010). Change in affect and needs satisfaction for amotivated students within the Sport Education Model. *Journal of Teaching in Physical Education, 29*, 433–445.

Perlman, D. (2011). Examination of self-determination within the Sport Education Model. *Asia-Pacific Journal of Health, Sport and Physical Education, 2,* 72–92.

Perlman, D. (2013). Influence of the social context on students' in-class physical activity. *Journal of Teaching in Physical Education, 32,* 46–60.

Perlman, D., & Goc Karp, G. (2010). A self-determined perspective of the sport education model. *Physical Education and Sport Pedagogy, 15,* 401–418.

Reeve, J. (2006). Teachers as facilitators: What autonomy-supportive teachers do and why their students benefit. *Elementary School Journal, 106,* 225–236.

Reeve, J., & Jang, H. (2006). What teachers say and do to support students' autonomy during a learning activity. *Journal of Educational Psychology, 98,* 209–218.

Rovegno, I. (1998). The development of in-service teachers' knowledge of a constructivist approach to physical education: Teaching beyond activities. *Research Quarterly for Exercise and Sport, 69,* 147–162.

Society of Health and Physical Education (SHAPE America). (2014). *National standards and grade-level outcomes for K-12 physical education.* Reston, VA: SHAPE America; Champaign, IL: Human Kinetics.

Spittle, M., & Byrne, K. (2009). The influence of Sport Education on student motivation in physical education. *Physical Education and Sport Pedagogy, 14,* 253–266.

Wallhead, T. L., & Ntoumanis, N. (2004). Effects of a sport education intervention on students' motivational responses in physical education. *Journal of Teaching in Physical Education, 23,* 4–18.

Widodo, A., & Duit, R. (2002). Conceptual change views and the reality of classroom practice. In S. Lehti & K. Merenluoto (Eds.), *Proceeding of the third European symposium on conceptual change: A process approach to conceptual change* (pp. 289–297). Turku, Finland: University of Turku.

Windschitl, M. (2002). Framing constructivism in practice as the negotiation of dilemmas: An analysis of the conceptual, pedagogical, cultural, and political challenges facing teachers. *Review of Educational Research, 72,* 131–175.

Chapter 11

Effects of the Reciprocal Teaching Style on skill acquisition, verbal interaction and ability to analyse in fifth grade children in physical education

Michael Goldberger and Brendan SueSee

This chapter presents new research completed by the authors on the Reciprocal Style. It demonstrates the importance of using the Reciprocal Style in the context of numerous syllabus documents from around the world and provides a brief literature review of the strengths of the Reciprocal Style. Finally, it presents the results of this latest research and draws conclusions.

Syllabus documents

SueSee and Barker (2018) have suggested that numerous physical education syllabus documents contain multidimensional goals relating to more than movement. For example, the Society of Health and Physical Educators (SHAPE, 2014) document has five standards, with standards four and five focusing on the social development of the individual through physical activity. More specifically the documents goals suggest that by the end of Year 8, students should be able to "cooperate with and encourage classmates; accept individual differences and demonstrate inclusive behaviors" (p. 21). Furthermore, standard S4.M3.8 requires students to "provides encouragement and feedback to peers without prompting from the teacher" (SHAPE, 2014, p. 30). Curriculum documents from other countries, such as the Scottish Qualifications Authority (2012) require students to be able to "reflect on the performance of self and/or others ..." (p. 4), value creativity, problem solving, independence and responsibility (Skolverket, 2011), while the Australian Curriculum for Health and Physical Education (AC: HPE) requires students to be able to respond to feedback from peers on their performance (The Australian Curriculum, Assessment and Reporting Authority [ACARA], 2016). Within each of these documents there is scant suggested advice on pedagogies that will enable these multi-dimensional aims to be met. A little like giving the destination but no map. Thus, we argue there is an underlying assumption that teachers will use appropriate pedagogies to meet prescribed aims (SueSee & Barker, 2018). Research has suggested however, that teachers do not always align pedagogies with aims, and that factors

such as teachers' previous experiences, teacher education and pragmatic concerns affect teachers' pedagogies (SueSee, 2012; Syrmpas & Digelidis, 2014;
Syrmpas, Digelidis, Watt, & Vicars, 2017; Thorburn & Collins, 2003). With
many of these aims and outcomes (ACARA, 2016; SHAPE, 2014; SQA, 2012;
Skolverket, 2011) focusing on the social development of the student how are
teachers able to achieve these goals? Is there a teaching style that focuses on the
social development of the student as well as the physical development? The
answer thankfully is 'yes' if learning experiences are created that target the
development of the social developmental channel. This chapter will outline
briefly research completed using the Reciprocal Style and the effects it had on
students. It will show how the Reciprocal Style created a learning episode that
improved motor performance, the amount of feedback given and the quality
of feedback given by the participants.

Reciprocal Style

The Reciprocal Style teaching style, from Mosston and Ashworth's Spectrum of Teaching Styles (2008), is particularly useful during early skill acquisition because it provides large amounts of feedback to learners about their
performance individually and in a timely fashion. In Reciprocal Style, learners operate in pairs with one performing the task while being observed by
and getting immediate feedback from her/his partner. The feedback is based
on skill criteria provided by the teacher. An example of a criteria sheet can be
seen in Figure 11.1 and Figure 11.2. Figure 11.1 is a teacher designed criteria
sheet for performing footwork in Netball. Figure 11.2 is a teacher designed
criteria sheet for writing a paragraph. Any content can be taught in this way
if there is identifiable concepts or movements to replicate. After the first
learner completes the task, they switch roles and reciprocate. In preparing
learners for Reciprocal Style they are taught how to observe and how to provide descriptive (not judgemental) feedback.

Reciprocal Style develops specific aspects from the developmental channels (social, physical, emotional, ethical/moral and cognitive). When a teacher
chooses to use Reciprocal Style it is likely to create a learning episode that
can develop socialisation skills, communication skills, giving and receiving
feedback from peers, allow the development of empathy and manners, build
trust interacting and socialising with others, allow students to experience the
reward of seeing others succeed and knowing you contributed and allow
students the experience the effect you have on others feelings and learning
(Mosston & Ashworth, 2008).

Research completed on the Reciprocal Style has demonstrated a number of positive aspects. For example, students taught with Reciprocal Style
scored significantly higher in attention, satisfaction and appropriate behaviours when being taught dance, and, the Reciprocal Style was better suited
to stimulate cognitive and affective responses than the experimental groups

YEAR 8 PHYSICAL EDUCATION-Netball

OBJECTIVE:	To learn the subroutine for netball footwork; To practice the subroutine for correct footwork in netball; and To observe and analyse a classmates technique and give feedback using criteria.
ACTIVITY 1:	Can I correctly perform my footwork?

Number done accurately out of 10: ....

ACTIVITY 2:	There will be 2 roles **for** you to play in the following activity. One role is the **DOER,** and the other role is the **OBSERVER.**
OBSERVERS ROLE:	Read the criteria Observe the DOER Give feedback based on the criteria, and information to improve.
DOER's ROLE:	Know the criteria Do you best to perform the skill correctly? Listen to feedback from the OBSERVER and respond

Criteria	Mostly	Sometimes	Not often
Takes off on correct foot.			
Hands out in front and fingers facing forward.			
Lands right/left (or left/right).			
Lands on balls of feet and sounds soft.			
Knees are bent and absorbs force.			
Stays low-low centre of gravity.			
Holds with no foot drag.			

Teacher ROLE: Speaks only to OBSERVER

The person I was observing was: ....

The feedback I gave was:

....
....
....
....
....
....

Figure 11.1 A Reciprocal Style criteria sheet for the students to use in a Reciprocal Style episode for footwork in netball

Year 12 physical education: writing a paragraph to justify a claim

Objective:	To write a paragraph to **justify** a claim
	To use the **CEEEQ** format correctly,
	To observe and analyse a classmates' use of the **CEEEQ** format and give feedback using criteria.
Activity 1:	Write your paragraph using the **CEEEQ** format.
Activity 2:	There will be 2 roles **for** you to play in the following activity. One role is the **DOER**, and the other role is the **OBSERVER**. As the observer you will provide feedback as per the criteria sheet.

Observers

Role:	Read the criteria
	Observe/read the DOER's work
	Give feedback (**appropriately**) based on the criteria, and
	Information to improve.
Doer's Role:	Know the criteria
	Do your best to perform the task correctly,
	Listen to feedback from the OBSERVER and respond appropriately.
Teachers Role:	Speaks only to the OBSERVER

The person I was observing was: ....

Criteria	Yes	Not Always Clear	No
S makes a claim that is clear.			
S uses **primary evidence** that supports the claim. ("*I would not feel....*".)			
S refers to **secondary evidence** ("*This is supported by Amezdroz, Dickens....*")			
S **references correctly** (i.e.- quote in inverted comas, Author/s, year, p).			
S **elaborates** by showing they know what the quote means by putting it in their own words and extending on the quote. ("*This means/shows/demonstrates that...*")			
S **qualifies** by making a prediction about the effect of this situation. ("*If this continues to happen then it is likely that . . .*".)			
S has correct spelling, grammar and punctuation.			

The feedback I gave was: ....
....
....

Figure 11.2 A Reciprocal Style criteria sheet to be used for paragraph writing

(Cuellar-Moreno, 2016). Students taught with Reciprocal Style outperformed the control group (taught with Self-Check Style) in chest pass accuracy and form (Kolovelonis, Goudas & Gerodimos, 2011), and Reciprocal Style has demonstrated to be as effective as Practice Style in developing students ability to perform a badminton stroke (Babatunde, 2014) and just as effective as Command Style when teaching psychomotor skills (Yoncalik, 2009). Yoncalik (2009) suggested that it is highly effective when working with females with low-ability. Iserbyt, Elen and Behets, (2010) found that students taught with a defined doer-observer relationship (and asked to switch roles every five minutes when prompted by the researcher) remembered and recalled all Basic Life Support skills better than a control group, and that error detection ability improved. Hennings, Wallhead and Byra (2010) also found that students taught using the Reciprocal Style were able to provide accurate error detection to their partners. While all of these findings show positive educational outcomes, it is understandable that teacher's may conclude that Reciprocal Style may detract from the learning of motor skills as time practicing the skill is reduced due to the social interaction provided by the peer teaching. This research addresses this concern.

The Practice Style was also utilised in this study along with a control group. In the Practice Style learners also practice a task but it is the teacher who provides feedback to the student/s. In comparing the conditions provided by Reciprocal Style and Practice Style in terms of frequency of feedback, under Reciprocal Style conditions, feedback is provided after every trial by the partner. In contrast, under Practice Style conditions, the teacher provides feedback only when, and if, s/he can.

The central question in the study was: Is Reciprocal Style more effective than Practice Style in fostering motor skill acquisition? Also of interest was a comparison of the amount and type of feedback provided. There was also an interest in assessing the benefit, if any, of observing and analysing the performance of another on one's own skill performance.

In this study it was hypothesised that:

(1)   Under Reciprocal Style conditions learners would perform better than Practice Style learners and a control group on a novel motor task;
(2)   Under Reciprocal Style conditions learners would offer more and better feedback than Practice Style learners or a control group when paired and asked to help their partners to learn another task; and
(3)   Under Reciprocal Style conditions learners would be better able to analyse a motor skill compared with their Practice Style and control group counterparts.

Method

This quasi-experimental study employed a pre-post control group design. There were two treatment groups, Reciprocal Style and Practice Style, and a control group. The participants came from two public middle schools in the Philadelphia (USA) area. Children from six heterogeneously grouped fifth grade classes, a total of 260 children, agreed to participate in this study. Informed consents were obtained from all the learners, parents, teachers and school administrators. Within each school three intact classes were randomly assigned to one of the two treatment groups or a control group.

The teachers who participated in this study were the two veteran physical education teachers from these schools, each with over 25 years of experience. Both teachers were highly trained and experienced in using The Spectrum of Teaching Styles.

The task

The task utilised in this study was a unique hockey accuracy skill.

Learners shot a series of plastic hockey pucks under a blind into a target area. The score was based on how close the shot ended to the target's bull's-eye. Two of these testing areas were set up in each school's gymnasium.

The treatments

Participants practiced this hockey accuracy task under the conditions provided by the condition assigned to their group. Learners in Reciprocal Style were paired and as one student practiced (the Doer) the skill her/his partner (the observer) provided immediate corrective feedback and positive reinforcement after each trial. They switched roles halfway through the trial period. Learners in the Practice Style took turns practicing the task and were provided feedback by the teacher less frequently, one feedback comment per ten trials. Learners under Practice Style conditions had 40 trials compared with only 20 trials under Reciprocal Style conditions.

Testing

All participants completed a pre-test and post-test hockey accuracy test, to see if performance improved. After the hockey testing was completed, 10 children from each treatment group were randomly selected to participate in the next phase of the study. These 20 children were partnered with someone from within their group, but, for the Reciprocal Style group, with someone other than whom they had been working during the first phase of the study. They were then asked to 'help' their partner learn a new and unique dart throwing skill. The interaction between the two partners were recorded for later analysis to see if Reciprocal Style children provided more and better feedback. An 'interaction analysis' type tool was used. Finally, all the children in the Reciprocal Style and Practice Style groups were asked to view a recording that displayed three lacrosse throws; each with an error purposely embedded within the performer's form. Participants were given criteria sheets and asked to identify the error in an effort to test their ability to analyse motor performance.

Results

As can be seen in Table 11.1, participants in both the Reciprocal Style and Practice Style groups improved their performance scores over the course of training and participants in the control group did not. Furthermore, using an analysis of covariance with the pre-test serving as the covariate, no significant difference was found between the two treatment groups. It is noted, again, that the Reciprocal Style group had half the number of actual practice trials, although they had better/richer feedback on the physical trials they had.

Table 11.2 shows the average number of both verbal and non-verbal interactions per minute for the two treatment groups as they tried to help their partners learn the new dart task. It can be seen that the Reciprocal Style group had more than double the number of interactions. This difference was found to be significant (p<.05).

Finally, Table 11.3 shows that children in the Reciprocal Style group were significantly better able to analyse videotaped motor performance in terms of identifying errors in skill form when compared to their Practice Style counterparts.

Table 11.1 Pre-and post-test motor performance scores for two treatment groups and a control group

Teaching Style	Pre-test			Post-test		
	n	M	s	M	s	Δ
Practice	125	18.17	5.56	25.64*	6.95	7.47
Reciprocal	89	17.65	7.49	25.04*	8.70	7.39
Control	46	18.22	6.20	17.74	6.51	0.48

*p < 0.05

Table 11.2 Number of verbal and non-verbal interactions per minute for the two treatment groups using the reciprocal coding system

	n	M	s
Practice Style B	10	7.9	4.01
Reciprocal Style C	10	17.5*	6.36

*p < 0.05

Table 11.3 Analytical scores for the two treatment groups

	n	M	s
Practice Style	100	4.69	2.86
Reciprocal Style	67	6.09*	3.17

*$p < 0.05$

Discussion

It was hypothesised that the conditions for learning provided by the Reciprocal Style, where corrective feedback and positive reinforcement are provided after every practice, would be an effective teaching approach to learn new skills. It was found that both teaching approaches proved to be effective in promoting skills acquisition. This was not surprising as numerous studies have shown that Practice Style is effective for learning motor skills (Beckett, 1990; Boyce, 1992; Chatoupis, 2000; Yoncalik, 2009).

These results are also similar to others (Babatunde, 2014) that have done comparative studies between Practice Style and Reciprocal Style and reported no significant difference in motor skill performance. Others, such as Boyce (1992) who found that when comparing Command Style, Practice Style and Reciprocal Style to teach a motor task that Reciprocal Style was not as effective as the other two styles. Interestingly, although the Reciprocal Style students received half the number of actual practice trials (20 trials) of their Practice Style counterparts (40 trials), the Reciprocal Style group did equally well. When improvements are compared for the two groups between pre-test and post-test the Practice Style group improved 7.47 while the Reciprocal Style group improved 7.39 with only half the attempts but clearly more feedback.

These findings reinforce the adage that practicing does not make perfect, unless the practice is correct. Otherwise it may be argued that all students are doing is practicing a motor pattern the 'wrong' way if they receive no corrective feedback, whether it is from a fellow student or a teacher seems to be irrelevant. It is assumed that the students being taught with Reciprocal Style had more feedback which allowed them to correct their performance in comparison to the students taught using Practice Style who had double the amount of practice attempts but significantly less feedback and therefore less opportunity to correct anything they may have been doing incorrectly. This result also may be comfort to teachers who valued the Reciprocal Style but felt they were using it at the detriment of developing physical skills. The results of this research can now allow teachers to know that they would be developing both the social skills and physical skills with students who were taught using this style. In conclusion it may be suggested that in the short term, incorrect practice trials do not foster skill improvement, something that may have been the case when Practice Style was used in this research.

The second research hypothesis was that Reciprocal Style learners would offer more and better feedback than Practice Style learners or a control group when paired and asked to help their partners to learn another task. It is important to remember here that all participants in this study were permitted to 'help' their partners learn the new skill. The results show that the Reciprocal Style group gave over twice the amount of feedback comments than the Practice Style group, clearly demonstrating that Reciprocal Style learners offered more and better feedback than the Practice Style group. These results are perhaps not surprising as the characteristics of Reciprocal Style are "social interaction, reciprocation, receiving and giving immediate feedback ... " (Mosston and Ashworth, 2008, p. 116). Research by some (Byra & Marks, 1993; Ernst & Byra, 1998) has already reported students taught with the Reciprocal Style leads to an increase in the number of positive interactions with their peers, and the feedback provided by the observers was perceived as specific and helpful. In contrast, research by Kolovelonis and Goudas (2012) found students taught with Reciprocal Style displayed moderate recording accuracy indicating room for improvement, and that analysing performance and giving accurate feedback are skills which need practice and development if they are to be accurate.

With regards to the amount of feedback given, Table 11.2 clearly shows that the Reciprocal Style group gave over double the feedback when helping compared to the Practice Style group, thus confirming the second hypothesis. With regard to better feedback, this conclusion may seem difficult to confirm as it can be suggested that even if feedback is accurate, if the learner does not understand it (and use it to improve performance) then it is of little value. This view is taking an outcome approach to feedback rather than a judgement about the quality of the feedback. However, given that the Reciprocal Style group had only half the amount of practice trials the Practice Style group had and that their improvement was nearly identical post-test (a difference of only 0.08) then it may be suggested that unless there are other factors at play the quality of feedback made a difference in improving performance.

The third and final research hypothesis was that Reciprocal Style learners would be better able to analyse a motor skill compared with their Practice Style and control group counterparts. The data displayed in Table 11.3 illustrates the difference between the Practice Style group and the Reciprocal Style group's ability to analyse a motor skill (a lacrosse throw) and identify an error. The results indicate that students taught with Reciprocal Style were significantly better at this task than the Practice Style group. The fact that the three learning episodes (hockey accuracy test, darts throw and a lacrosse throw) are all quite different means that it is unlikely that the Reciprocal Style group brought experience in analysing the lacrosse throw to the last task. It may indicate that the Reciprocal Style students had undoubtedly become more focused on analysing movement given the two previous learning experiences required them to do so.

In addition, it was hypothesised that these conditions would foster collaborative learning and would help children improve their analytical skills. In terms of social development, the Reciprocal Style learners behaved more socially than their Practice Style counterparts, at least in terms of their ability to provide feedback. These findings support the notion that children can learn how to provide feedback that is more effective and will do so if the situation allows this. Giving and receiving feedback are 'teachable' social skills. The possible benefits of other aspects of socialisation must be examined more closely in other studies.

Conclusion

Numerous syllabus documents have goals that reflect a valuing of more than just the psychomotor domain. The Reciprocal Style would be a very appropriate teaching style to meet the outcomes listed here:

- Listens respectfully to corrective feedback from others (e.g. peers, adults) (SHAPE, 2013, p. 18);
- Describes the positive social inter- actions that come when engaged with others in physical activity (SHAPE, 2013, p. 20);
- Examining how individuals, family and peer groups influence people's behaviours, decisions and actions (ACARA, 2014, p. 46);
- Exploring skills and strategies needed to communicate and engage in relationships in respectful ways (ACARA, 2014, p. 46);
- Using knowledge of results feedback to support another student in performing a skill with greater accuracy or control (ACARA, 2014, p. 58); and
- Using knowledge of results feedback to support another student in performing a skill with greater accuracy or control (Skolverket, 2018, p. 48).

The examples from the aforementioned documents demonstrate the requirement for the social development of students and the Reciprocal Style is one teaching style that should be employed regularly as it allows for the development of the social domain of the student. It does this by creating an environment where social skills such as giving and receiving feedback, and the effect that we have on others participation, can be taught through a lived experience. The study we outlined in this chapter provides support for the suggestion that developing in students 'an eye' for analysing motor performance can be accomplished using this style. In this study, students were taught how to hold criteria in mind while observing performance and being able to compare actual performance against the criteria.

This chapter has showed that Reciprocal Style was just as effective as Practice Style in developing a motor skill, with only half the number of practice trials. This research has also demonstrated that Reciprocal Style increased the number of both verbal and non-verbal interactions between participants, and that students taught with Reciprocal Style were better at error identification than those taught with Practice Style. When these results are considered in light of Spectrum theory, two of the three are not surprising – those being that error identification was improved and that more feedback was given as these are decisions that are shifted to the learner from Practice Style. It is not surprising because Reciprocal Style requires students to practice observing a motor task and to give feedback about how well that task is being performed when compared to a task sheet. What perhaps is surprising is that motor performance was not less than the Practice Style group even though the number of practice tasks for the group taught with Reciprocal Style were half that of Practice Style. Finally, we have shown that Reciprocal Style also allows for many of the values and objectives (particularly of the social nature) of a range of syllabus documents to be taught.

References

Australian Curriculum, Assessment and Reporting Authority. (2016). *The Health and Physical Education Curriculum*. Version 8.2, Sydney, Australia. Retrieved from www.australiancurriculum.edu.au/download?view=f10

Babatunde, E., (2014). Effects of two methods of teaching badminton strokes on skill performance of children. *Journal of Emerging Trends in Educational Research and Policy Studies* (JETERAPS) 5(8), 118–123.

Beckett, K.D. (1990). The effects of two teaching styles on college students' achievement of selected physical education outcomes. *Journal of Teaching in Physical Education, 10*(2), 153–169.

Boyce, B.A. (1992). The effects of three styles of teaching on university student's motor performance. *Journal of Teaching in Physical Education, 11*(4), 389–401.

Byra, M., & Marks, M. (1993). The effect of two pairing techniques on specific feedback and comfort levels of learners in the reciprocal style of teaching. *Journal of Teaching in Physical Education, 12*, 286–300.

Chatoupis, C. (2000). *The effects of two teaching styles on physical fitness and perceived athletic competence of fifth grade students*. Unpublished doctoral dissertation. University of Manchester, UK.

Cuellar-Moreno, M. (2016). Effects of the command and mixed styles on student learning in primary education. *Journal of Physical Education & Sport, 16*(4), 1159–1168.

Ernst, M., & Byra, M. (1998). Pairing learners in the reciprocal style of teaching: Influence on students' skill, knowledge, and socialization. *The Physical Educator, 55*, 24–37.

Hennings, J., Wallhead, T., & Byra, M., (2010). A didactic analysis of student content learning during the reciprocal style of teaching. *Journal of Teaching in Physical Education, 29*(3), 227–244.

Iserbyt, P., Elen, J., & Behets, D. (2010). Instructional guidance in reciprocal peer tutoring with task cards. *Journal of Teaching in Physical Education, 29*, 38–53.

Kolovelonis, A., & Goudas, M. (2012). Students' recording accuracy in the reciprocal and the self-check teaching styles in physical education. *Educational Research and Evaluation, 18*, 733–747.

Kolovelonis, A., Goudas, M., and Gerodimos, I. (2011). The effects of the reciprocal and the self- check styles on pupils' performance in primary physical education. *European Physical Education Review*, 17(1), 35–50.

Mosston, M., & Ashworth, S. (2008). *Teaching physical education*: First online edition. Retrieved from www.spectrumofteachingstyles.

Spectrum Institute for Teaching and Learning. (United States). [E-Book Download]

SHAPE America – Society of Health and Physical Educators. (2014). *National standards and grade-level outcomes for K–12 physical education*. Champaign, IL: Human Kinetics.

SHAPE America. (2013). *Grade-level outcomes for K-12 physical education*. Reston, VA: Author.

Skolverket. (2011). *Curriculum for the compulsory school, preschool class and the leisure-time centre*. Retrieved from www.skolverket.se/publikationer

Scottish Qualifications Authority. (2012). National 3 physical education course specification (Scotland). Retrieved from www.sqa.org.uk

SueSee, B. (2012). *Incongruence between self-reported and observed senior physical education teaching styles: An analysis using Mosston and Ashworth's Spectrum* (Unpublished doctoral dissertation). Queensland University of Technology, Brisbane, QLD.

SueSee, B., & Barker, D. (2018). Self-reported and observed teaching styles of Swedish physical education teachers, *Curriculum Studies in Health and Physical Education*, 10(1), 34–50.

Syrmpas, I., & Digelidis, N. (2014). Physical education student teachers' experiences with and perceptions of teaching styles. *Journal of Physical Education and Sport*, 14, 52–59.

Syrmpas, I., Digelidis, N., Watt, A., & Vicars, M. (2017). Physical education teachers' experiences and beliefs of production and reproduction teaching approaches. *Teaching and Teacher Education*, 66, 184–194.

Thorburn, M., & Collins, D. (2003). Integrated curriculum Models and their effects on teachers' pedagogy practices. *European Physical Education Review*, 9, 185–209.

Yoncalık, O. (2009). The effects of three teaching styles on elementary sixth grade students' achievement in physical education lesson. *Selçuk University Journal of Physical Education and Sport Science*, 11(3), 33–46.

Chapter 12

Teachers' and students' experiences with and perceptions of the Teaching Styles

Donetta J. Cothran and Pamela Hodges Kulinna

The single unifying principle (the Axiom) that governs the theoretical structure of The Spectrum states that *teaching is a chain of decision making* (Mosston & Ashworth, 1994, p. 11). Traditionally, understanding and using The Spectrum means understanding decisions made at the pre-impact, impact, and post-impact stages, and those decisions are framed by the desired end point of an educational outcome. In this chapter, we seek to add to the field's understanding of that decision making chain by expanding the conversation about participants' decision making. Specifically, we are interested in participants' broader beliefs about the teaching styles and their class goals that may or may not be strictly educational. For example, numerous studies have shown that both teachers and students have fun as a primary goal of physical education (e.g. Cothran & Ennis, 1996; Garn & Cothran, 2006). Does that goal influence teacher and student decision making about and perspectives on The Spectrum? We also believe that the decision making chain can only be understood fully when we understand who our participants are and in what contexts are they operating.

This chapter will briefly review a series of three related investigations conducted by our research team that broke new ground in exploring what styles were being used, by whom and what those individuals believed about the styles. We then expand that discussion to other researchers' work around the central themes of our findings in an attempt to capture a more complete picture of The Spectrum decision making chain and to suggest new paths of inquiry regarding The Spectrum and its use.

The Spectrum use and perceptions

Overview

With our colleagues, we conducted a series of three investigations guided by the overarching goals of understanding participants' experiences with and perspectives on The Spectrum. All three studies shared similar research questions of: (a) What styles have the participants experienced? (b) Do participants differentiate among the potential style characteristics (e.g. fun, learning and motivation)? and, (c) Are there demographic influences on the participants' experiences and perceptions? Each investigation focused on a different participant group: students (Cothran, Kulinna, & Ward, 2000); teachers (Kulinna & Cothran, 2003), and an international group of teachers (Cothran et al., 2005).

Using the Mosston and Ashworth (1994) text as a guide, a short descriptive scenario was written for each of the 11 teaching styles on The Spectrum (see Table 12.1). After a content validation process, the scenarios were then integrated into a survey instrument to explore both participants' experience with, as well as perceptions of, the potential benefits of the various styles. The original student focused survey statements were: (a) I had a physical education teacher that taught this way; (b) I think this way of teaching would make class fun; (c) I think this way of teaching would help students learn skills and concepts; and, (d) I think this way of teaching would motivate students to learn. The wording of the questions was changed slightly for the teacher surveys. For example, the first item became, "I have used this way to teach physical education". Each item was followed by a 5-point Likert-like scale. For the first experience statement the end points were "never" and "always". The other three statements had ranges with "strongly disagree" and "strongly agree" as the anchors.

Table 12.1 Teaching Style scenarios

A	Command	The teacher breaks down the skills into parts and demonstrates the right way to perform the skill. Students try to move when and exactly how the teacher tells them. The teacher provides feedback and the students try to look like the teacher's model.
B	Practice	The teacher makes several stations in the gym where students work on different parts of a skill or different skills. Students rotate around the stations and do the tasks at their own pace. The teacher moves around and helps students when needed.
C	Reciprocal	Two students work together on a task that the teacher has designed. One student practices, while the other student gives feedback to the partner. The students might use checklists to help them give good feedback to each other.
D	Self-check	Students work alone on a task and check their own work. The teacher might give them a checklist so that the students can provide feedback to themselves while they learn the task.
E	Inclusion	The teacher designs a learning task and there are several levels of difficulty. Students choose the level at which they want to work. Students can decide to make the task easier or harder by changing levels of the task to match their ability.

continued

Table 12.1 continued

F	Guided Discovery	The teacher asks students to discover a solution to a movement problem. The teacher asks students a series of specific questions and the students try out their answers until they discover the right answer that the teacher wanted them to discover.
G	Convergent Discovery	Students try to learn a skill or concept by using logical reasoning. The teacher asks a question and students try to reason and think about different solutions. By critically thinking about the question and trying solutions, students can discover the single, right answer.
H	Divergent Production	The teacher asks students to solve a movement question. The students try to discover different movement solutions to the teacher's question. There are multiple ways for the students to answer the question correctly.
I	Learner's Designed Individual Program	The teacher picks the general subject matter, but the student makes most of the decisions about the learning experience. The student decides what will be learned within the teacher's guidelines, and then designs a personal learning program with consultation from the teacher.
J	Learner Initiated	The student decides what will be learned as well as how it will be learned. The teacher and student set some basic criteria, but the student is responsible for all the decisions about how and what to learn. The teacher can help with information if the student needs it.
K	Self Teaching	The student decides everything about learning something new. They even decide if they want to involve the teacher or not. The teacher accepts the student's decisions about learning.

Reprinted from Learning and Instruction, Kulinna, P. H., & Cothran, D. J. (2003). Physical Education Teachers' Self-Reported Use and Perception of Various Teaching Styles, 597–609. (Copyright, 2003), with permission from Elsevier.

Each survey had slightly different demographic questions to reflect the specifics of each population. Minimally the instrument asked about sex, ethnicity, age (students) or experience (teachers) and self-rated ability in learning (student) or teaching (teachers). For full details on each study as well as the extensive instrument development and validation procedures, please refer to the original papers.

The first investigation focused on students and involved 438 college students that were predominantly (82 per cent) Caucasian and evenly divided between male and female.

The students were enrolled in elective physical education classes (team sports, fitness, individual and dual sports) at a large university in the United States. The United States was also the setting for the next investigation that focused on physical education teachers (N=212). The population was once again predominantly Caucasian (90 per cent) and relatively balanced across sex, school level and experience. To examine the possible influence of culture on Spectrum use, the third investigation recruited 1,436 teachers from seven countries: Australia,

Canada, England, France, Korea, Portugal and the United States. This group was also relatively balanced across experience and grade level, but there were more male participants (753) than female participants (445).

In the section that follows all three studies are summarised for their major trends in answering the research questions. Due to the larger number of participants from different settings and a desire to focus on potential cultural effects on teacher use of styles, direct comparisons of some of the data points between the three sets is not possible.

How many styles are being used?

From the participants' perspectives, physical education is a course where multiple teaching styles are used. On average, students reported experience with slightly more than five styles with those experiences being dominated by the Reproduction cluster. The teacher sample from the United States reported using eight styles on average with the reproduction cluster again being the most commonly used. In the United States samples there were two exceptions to the trend of reproduction styles as the most commonly used. Both teachers and students reported that Self-Check Style was not as commonly used as other styles from that cluster. Both groups also reported that Divergent Production Style was one of the top five most commonly used styles although they did differ slightly in their ordering of the top five.

The international teacher data was reported slightly differently, but a ranking of style use is still possible. The percentage of teachers who reported using a style "sometimes to always" was reported in percentages. For example, 94.2 per cent of Korean teachers reported implementing Command Style, "sometimes to always" while 37.3 per cent of French teachers did. For each country, the three highest rated styles for percentage of teachers who reported using the style "sometimes to always" was: Australia (Command Style, Practice Style and Reciprocal Style) Canada (Practice Style, Guided Discovery Style and Command Style), England (Reciprocal Style, Inclusion Style and Guided Discovery Style), France (Practice Style, Inclusion Style and Reciprocal Style), Korea (Command Style, Practice Style and Inclusion Style) and the United States (Practice Style, Command Style and Reciprocal Style). Although the top three styles were dominated by the reproduction style cluster, there were other trends of note. Once again, Self-Check Style was the exception in the reproduction cluster with no country ranking it in their top five used styles. Additionally, each country placed at least one style from the production cluster (e.g. Guided Discovery Style, depending on the country) in the top five use ratings.

What are participants' perspectives on the styles?

All styles were perceived as having some value, but there were clear trends in evaluating potential positive outcomes of the styles. In the United States samples, both teachers and students preferred the reproduction styles over the production styles as both groups placed Command Style, Practice Style, Reciprocal Style and Inclusion Style, in their top five styles for perceived benefits with regard to learning, fun and motivation. Practice Style, was top ranked for both groups. The remaining styles in the top five ratings were Learner's Individual Designed Program Style, for the students and Divergent Discovery Style, for the teachers.

For the international sample, the cultural influences on teachers' beliefs were evident showing that all countries were significantly different in their beliefs about styles. The general trend of an overall more positive view of the reproduction cluster held true in the international group. Each country, however, had a unique perspective on the styles. For example, Portugal tended to view the collective styles on The Spectrum less positively overall than did the other countries, while England was the most positive towards a range of styles. There were also national differences in the range of scores given the various styles. Korea reported similar perceptions scores for most styles while countries like England and France showed more variability in their ranking of the styles on the potential outcomes of learning, fun and motivation.

Do participant characteristics influence their perspectives?

Individual and contextual factors both influenced participants' perspectives on the styles. For the student participants, sex, self-rated ability and the type of elective course (team sports, individual and dual sports, fitness) enrolled in all affected their ratings to a certain degree. For example, female students held significantly higher ratings for Inclusion Style, Divergent Discovery Style and Learner's Individual Designed Program than did their male counterparts. Divergent Discovery Style, was also perceived more highly by students in the fitness classes than the sports-based courses, a trend also true for Self-Check Style. The interplay between the sex of the student and the course enrolment pattern complicates these findings as the fitness classes were predominantly female. Self-rated ability also played a role in student ratings. Students who reported themselves to be high ability rated Command Style higher than did other students. At the other end of the self-rated ability spectrum, students who considered themselves low ability perceived Self-Check Style more favourably.

For the United States based teachers, self-rated ability to teach was also an influence on their style perceptions. Teachers who rated themselves in the high ability group perceived the styles, particularly the production styles, more positively. Interestingly, teacher ratings of the styles' potential outcomes were not influenced by their sex, age, experience, class size and length of class session, nor by school environment (urban, suburban, rural) or grade level.

In contrast to the United States teacher sample, the international teachers' perceptions of the styles became more positive with more years of teaching experience. Their perceptions of the styles' potential outcomes were also influenced by self-rated ability and sex. Interestingly, how teachers learned to use styles was quite different across countries. For example, teachers in Portugal indicated that they learned about styles in graduate school (94.2 per cent), while Korean teachers reported that they learned to use styles through books (82.1 per cent), and 91.3 per cent of Australian teachers reported that they used to learn the styles from other teachers.

One trend that held true for all the participant groups is that familiarity with a style was contributing factor to the participants' style ratings. There was a small, but significant correlation between experience and rating. Although significant, the correlations were not strong which suggests other factors were involved in the participants' perspectives.

Discussion

These three investigations provided new insights into participants' experiences with and perceptions of the styles. When viewed in combination with other work in the field, the findings offer some insights into the decision making chain that is at the heart of The Spectrum. Those insights also suggest the need for more work in this area as critical questions and tensions are clear.

Teachers reported using a variety of different styles and other investigators report similar findings. Using a version of the same instrument from the Cothran and Kulinna trilogy, Syrmpas and Digelidis (2014) surveyed over 280 physical education student teachers about their experiences as students in Greece and those students reported their teachers primarily used the reproduction cluster with Guided Discovery Style being the one production style that was rated as frequently used. In a related paper, the authors focused on 219 Greek teachers and reported similar patterns to the teacher education student reports (Syrmpas, Digelidis, & Watt, 2016). Working with a Finnish sample of nearly 300 teachers and a similar instrument, Jaakkola and Watt (2011) found comparable use trends.

A partial level of support for the basic trend of teachers incorporating a variety of styles, particularly from the reproduction cluster, is provided by other researchers using other methods. Curtner-Smith, Todorovich, McCaughtry and Lacon (2011) reported on direct systematic observations of 18 teachers in England. A range of styles were observed but the teaching segments were dominated by the reproduction styles, primarily Practice Style. Working in Australia, SueSee and Edwards (2015) offer a unique and important research design in which a larger group of teachers (N=110) self-reported their style use and then a small group (n=27) from that sample was followed up with a systematic observation of multiple lessons. The teachers, including the ones observed, indicated they used a range of styles. Direct observation of the sub-sample teaching, however, revealed a much different profile. The researchers did find five different styles in use, however, Practice Style dominated. They also found that five of their participants used only one style. This phenomenon is not restricted to findings with PE teachers; it has also been seen with tennis coaches (Hewitt & Edwards, 2015).

Clearly, additional work is needed in this area of style use as teachers and theorists seem to think about style use differently. Some level of social desirability bias may be in play in the self-reports as perhaps teachers sought to present the best possible professional image. Given the consistency of the responses, though, across countries, the anonymity of the survey, and the fact that student survey results support teacher reports of multiple style use; it seems more than just social desirability is affecting teacher reports. Combining the results of all the studies that used some version of the Kulinna and Cothran (2003) instrument, well over 2,000 teachers from around the world report using multiple styles, yet theorists often discount these reports. It is important to understand these differences. Do teachers, from their perspective of praxis, understand the styles differently than do researchers? Perhaps teachers are reporting on "micro-teaching" episodes that involve individual or small group interactions different from the primary thrust of the lesson style. For example, in a volleyball lesson that is primarily presented to the class in a Practice Style, the teacher may stop and ask a partner group to each identify what their partner is doing well and needs to work on leading the teacher to indicate on a survey that they have used both Practice and Reciprocal style in a lesson. Meanwhile, the external observer was focused on more global class pedagogy and perhaps did not even hear what the teacher asked the volleyball pair to reflect on, and thus they recorded the primary teaching style of Practice but not the micro-teach of varied instruction that involved a small scale reciprocal approach. Much more work is needed in this area of theorist-practitioner differences and how each are interpreting style use.

Perhaps a more basic and important question that has been largely unaddressed is if teachers should even be expected to use a variety of styles. Mosston theorists often speak of a "'mobility ability', the skill of easily moving from one teaching style to another as the circumstances suggest" (Goldberger, Ashworth, & Byra, 2012, p. 274) and with that comes the implied at least assumption that more style use is better. That assumption also suggests that teachers are seeking to meet a range of educational goals in different domains thus needing different styles. Jaakkola and Watt (2011) offer an interesting counterpoint and suggest that Finnish teachers' reliance on reproduction styles may indicate a clear preference for motor skill learning and from that perspective their narrow style use is appropriate in light of their more singular focus on psychomotor mastery. Working from a critical pedagogical perspective, Sicilia-Camacho and Brown (2008) offer an important, alternate theoretical discussion of why 'mobility ability' should be questioned. SueSee, Pill and Edwards (2016) discuss why games-based approaches do not need to be seen as in conflict with The Spectrum since they are both guided by pedagogical decision making.

Overall both students and teachers see some value for all the styles, although the reproduction styles were generally rated higher on the outcomes of fun, learning and motivation than were the production cluster styles. We suggest one of the next steps for this area of research is to examine the trends at a more granular level, perhaps starting with the interesting "mismatches" and considering other outcomes that may be driving the teacher decision making chain. One example is from the international teacher data set. Why is England the one country that does not rate Practice Style in their top five? Is their teacher training or national curriculum that different from other countries? Other research (e.g. Curtner-Smith, 1999; SueSee et al., 2018) suggests that a national curriculum may not have that much influence on practice so what is influencing English teachers? Another example is the clear anomaly in the reproduction cluster for Self-Check Style. What makes this teacher centred style less attractive than the other styles in that cluster Self-Check Style is the least experienced by students so does that early inexperience lend itself to later non-use as a teacher thus continuing the cycle? Syrmpas and Digelidis (2014) found a significant relationship between their physical education student teachers' experience with and intent to use several of the styles when teaching.

Alternately, perhaps the decision to not implement Self-Check Style is not about familiarity, but about matching the teaching environment to student preferences.

Students rated Self-Check Style low compared to other reproduction styles so perhaps teachers are merely responding to their partners in the classroom and avoiding a disliked style. In a mixed methods design with middle school students, Cothran and Kulinna (2006) found that students held very clear and unique perspectives on the effectiveness of various teaching strategies. They desired positive social interaction and a significant number of the students questioned if anyone other than the teacher is qualified to lead learning … two traits that may explain the rating profile for Self-Check Style and teachers' decision to avoid using it relative to the other styles in the reproduction cluster. Students' views may be related to them becoming institutionalised with expectations about normal lessons and normal relationships.

Another avenue of future inquiry is that of outcomes outside the measured learning, fun and motivation factors that may influence the decision-making chain. Given that class management is the most pressing concern for teachers of all experience levels, it seems likely that teacher control of students, or at least teacher comfort with student choice and option is at play in these ratings and use. Generally speaking, the lowest rated styles are those with the most student choice and potential variance in engagement. Cothran and Kulinna (2008) found that teacher decision making about teaching model selection was based on the factors of control, time and expertise.

In their United States sample, teachers feared that more production cluster styles would have more off task students and even when learning might be occurring in a more student-centred style, the learning would take longer. The final factor related to teacher decision making was in the area of expertise and who had the knowledge necessary for student learning to occur. For this group of 32 teaches from the United States, there was a strong belief that only teachers had the knowledge necessary for accurate student learning to occur and styles like peer teaching or inquiry models would lead to missing or inaccurate learning. Syrmpas, Digelidis, Watt and Vicars (2017) reported similar teacher concerns from Greece about class control and time use when using different styles. Ironically as Jaakkola and Watt (2011) note, the teachers' preference for more teacher-centred styles to increase on task behaviour and learning may be actually working against those goals. They comment that autonomy is central to student motivation and by removing that autonomy teachers may be decreasing involvement instead of increasing it. The motivational environment created by style choice has largely been overlooked as a primary focus of Mosston investigations but some more recent work in the area suggests it is important to do so (e.g. Kirby, Byra, Riley, & Wallhead, 2015; Morgan, Kingston, & Sprule, 2005).

The impact of The Spectrum on the field has been, and continues to be significant. Given that importance, it is critical that the field more closely examines and understands the decision making chain that lies at its heart. This chapter offers clear evidence that those decisions are multi-faceted, connected, and are individually and culturally influenced. This broader perspective on the teacher decision making chain is still not fully understood and much work is needed to clarify key decision making influences that result in important findings like the dominance of the reproduction styles and teacher-practitioners' different understandings of style use. We hope that these initial insights and the insights yet to come on teacher use and perceptions of The Spectrum provide guidance that can help us better understand and assist teachers in their complicated work with students.

References

Cothran, D. J., & Ennis, C. D. (1998). Curricula of mutual worth: Comparisons of students' and teachers' curricular goals. *Journal of Teaching in Physical Education*, 17, 307–327.

Cothran, D. J., & Kulinna, P. H. (2008). Teachers' knowledge about and use of teaching models. *The Physical Educator*, 65, 122–133.

Cothran, D. J., & Kulinna, P. H. (2006). Students' perspectives on direct, peer, and inquiry teaching strategies. *Journal of Teaching in Physical Education*, 25, 166-181.

Cothran, D. J., Kulinna, P. H., Banville, D., Choi, E., Amade-Escot, C., MacPhail, A., Macdonald, D., Richard, J. F., Sarmento, P., & Kirk, D. (2005). A cross-cultural investigation of the use of teaching styles. *Research Quarterly for Exercise and Sport*, 76, 193-201.

Cothran, D. J., Kulinna, P. H., & Ward, E. (2000). Students' experiences with and perceptions of Mosston's teaching styles. *Journal of Research and Development in Education, 34*, 93–103.

Curtner-Smith, M. D. (1999). The more things change the more they stay the same: Factors influencing teachers' interpretations and delivery of national curriculum physical education. *Sport, Education and Society, 4*, 75–97.

Curtner-Smith, M. D., Todorovich, J. R., McCaughtry, N. A., & Lacon, S.A. (2001). Urban teachers' use of production and reproduction teaching styles within the confines of the National Curriculum for Physical Education. *European Physical Education Review, 7*, 177–190.

Garn, A. C., & Cothran, D. J. (2006). The fun factor in physical education. *Journal of Teaching in Physical Education, 25*, 281–297.

Goldberger, M., Ashworth, S., & Byra, M. (2012) Spectrum of teaching styles retrospective 2012, *Quest, 64*(4), 268–282.

Harmes, M. K., Hauijser, H., & Danaher, P. A. (Eds.) (2015). *Myths in education, learning and teaching.* London: Palgrave Macmillan.

Hewitt, M., & Edwards, K. (2015) *Self-identified teaching styles of junior development and club professional tennis coaches in Australia.* In P. A. Danaher, K. Noble, K. W. Larkin, M. Kawka, H. van Rensburg, L. Brodie, & H. Rensburg (Eds.), *Empowering Educators: Proven Principles and Successful Strategies* (pp. 127–154). London: Palgrave Macmillan.

Jaakkola, T., & Watt, A. (2011). Finnish physical education teachers' self-reported use and perceptions of Mosston and Ashworth's teaching styles. *Journal of Teaching in Physical Education, 30*, 248–262.

Kirby, S., Byra, M., Riley, T., & Wallhead, T. (2015). Effects of spectrum teaching styles on college students' psychological needs satisfaction and self-determined motivation. *European Physical Education Review, 21*, 521–540.

Kulinna, P. H., & Cothran, D. J. (2003). Physical education teachers' self-reported use and perceptions of various teaching styles. *Learning and Instruction, 13*, 597–609.

Morgan, K., Kingston, K., & Sprule, J. (2005). Effects of different teaching styles on the teacher behaviours that influence motivational climate and pupils' motivation in physical education. *European Physical Education Review, 11*, 257–285.

Mosston, M., & Ashworth, S. (1994). *Teaching physical education* (4th ed.). New York, NY: Macmillan.

Sicilia-Camacho, A., & Brown, D. (2008). Revisiting the paradigm shift from the *versus* to the *non-versus* notion of Mosston's Spectrum of teaching styles in physical education pedagogy: A critical pedagogical perspective. *Physical Education and Sport Pedagogy, 13*, 85–108.

SueSee, B., & Edwards, K. (2015). Self-identified and observed teaching styles: A case study of senior physical education teachers in Queensland schools. In M. K. Harmes, H. Huijser, & P. A. Danaher (Eds.), *Myths in Education, Learning and Teaching* (pp. 73–93). New York, NY: Palgrave Macmillan.

SueSee, B., Pill, S., & Edwards, K. (2016). Reconciling approaches: A game centered approach to sport teaching and Mosston's Spectrum of Teaching Styles. *European Journal of Physical Education and Sport Science, 2*(4), 69–96.

Suesee, B., Edwards, K., Pill, S., & Cuddihy, T. (2018). Self-reported teaching styles of Australian senior physical education teachers. *Curriculum Perspectives, 38*(1), 41–54.

Syrmpas, I., & Digelidis, N. (2014). Physical education student teachers' experiences with and perceptions of teaching styles. *Journal of Physical Education and Sport, 14,* 52–59.

Syrmpas, I., Digelidis, N., & Watt, A. (2016). An examination of Greek physical educators' implementation and perceptions of Spectrum teaching styles. *European Physical Education Review, 22,* 201–214.

Syrmpas, I., Digelidis, N., Watt, A., & Vicars, M. (2017). Physical education teachers' experiences and beliefs of production and reproduction teaching approaches. *Teaching and Teacher Education, 66,* 184–194.

Chapter 13

Examining physical education teachers' and pre-service physical education teachers' knowledge related to reproduction and production Teaching Styles through the Framework Theory of Conceptual Change

Ioannis Syrmpas and Nikolaos Digelidis

To date, studies have focused on examining the effect of teaching styles on specific outcomes (Chatoupis, 2009). Most of these studies examined the effectiveness of reproduction teaching styles on students' skills development (e.g. Kolovelonis & Goudas, 2012), and students' motivation (e.g. Digelidis, Byra, Mizios, Syrmpas, & Papaioannou, 2018). Additionally, studies have examined the influence of the production teaching styles on students' critical thinking, (e.g. Chen & Cone, 2003), and students' skill development (Dyson, 2002). Studies have also focused on exploring, through PE teachers' reports (Cothran et al. 2005; Jaakkola & Watt, 2011; Kulinna & Cothran, 2003; Syrmpas, Digelidis, & Watt, 2015), to what extent teaching styles located on The Spectrum were used in the physical education (PE) context. The findings of these studies consistently indicated that PE teachers tend to implement a variety of teaching styles. However, they use teaching styles from the reproduction cluster more frequently than the production cluster. Similarly, studies with college students (Cothran, Kulinna, & Ward, 2000) and pre-service PE teachers (Syrmpas & Digelidis, 2014) reported that they are more frequently exposed to the reproduction teaching styles in their PE classes.

To date, there is little evidence of the most profound reasons that urge PE teachers and pre-service teachers to adopt reproduction teaching styles into their repertoire. Previous studies indicated that PE teachers (Cothran et al., 2005; Jaakkola & Watt, 2011; Kulinna & Cothran, 2003; Syrmpas et al., 2015) and pre-service teachers' (Syrmpas & Digelidis, 2014) beliefs influence their teaching repertoire. However, there is a need for further research to clarify the reasons that urge them to form these beliefs. Accordingly, the examination of pre-service teachers and PE teachers' knowledge about teaching could be especially useful in understanding the more profound reasons that urge them to adopt a teaching style. Perhaps, that way we can effectively promote PE teachers' knowledge development. A prominent approach to examine knowledge development and explore the complexity of the learning process is the Framework Theory of Conceptual Change (FTCC) developed by Vosniadou (1994).

Framework Theory of Conceptual Change

Since 1994 the Framework Theory of Conceptual Change (FTCC) has been applied in many educational contexts, such as astronomy (Vosniadou, Skopeliti, & Ikosipentaki, 2004), mathematics (e.g. Christou, Vosniadou, & Vamkoussi, 2007), physics (e.g. Stathopoulou & Vosniadou, 2007), biology (e.g. Hatano & Inagaki, 2003) and physical education (Pasco & Ennis, 2015). Vosniadou (1994) articulated the FTCC based on constructivist learning theories (Piaget, 1929; Vygotsky, 1978). However, in contrast with the Piagetian and Vygotskian domain general approach, Vosniadou adopted Carey's (1985) specific domain approach.

Vosniadou (1994) suggested that learners during infancy in their attempt to explain a specific phenomenon based on daily observation and interaction with social, cultural and contextual factors developed their prior knowledge. This initial attempt to decipher the structure and operation of their surroundings is the foundation in which learners construct new knowledge. Thus, it can be argued that learners coming to school having already developed an explanatory framework theory for interpreting a specific phenomenon. However, Vosniadou (1994) suggested learners' initial conceptions are in contrast with the scientific theories. Additionally, she articulated that learning is a gradual, slow and longitudinal process and occurs through conceptual change (Vosniadou, 2013).

Conceptual change is a process with which learners gradually enrich and/ or modify their prior beliefs towards more scientifically accurate theories (Murphy, 2007). Alexander (2006) stressed conceptual change may occur in all academic domains. However, learners may cope with different learning constraints in each domain. Vosniadou (1994) suggested that knowledge is organised to a general explanatory framework theory and a specific theory.

General explanatory framework theory. This framework consists of ontological and epistemological presuppositions. Learners' assumptions about the nature of a specific phenomenon in the world (e.g. physical objects are stable and solid) are called ontological presuppositions (Vosniadou, 1994). They reflect learners' assumptions about the categories and properties of knowledge in the world (Chinn & Brewer, 1993). Additionally, presuppositions reflect learners' perceptions about the nature and the development of the knowledge, and include several dimensions as the justification of the knowledge and the source of the authority called epistemological presuppositions (Vosniadou, 2007a).

Specific theory. Learners' beliefs are formed through the daily observation of the world or information received from their cultural context or during their instruction in the educational context. These beliefs are called specific theory, and refer to properties or behaviours that learners attribute to a physical object.

Learners' initial perceptions about a specific phenomenon (called preconceptions) that are contradictory to the scientific theory are formed before learners' exposure to scientific knowledge (Vosniadou, 2012). Later, during learners' exposure to scientific knowledge a variety of misconceptions can be developed. These misconceptions reflect learners' attempt to add new information to their existing prior knowledge about a specific phenomenon and are contradictory to scientific knowledge.

Vosniadou (1994) emphasised the mediating role of mental models on the learning process. Learner's mental representations of a specific phenomenon, mediating in knowledge's enrichment and reconstruction process, are called mental models. They are developed on the spot or retrieved from the memory based on presuppositions and beliefs as learners try to solve a problem or to cope with an unfamiliar situation. There are three kinds of mental models (Vosniadou, 1994). 1) *Intuitive or initial:* Formed mainly during infancy or before learners' exposure to typical education and reflect learner's initial attempt to interpret a phenomenon based on the observation (Vosniadou, 1991). 2) *Synthetic:* Formed during learner's attempt to integrate new information counter-intuitive to their prior knowledge. Most of the times learner distort the new information in order to be compatible with their prior knowledge (Vosniadou, 1994). 3) *Scientific:* Reflects the evolution of synthetic mental models and represent learner's ability to understand scientific concepts (Vosniadou, 2007b).

Conceptual Change and implications to curriculum design

From the perspective of FTCC, teaching is a demanding process. Curriculum developers and professional developers should be aware of the fact that the provided information could be consistent or inconsistent with students' prior knowledge. In the case that the new information is consistent with learners' prior knowledge, then it can be easily incorporated into their existing conceptual structures. This type of information will most likely be understood, even if it is presented as a fact without any further explication (Vosniadou, 1994). On the contrary, when the new information is contradictory to learners' existing conceptual structures, instructors must help learners not simply to restructure their naive theories but their modes of learning (Vosniadou, 2007b).

Vosniadou, (1994) suggested that learners' prior experience influence their knowledge. Thus, instructors should be aware of learners' naïve theories in order to generate important feedback to better train learners. Therefore, curriculum developers would be useful to create educational programs that will incorporate information relative to pre-service and PE teachers' knowledge in order to help them reconstruct their existing knowledge (Vosniadou, 2007b). The Spectrum is a universal model of teaching that can help teachers effectively plan and assess the learning process (Mosston & Ashworth, 2008). Additionally, The Spectrum has been described as a 'tool box' that can help PE teachers to cope with students' diversity (Sanchez, Byra, & Walhead, 2012).

Pre-service physical education teachers and physical education teachers' knowledge development of teaching styles

The Spectrum is taught in many countries around the world and many PE teachers are familiar with it. However, there are questions concerning their knowledge development in relation with The Spectrum and furthermore, because there is evidence of not using the whole range of The Spectrum and reliance on mostly reproduction cluster, about the impact or the efficiency of their education with The Spectrum. Arguably, it is important to understand pre-service PE teachers and PE teachers' knowledge about The Spectrum.

So far, two qualitative studies conducted to examine pre-service PE teachers (Syrmpas, Chen, Pasco, & Digelidis, 2019) and PE teachers' mental models (Syrmpas & Digelidis, 2015) of reproduction and production teaching styles. The pre-service PE teachers were second year pre-service PE teachers that they have not introduced to reproduction and production teaching styles. However, they have been exposed to scientific concepts (i.e. motivation, autonomy, PE lesson goals, etc.). Similarly, PE teachers have not been exposed to The Spectrum during their undergraduate studies. However, they were introduced to The Spectrum through seminars and PE textbooks. The findings of both studies revealed that pre- service PE teachers and PE teachers held two similar mental models; an initial and a synthetic mental model.

Initial mental model

Five pre-service PE teachers and three PE teachers categorised within this initial mental model based on their reports (see Figure 13.1). This initial mental model (Figure 13.1) that generated under the constraint of a set of ontological and epistemological presuppositions and beliefs (Vosniadou, 1994). These presuppositions and belief formed by pre-service prior experiences and backgrounds and PE teachers' prior experiences and knowledge acquired through informal education. Participants within this initial mental model formed the ontological presupposition that PE teacher's authority promotes students' learning which is unidimensional and transmissive. They also formed the epistemological presupposition that each cluster of teaching styles leads to a specific outcome. Finally, participants within this initial mental model held the specific beliefs that the reproduction cluster of teaching styles promotes students' effective learning, skills development and discipline, class control and safety. On the other hand, pre-service PE teachers formed the specific beliefs that production teaching styles promote students' autonomy, critical thinking and motivation (Syrmpas et al., 2019). PE teachers held similar beliefs with the exception of motivation. In contrast with pre- service, they believed that the reproduction cluster of teaching styles promotes students' motivation (Syrmpas & Digelidis, 2015). These teachers constituted a negative case. These teachers have not participated in seminars and they stated that they formed their knowledge through PE textbooks.

Participants within the initial mental model (Figure 13.1) appear to form preconceptions. More specifically, they perceived that learning is a transmissive process that is a common finding in previous studies (Stylianou, Kulinna, Cothran, & Kwon, 2013). They also formed the preconception that learning in the PE related to skill development and thus is a unidimensional process. These preconceptions may be formed based on participants' prior experiences during schooling. It is likely their PE teachers in school to emphasise only on skill development. If that is the case, then arguably they urge their students to reproduce and practice skills. These prior experiences urge pre-service PE teachers and PE teachers to form these specific preconceptions that constrain the learning process (Vosniadou, 2012). In this specific case, these preconceptions constrain the understanding of the multidimensional structure of the PE curriculum. Additionally, since they perceived learning as a skill development process then arguably attributed to learning transmissive characteristics. Finally, PE teachers' belief that reproduction teaching styles promote students' motivation may appear to be contradictory to previous research that suggested that autonomy plays an important role in the facilitation of students' motivation to participate in physical education (Reeve, Bolt, & Cai, 1999).

However, based on PE teachers' reports:

> In the case that some students do not want to participate in the PE lesson and use as an excuse that for example, I do not like basketball then I try to convince them to participate and as a reward another time or at the last period of the lesson they can do the activity that they prefer. (Syrmpas & Digelidis, 2015, p. 23)

It can be concluded that the authors referred to extrinsic motivation. Furthermore, it can be assumed that since PE teachers within this mental model perceived that teachers' authority plays a pivotal role on the learning

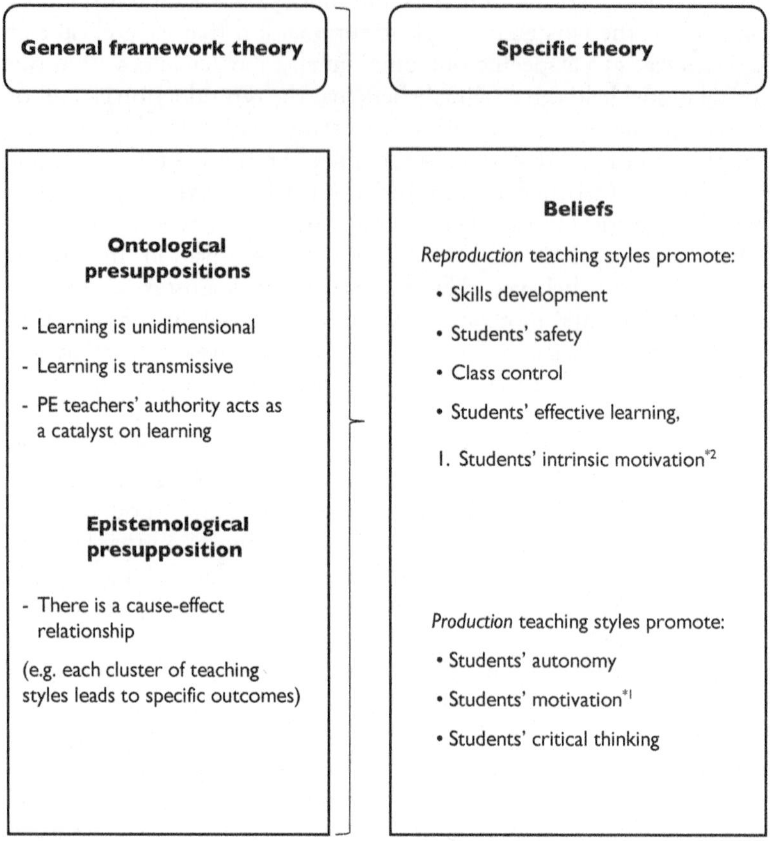

Figure 13.1 Hypothetical conceptual structure underlying preservice teachers and PE teachers' initial mental model of reproduction and production teaching styles

Note:
PE teachers share common beliefs with pre-service teachers. However, the asterisk (*[1]) declares that only pre-service PE teachers held this belief. Similarly, the asterisk (*[2]) declares that only PE teachers held this belief.

process then arguably, they prioritise PE teachers' rewards than the promotion of students' praise of internal rewards such as satisfaction.

Interestingly, participants guiding from the preconception that teacher plays a pivotal role on the learning process attributed to the structure of production and reproduction teaching styles such as Self-Check Style lack of class control, and ineffective learning. For example, a PE teacher reported "I tried two or three times to deliver my lesson through Self-Check Style and I created criteria sheets. Unfortunately, students make noise, the active time was decreased, and the lesson was not effective" (Syrmpas, 2015, p. 153).

Similarly, a pre-service stated, "I do not intend to use it (production teaching styles) because I am not convinced that it is effective in class control and skill development" (Syrmpas, 2015, p. 98).

Synthetic mental model

Eleven pre-service PE teachers and seven PE teachers were categorised within this synthetic mental model based on their reports (see Figure 13.2). This mental model was characterised as synthetic because participants appear to hold similar epistemological presuppositions and beliefs with those of participants within the initial mental model. However, they formed ontological presuppositions and beliefs more relative to the scientific domain knowledge. More specifically, participants within this synthetic mental model formed the ontological presupposition that students' role acts positively to students' learning that is multidimensional and constructivist. They held the same epistemological presupposition with participants of the initial mental model (Syrmpas et al. 2019; Syrmpas & Digelidis, 2015). This specific general framework urges participants within this synthetic mental model to attribute common and different characteristics to the production and the reproduction teaching styles compared to pre-service teachers and PE teachers who held the previous mental. More specifically, they perceived that the reproduction teaching styles foster class control and students' safety. Additionally, the PE teachers perceived that reproduction teaching styles promote students' skills. On the contrary, they perceived that production teaching styles foster students' autonomy, motivation, discipline, students' responsibility, critical thinking, effective learning and satisfaction. Additionally, the PE teachers perceived that the production teaching styles promote students' socialisation and a sense of belonging and the adoption of PE as a lifelong habit (Syrmpas & Digelidis, 2015).

Pre-service teachers and PE teachers within the synthetic mental model, in their attempt to incorporate the new information received by educators and professional developers respectively into their existing knowledge structure and appeared to form a misconception. They considered that the multidimensional nature of learning could be achieved effectively through the production approach (Syrmpas et al., 2019). However, this perception is in contrast with The Spectrum, which stipulates that each teaching style leads to specific outcomes (Mosston & Ashworth, 2008). For example, curriculum goals such as students' socio-moral development, cognitive and affective learning could be effectively promoted through the production teaching styles (Garn & Byra, 2002). On the contrary, curriculum goals such as students' skills and physical development could be effectively promoted through the reproduction teaching styles (Garn & Byra, 2002). This finding suggests that pre-service teachers and PE teachers' exposure to the new information during their first year of undergraduate studies and seminars respectively urge them to misinterpret the

General framework theory		Specific theory

		Beliefs
Ontological presuppositions		*Reproduction* teaching styles promote:
		• Students' safety
- Learning is multidimensional		• Class control
- Learning is constructivist		• Skills' development*[1]
- Students' role acts as a catalyst on learning		*Production* teaching styles promote:
		• Students' autonomy
		• Students' motivation
Epistemological presupposition		• Students' discipline
		• Students' responsibility
- There is a cause-effect relationship		• Students' critical thinking
		• Students' effective learning
(e.g. each cluster of teaching styles leads to specific outcomes)		• Students' satisfaction
		• Students' socialization*[1]
		• PE for life*[1]
		• Students' socialization

Figure 13.2 Hypothetical conceptual structure underlying preservice teachers and PE teachers' synthetic mental model of reproduction and production teaching styles

Note:
PE teachers share common beliefs with pre-service teachers. However, the asterisk (*) declares that only PE teachers held this belief.

effectiveness of production teaching styles and formed this synthetic mental model.

Implications

Up to now it seems that university students come with a variety of ideas about physical education and how we teach. Unfortunately, these beliefs are not exactly consistent with knowledge produced in the discipline of PE and sport pedagogy. The findings so far confirm Vosniadou's (2012) suggestion that learners coming to the educational context, not as a "tabula rasa" but having already formed a prior understanding of various concepts. Pre-service PE teachers' prior knowledge is inconsistent with scientific knowledge and seems possibly influenced by their schooling experiences. More specifically, pre-service teachers' initial understanding of reproduction and production teaching styles is very robust because is constantly reconfirmed by learners' participation in PE context. Additionally, the influence of the content of the first-year courses (includes general information about the goals of PE curriculum and concepts such as autonomy, motivation and goal orientation) appears to be weak and does not help very much in overcoming preconceptions. As a result, in a few cases, the curriculum seemed to not influence their knowledge and arguably they held an initial mental model. However, the first-year curriculum urges the majority of the pre-service PE teachers to form a synthetic mental model. At this point, it must be stressed that the pre-service teachers of this study have not yet been formally exposed to The Spectrum and thus the effectiveness of the curriculum cannot be questioned by the aforementioned findings. However, findings of previous studies (Stylianou et al., 2013; Syrmpas & Digelidis, 2014) imply that the curriculum has rather a weak influence on teachers and pre-service teachers' teaching perceptions and preferences. So, unless they gain a better understanding through appropriate learning experiences at university, there is always a possibility they will reject new knowledge (and during their teaching in the future) they will replicate ideas and/or experiences they had before coming to university.

Similarly, PE teachers reported that they have not been exposed to The Spectrum during their undergraduate studies. However, they have been informed by this theory either through seminars or textbooks. The findings of this study (Syrmpas & Digelidis, 2015) support that PE teachers' knowledge is contradictory to scientific knowledge. Three PE teachers reported that they were only exposed to The Spectrum through textbooks. Interestingly, these PE teachers were categorised within the initial mental model. This finding confirmed Duit and Treagust's (2012) suggestion that many instructors are not aware of the prevailing theories in teaching and learning. This finding also suggests that textbooks may not influence PE teachers' knowledge. On the other hand, PE teachers within synthetic mental model reported that they have been exposed to The Spectrum through seminars and textbooks. Taking into consideration Vosniadou's (2007b) suggestion that learning is a slow, gradual and longitudinal process then arguably it can be assumed that PE teachers' exposure to The Spectrum through these sources has rather a weak influence on them to form synthetic mental models.

The aforementioned findings indicated that curriculum developers in higher education should develop courses related to The Spectrum throughout undergraduate and/or postgraduate studies. Additionally, it is useful to follow Vosniadou and his colleagues' suggestions (Vosniadou & Scopeliti, 2014). More specifically, they proposed that curriculum developers have to incorporate in to courses' content information relative to learners' explanatory framework (Vosniadou, 2007b). Additionally, the content of undergraduate courses and seminars should not be limited to present The Spectrum to pre-service teachers and PE teachers (Vosniadou & Scopeliti, 2014). According to Mosston and Ashworth (2008), The Spectrum should be presented accompanied by practice. This suggestion is aligned with Vosniadou and his colleagues (2001) recommendations that learning occurs in a broader social and cultural context and therefore curriculum developers should plan by presenting progressively each teaching style in a context similar to the subject matter.

During their undergraduate studies, pre-service PE teachers should be informed that each teaching style has specific structure and characteristics that lead to specific outcomes. Then a period of practice should be followed in which the pre-service teachers will have the opportunity to convert the theory into practice. As scholars (Guskey, 2002; Stylianou et al., 2013) stressed physical educators will adopt an innovative teaching style only in the case that they experience tangible evidence of the effectiveness of these styles on students' learning by participating in a course that combines the information and the implementation of these styles.

Changing the way we teach is always challenging because, as teachers, we all try to be effective and follow every possible tip or strategy we know. Pre-service teachers should also be informed that the transition from a traditional teaching approach to an innovative style, when needed, is not a smooth process, on the contrary, requires effort, persistence and patience from teachers and students (Dyson, 2002). It is almost certain that when one tries something new during his/her teaching there will be failures that might disappoint us from evaluating and further improving our approach.

Additionally, the design of an effective curriculum and seminar requires curriculum developers and professional developers to be aware of pre-service and PE teachers' prior knowledge in order to help them to understand that there is a mismatch between their beliefs about the teachers and learner's role on the learning roles. Thus, participants within the initial mental model should be informed of the importance of the learner's role in the learning process. For example, they should be educated that students' critical thinking could be more effectively promoted by students' active participation in the learning process. Similarly, participants within the synthetic mental model should be informed that teachers' authority plays an important role in the learning process. For example, in the case that the lesson objective is to help students to reproduce a model and/or to perform accurately a skill then teachers' authority plays a pivotal role. Finally, pre-service and PE teachers should be aware that the development of students' skills is one of the PE lesson goals, but not the sole one. On the contrary, a variety of goals should be accomplished during a PE lesson. It is important for pre-service and PE teachers to understand that they can apply the most appropriate teaching styles that suits the specific subject matter. For example, in the case that students have to reproduce knowledge or skills then a reproduction teaching style can be applied (Mosston & Ashworth, 2002). On the contrary, when students have to produce new skills or knowledge then a production teaching style can be used. Arguably, the seminars can last for a long period, however PE teachers can be progressively introduced to the aforementioned information and then they will apply this theory into practice. Seminars should also include information about key concepts of educational psychology.

The findings of the present studies describe participants' specific perceptions about a particular phenomenon and cannot be generalised. Both studies represent an early attempt to reveal pre-service teachers and PE teachers' presuppositions, beliefs and mental models related to reproduction and production teaching styles. Future research would be useful to examine curriculum effectiveness on pre-service knowledge development by exploring pre-service teachers' beliefs about the reproduction and production teaching styles throughout the duration of their studies. Similarly, future studies may examine seminars' effectiveness on the development of PE teachers' knowledge.

References

Alexander, P. A. (2006). *Psychology in learning and instruction*. Upper Saddle River, NJ: Pearson Prentice Hall.

Carey, S. (1985). *Conceptual change in childhood*. Cambridge, MA: MIT Press.

Cothran, D., Kulinna, P. H., & Ward, E. (2000). Students' experiences with and perceptions of teaching styles. *Journal of Research and Development in Education, 34*(1), 93–103.

Cothran, D. J., Kulinna, P. H., Banville, D., Choi, E., Amade-Escot, C., MacPhail, A., and Kirk, D. (2005). Cross-cultural investigation of the use of teaching styles. *Research Quarterly for Exercise and Sport, 76*, 193–201

Chatoupis, C. (2009). Contributions of the spectrum of teaching styles to research on teaching. *Studies in Physical Culture & Tourism, 16*(2), 193–205.

Chen, W., & Cone, T. (2003). Links between children's use of critical thinking and an expert teacher's teaching in creative dance. *Journal of Teaching in Physical Education, 22*(2), 169–185.

Chinn, C. A., & Brewer, W. F. (1993). The role of anomalous data in knowledge acquisition: A theoretical framework and implications for science instruction. Review of educational research, *63*(1), 1–49.

Christou, K. P. (2007). Students' Interpretations of Literal Symbols in Algebra. In: S. Vosniadou, A. Baltas & X. Vamvakoussi (Eds.). *Re-Framing the Conceptual Change Approach in Learning and Instruction. Advances in Learning and Instruction Series* (pp. 283–297). Oxford: Elsevier Press.

Digelidis, N., Byra, M., Mizios, D., Syrmpas, I., & Papaioannou, A. (2018). The reciprocal and self-check teaching styles in physical education: Effects in basketball skills' performance, enjoyment and behavioural regulations. *International Journal of Physical Education, 4*(4), 13–22.

Duit, R., & Treagust, D. F. (2012). How can conceptual change contribute to theory and practice in science education? In B. J. Fraser, K. Tobin & C. J. McRobbie (Eds.), *Second international handbook of science education* (pp. 107–118). Dordrecht: Springer.

Dyson, B. (2002). The implementation of cooperative learning in an elementary physical education program. *Journal of Teaching in Physical Education, 22*(1), 69–85.

Goldberger, M., Ashworth, S., & Byra, M. (2012). Spectrum of teaching styles retrospective 2012. *Quest, 64*(4), 268–282.

Hatano, G., & Inagaki, K. (2003). When is conceptual change intended? A cognitive–sociocultural view. In G. M. Sinatra & P. R. Pintrich (Eds.), *Intentional Conceptual Change* (pp. 407–427). Mahwah, NJ: Lawrence Erlbaum Associates.

Jaakkola, T., & Watt, A. (2011). Finnish physical education teachers' self-reported use and perceptions of Mosston and Ashworth's teaching styles. *Journal of Teaching in Physical Education, 30*(3), 248–262.

Jenkins, J., & Byra, M. (1996). An exploration of theoretical constructs associated with the Spectrum of teaching styles. In C. de Costa et al. (Eds.), *Research on teaching and research on teacher education* (pp. 103–108). Lisbon: Faculdade de Motricidade Humana, Universidade Tecnica de Lisboa.

Kolovelonis, A., Goudas, M., & Dermitzaki, I. (2012). The effects of self-talk and goal setting on self-regulation of learning a new motor skill in physical education. *International Journal of Sport and Exercise Psychology, 10*(3), 221–235.

Kulinna, P. H., & Cothran, D. J. (2003). Physical education teachers' self-reported use and perceptions of various teaching styles. *Learning and Instruction, 13*, 597–609

Mosston, M. & Ashworth, S. (2008). Teaching Physical Education (1st online edition). Buckeystown, MD: Spectrum Institute for Teaching and Learning. Retrieved from www.spectrumofteachingstyles.org/pdfs/ebook/Teaching_Physical_Edu_1st_Online_old.pdf

McBride, R. E., Gabbard, C. C., & Miller, G. (1990). Teaching critical thinking skills in the psychomotor domain. *The Clearing House, 63*(5), 197–201.

Pasco, D., & Ennis, C.D. (2015). Third grade students' mental models of blood circulation related to exercise. *Journal of Teaching in Physical Education, 34*(1), 76–92.

Piaget, J. (1929). *The child's conception of the world.* New York, NY: Harcourt-Brace.

Reeve, J., Bolt, E., & Cai, Y. (1999). Autonomy-supportive teachers: How they teach and motivate students. *Journal of Educational Psychology, 91*(3), 537–548.

Sanchez, B., Byra, M., & Wallhead, T. L. (2012). Students' perceptions of the command, practice, and inclusion styles of teaching. *Physical Education & Sport Pedagogy, 17*(3), 317–330.

Stathopoulou, C., & Vosniadou, S. (2007). Exploring the relationship between physics-related epistemological beliefs and physics understanding. *Contemporary Educational Psychology, 32*(3), 255–281

Stylianou, M., Kulinna, P. H., Cothran, D., & Kwon, J. Y. (2013). Physical education teachers' metaphors of teaching and learning. *Journal of Teaching in Physical Education, 32*(1), 22–45.

Syrmpas, I. (2015). *An examination of PE student teachers' and PE teachers' experiences with and beliefs of teaching styles.* (Unpublished doctoral dissertation). University of Thessaly, Trikala, Greece.

Syrmpas, I., & Digelidis, N. (2014). Physical education student teachers' experiences with and perceptions of teaching styles. *Journal of Physical Education and Sport, 14*(1), 52–59.

Syrmpas, I., & Digelidis, N. (2015). PE teachers' mental models of reproduction and production teaching styles. Unpublished manuscript.

Syrmpas, I., Digelidis, N., & Watt, A. (2016). An examination of Greek physical educators' implementation and perceptions of Spectrum teaching styles. *European Physical Education Review*, 22(2), 201–214.

Syrmpas, I., Chen, S., Pasco, D., & Digelidis, N. (2019). Greek preservice physical education teachers' mental models of production and reproduction teaching styles. *European Physical Education Review*, 25(2) 544–564.

Vosniadou, S. (1991). Designing curricula for conceptual restructuring: Lessons from the study of knowledge acquisition in astronomy. *Journal of Curriculum Studies* 23(3), 219–237.

Vosniadou, S. (1994). Capturing and modelling the process of conceptual change. *Learning and Instruction* 4(1), 45–69.

Vosniadou, S. (2002). On the nature of naïve physics. In M. Limon & L. Mason (Eds), *Reconsidering Conceptual Change: Issues in Theory and Practice* (pp. 61–76). Dordrecht: Kluwer.

Vosniadou, S. (2003). Exploring the relationships between conceptual change and intentional learning. In G. M. Sinatra & P.R. Pintrich (Eds.), *Intentional Conceptual Change* (pp. 377–406). Mahwah, NJ: Lawrence Erlbaum Associates.

Vosniadou, S. (2007a) The conceptual change approach and its re-framing. In S. Vosniadou S, A. Baltas & X. Vamvakoussi (Eds.), *Reframing the Conceptual Change Approach in Learning and Instruction* (pp. 1–15). Oxford: Elsevier.

Vosniadou, S. (2007b). Conceptual change and education. *Human Development*, 50(1), 47–54.

Vosniadou, S. (2012). Reframing the classical approach to conceptual change: Pre-conceptions, misconceptions and synthetic models. In B. Frazer, K. Tobin, & C. McRobbie (Eds.), *Second International Handbook of Science Education, Volume 2* (pp. 119–130). New York, NY: Springer.

Vosniadou, S., Ioannides, C., Dimitrakopoulou, A., & Papademetriou, E. (2001). Designing learning environments to promote conceptual change in science. *Learning and Instruction*, 11(4–5), 381–419.

Vosniadou, S., & Skopeliti, I. (2014). Conceptual change from the framework theory side of the fence. *Science & Education*, 23(7), 1427–1445.

Vosniadou, S., Skopeliti, I., & Ikospentaki, K. (2004). Modes of knowing and ways of reasoning in elementary astronomy. *Cognitive Development*, 19(2), 203–222

Vygotsky, L. (1978). Interaction between learning and development. *Readings on the Development of Children*, 23(3), 34–41.

Chapter 14

The teaching continuum

A framework for generalist trained elementary school teachers in physical education

Brent Bradford, Clive Hickson and Stephen Berg

For student learning to occur, teachers require knowledge of the subject area content being taught and pedagogical expertise to support student understanding and knowledge acquisition. How a teacher chooses, designs and sequences such student learning opportunities can influence the potential of learning experiences (Mosston & Ashworth, 2008). Being effective in lesson planning and the delivery of developmentally appropriate learning opportunities in physical education settings is a critical task for teachers in elementary (also known as 'primary') schools. Specifically, generalist trained (GT) elementary school teachers are faced with a myriad of decisions about which teaching style to choose. Especially, as they transition between subject areas throughout the school day along with varying locations (e.g. classrooms, libraries, gymnasia). Therefore, developing a thorough knowledge about the influence that the choice of teaching style can have on the learning process is critically important for GT teachers as they consider the learning environment they intend to foster.

As GT teachers are immersed in a teaching world encompassing a multitude of venues and subject areas, it can be overwhelming to fully understand, implement and reflect on teaching style frameworks for learning in physical education. With the present-day emphasis of high stakes performance in school environments that focus on test scores in subject areas such as language arts and mathematics, it could easily be argued that GT teachers spend more time immersed in fully understanding how best to teach those subject areas rather than areas, such as physical education. Therefore, simplifying the pedagogical choices presented to GT teachers and easing the pressure of understanding pedagogical complexity across all subject areas can be of value.

To support this simplification, this chapter presents *The Teaching Continuum*, an interpretation of the theoretical premise surrounding The Spectrum (Mosston & Ashworth, 2008) and other teaching style frameworks in a manner that aims to resonate with GT teachers and assist in understanding the choice of teaching style available when teaching physical education.

Importance of effective teaching in elementary school physical education

When planning for effective physical education lessons, research has clearly shown that a wide range of teaching style choices is available for teachers to create the most productive learning environments for student learning (SueSee, Pill, & Edwards, 2016; Syrmpas, Digelidis, & Watt, 2015). According to SueSee et al. (2016), it is worth remembering that no one teaching style is superior to another; each has its own uses in a non-versus approach. Although Fishburne (2005) contended that specific learning outcomes are best achieved through different pedagogical approaches, not all GT teachers may know the range of choices available to them or actually be aware that there are choices of how to best teach their physical education lessons. As the choice of what particular approach to adopt when presenting learning opportunities to students is a critical decision that can impact student learning opportunities, teachers need to fully understand their possible choices.

The first section of this chapter considers two issues. First, it outlines the importance of effective physical education programming as it relates to physical literacy, fundamental movement skills and the sensitive period of time for elementary school students' learning (Fishburne, 2005; Gleddie, Hickson, & Bradford, 2018). Second, it identifies and explains a 'teaching styles framework,' that closely aligns with and resembles The Spectrum, entitled *The Teaching Continuum*. When the importance of effectively teaching physical education and the choice of teaching framework are considered together, a potential solution is proposed to assist GT teachers – The Teaching Continuum.

Critical components of an elementary school physical education experience

The experiences presented to elementary school students in physical education programming can potentially influence their relationship with physical activity throughout their lives (Gleddie et al., 2018; Haywood & Getchell, 2014). In particular, the notion of recognising the early years of students' lives for the development of physical literacy and basic fundamental motor skills is of crucial importance.

Physical literacy. Margaret Whitehead is a physical education philosopher from the United Kingdom who pioneered the use of the term 'physical literacy' and its critical importance to children and youth. Margaret stated that physical literacy is a disposition in which individuals have the motivation, confidence, physical competence, knowledge and understanding to value and take responsibility for maintaining purposeful physical activities throughout their lives (Whitehead, 2010). A life-long physical literacy journey will prepare individuals to meet the challenges of physical inactivity, poor health and sedentary lifestyles. As part of an individual's physical literacy journey, the development of fundamental movement skills is essential for more complex skills (e.g. sport-based skills) during the elementary school years. Undoubtedly, Whitehead's (2010) influence on the world of physical education and interpretation of the importance of movement in an individual's life has been crucial during a time when sedentary behaviour is arguably at its highest levels in our society (ParticipACTION, 2018).

Fundamental movement skills. In a similar manner to physical literacy, fully understanding that fundamental movement skills are essential for performance in all sport and physical activity is also crucial for GT teachers. When considering complex physical activities such as rugby, skating, or kayaking, many fundamental movements are fused and, therefore, must all be taught with progression in mind (Gleddie et al., 2018). With the physical literacy movement worldwide, fundamental movement skills have continued to receive critical attention (Gleddie et al., 2018; Jaakkola, Yli-Piipari, Huortari, Watt, & Liukkonen, 2015; Lander, Eather, Morgan, Salmon, & Barnett, 2017; Liong, Ridgers, & Barnett, 2015;). Referred to as a building block to further student development of physical skills as well as a precursor to life-long attitudes towards physical activity (Fishburne 2005; Gleddie et al., 2018), fundamental movement skills must remain a focal point of teaching in elementary school physical education programming.

Mastery of fundamental movement skills can also be seen as an important motivational factor. For example, students will most likely not want to play soccer if they are unable to kick a ball. Or rather, if a student cannot run effectively, combining these actions with other fundamental movements such as dodging may become frustrating even within a basic game of tag. It is this opportunity as elementary school teachers to inspire our students with effective and progressive movement opportunities in quality physical education programming. Fundamental movement skills can be broken down into three types of categories: locomotor, balance and stability, and ballistic and manipulative (Gleddie et al., 2018; Haywood & Getchell, 2014). These skills can be described as all action words; bodies are in motion or in motor control.

- Locomotor Skills move the body from one place to another (e.g. Point A to B) or can project the body upward (Haywood & Getchell, 2014; Pangrazi & Beighle, 2013). Walking, running, skipping, galloping and jumping are all examples of skills to be taught at an early age (during students' sensitive period of time [i.e. fundamental stage]);
- Balance and Stability Skills are performed in place and with control (Haywood & Getchell, 2014; Pangrazi & Beighle, 2013). Bending, stretching, pushing, pulling, balancing, curling and twisting are all examples of skills to be taught at the fundamental stage; and
- Manipulative and Ballistic Skills typically describe movements used within games and more specifically how one handles objects (Haywood & Getchell, 2014; Pangrazi & Beighle, 2013). For example, throwing, catching,

dribbling with your hands or feet and striking are examples of skills to be taught at the fundamental stage.

Sensitive period of time. The elementary school years mark a sensitive period of time for student learning in physical education (Fishburne, 2005; Gleddie et al., 2018). The need for physical education during these years is more evident than ever before as it affords a unique and valuable contribution towards 'holistic' student development. According to Fishburne (2005), "although much research remains to be done in the area of sensitive time frames, the one common feature of all studies conducted thus far is the finding that sensitive times appear early in life and certainly not after puberty" (p. 35). Participation in elementary school physical education provides a range of learning opportunities and benefits that are vital for growth and development, including: the acquisition of fundamental movement skills and advancement along physical literacy journeys (Gleddie et al., 2018; PHE Canada, 2019; Sport for Life, 2018); social and emotional learning (Iannotti, Kogan, Janssen, & Boyce, 2009; ParticipACTION, 2018); and the joy of movement (Almond & Whitehead, 2012; Beni, Fletcher, & Ní Chróinín, 2016).

Teaching Styles available for GT teachers

As mentioned in the introduction of this chapter, GT teachers in elementary schools are faced with a very diverse set of teaching expectations. They are required to comprehend a range of curricular material, develop engaging and challenging learning objectives that meet curricular outcomes and, wherever possible, develop cross-curricular links to enhance the meaningfulness of learning opportunities for students. The task of creating such learning opportunities for students when teaching across subject areas that range from mathematics, language arts and science to art, music and physical education, is immense and for many can be quite overwhelming.

However, in regard to the teaching of physical education, it is essential for GT teachers to understand there are varying teaching styles available that can support student learning, and their adoption of a particular teaching style can influence the type of learning experienced by students and support their teaching.

Benefits of variety (Non-versus approach). It is important to recognise that the variety of choice of teaching style allows a teacher to choose and move between styles. Variety allows for flexibility and supports teachers in creating positive and meaningful learning opportunities for students. Having a repertoire of teaching styles and recognising how and when to employ them to facilitate student learning can promote effective learning environments (Mosston & Ashworth, 2008; Pangrazi & Beighle, 2013) and can benefit teachers, including of course GT teachers in elementary schools. Because different teaching styles have distinctive purposes in the learning environment, it is important that teachers can call on several different styles during a lesson in order to meet all student learning needs. Teachers who are aware of the strengths, weaknesses and challenges of different teaching styles will experience greater ease in reaching learning objectives (Bradford & Hickson, 2014; Fishburne, 2005; Mosston & Ashworth, 2008; Pangrazi & Beighle, 2013).

Relative to how much control teachers desire to hold in the learning environments, different teaching styles promote various types of learning (Bradford & Hickson, 2014; Gleddie et al., 2018; Mosston & Ashworth, 2008). Teachers who employ different teaching styles within their repertoire are likely to be more effective in specific learning environments and may provide learning opportunities that benefit students. When a teacher-centred teaching style, for example, is adopted in a gymnastics-type lesson, a student can benefit from observing and attempting to replicate specific skill demonstrations such as a forward roll. Whereas, in a creative dance lesson, a more student-centred and less teacher directed style can enhance student learning as students are encouraged to create and explore a range of possibilities. Teachers can create conducive learning environments through the employment of different teaching styles in accordance to varying learning needs.

GT teachers' background of physical education

When considering the preparation of future teachers, it has been noted in several cases that teacher education programming may not focus in physical education. Several teacher education programs have included minimal, if any, education for the teaching of elementary school physical education. That said, both teachers and learners can benefit when teachers understand how to teach physical education effectively. However, in a review of the possible barriers to effectively teaching physical education, Jenkinson and Benson (2010) summarised that school teachers exhibit low levels of confidence or interest in teaching physical education, are often unable to provide lessons that are structured and safe, and lack the training, knowledge and expertise to provide quality physical education experiences to students. If unchecked, such issues can be of great consequence to the physical education teaching and learning environment. Therefore, it seems critical that GT teachers become aware of how their decision making and choices of learning experiences might be enhanced for student learning in elementary school physical education.

While teaching physical education, knowing when a student requires opportunities to explore and to discover or when to be presented with more concrete direction and demonstration to follow can be a difficult task for a GT teacher with little, if any, formal training in teaching physical education. This dilemma raises the question: *How can a GT teacher best support student learning in elementary school physical education?* To help answer this question, we wish to introduce The Teaching Continuum.

The Teaching Continuum

Purpose of the Teaching Continuum. The Teaching Continuum was created in recognition of the immensity of tasks facing GT teachers in elementary schools on a daily basis and to support their teaching of physical education. It builds upon the foundational work of The Spectrum and employs the framework to simplify and build success for non-specialist (GT) teachers' understanding of physical education teaching.

How it originated. According to Mosston and Ashworth (2008), it is critical for teachers of physical education to realise students can develop their cognitive skills during effective physical education lessons which include varying teaching styles. Bradford and Hickson (2018) aimed to simplify the understanding of utilising various teaching styles in elementary school physical education. As GT teachers are deeply immersed in a teaching world that extends far beyond the gymnasium and the teaching of physical education, we contend that it can be difficult for teachers to fully understand and implement highly researched theoretical frameworks into their daily practice. For example, it may well be problematic to expect a GT teacher to decide upon Convergent Discovery Style as opposed to Divergent Discovery Style (although both are recognised as Landmark Styles [Mosston & Ashworth, 2008]). Hence, what is presented in this section is a modified interpretation of The Spectrum's theoretical underpinnings in a GT teacher-friendly manner. The Teaching Continuum includes three general styles for teaching: Teacher as a Guide; Shared Guides; and Student Self-Guide (Figure 14.1).

Teacher as a Guide. Specific learning outcomes in physical education require finite learning opportunities. An array of skills, such as learning to perform a forward roll in gymnastics, has minimal room for discovery and exploration due to safety issues. Therefore, the Teacher as a Guide approach to teaching particular skills that require teacher specialisation, thorough demonstrations and specific assessment criteria must become a regular part

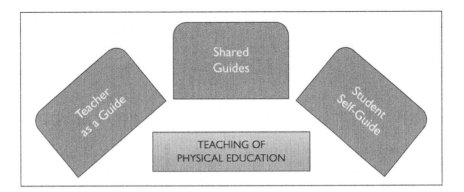

Figure 14.1 The Teaching Continuum

of teacher's repertoire and should become easy for teachers to understand and implement when required. When employing the Teacher as a Guide approach, the teacher makes all the decisions in the learning environment. Similar to The Spectrum's Command Style and other reproduction cluster styles (Mosston & Ashworth, 2008), a defining characteristic of Teacher as a Guide includes "precision performance – reproducing a predicted response or performance on cue" (p. 76). For example, the teacher plans out the activities, demonstrates how to perform the activities, and assesses and evaluates student learning on pre-determined criteria.

Shared Guides. Some learning outcomes in physical education allow for opportunities for teachers and students to work in a concerted manner; a partnership helps to meet learning outcomes through co-created knowledge. Certain skills, such as performing a gymnastics sequence, can call upon a teacher-learner partnership in decision making. Performing forward rolls in a gymnastics sequence may require the Teacher as a Guide approach for safety purposes, while other components of the sequence can be installed through student innovativeness, creativity, etc. The teacher allows for students to make specific decisions in the learning environment while maintaining a level of influence over various aspects of the learning episode (Mosston & Ashworth, 2008). Similar to styles on The Spectrum such as the Self-Check Style (Mosston & Ashworth, 2008), a defining characteristic of Shared Guides includes "performing a task and engaging in self-assessment guided by specific teacher provided criteria" (p. 141). The students, for example, can plan out the activities, discover ways to perform the activities, with the teacher incorporating pre-determined assessment criteria.

Student Self-Guide. Specific physical education learning outcomes allow for additional room for students to explore, discover, create, innovate, etc. Certain skills, such as creative movement, can afford students plenty of opportunities to create their own story through movement whilst listening to a song and should become easy for teachers to understand and implement when required. The students are provided with ample opportunities to make decisions within the learning environment. Similar to styles on The Spectrum such as Learner Designed Individual Program Style (Mosston & Ashworth, 2008), a defining characteristic of Student Self-Guide includes "the independence of each learner to discover a structure that resolves an issue or problem" (p. 274). For example, the students are able to plan out the activities, discover ways to perform the activities and assess their learning based on their pre-set criteria.

The Teaching Continuum – examples

As with The Spectrum, the premise behind The Teaching Continuum is focused on deliberate teaching. In this section, three examples of The Teaching Continuum are shared with a focus on using dance to develop student understanding of how their bodies can move. Although there are several modifications that can be implemented when considering various teaching styles for student learning, we wish to impart some simple lesson examples that GT teachers can employ as they embark on their journey towards more effective teaching in physical education. For each of the three lesson examples, an explanation follows that supports the reason behind the teaching style choice.

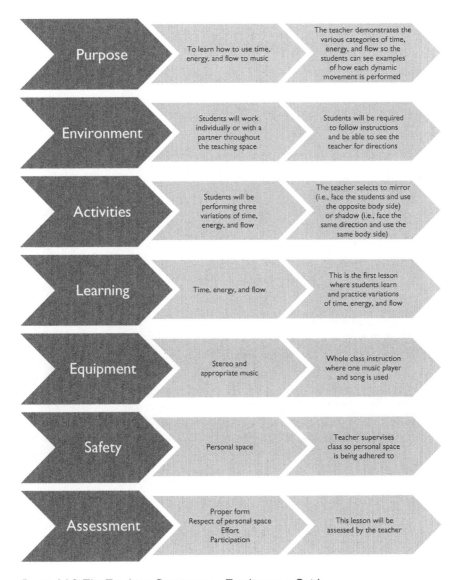

Figure 14.2 The Teaching Continuum – Teacher as a Guide

Teacher as a Guide. For this lesson example, the teacher facilitates the entire learning experience for students. That is, the teacher provides the modelling of the movement and skills to be practiced and performed. Here, the students perform the skills at the same time as the teacher (see Figure 14.2). The teacher is more or less 'the centre of attention' and when the teacher stops doing the movement or steps, so too do the students. The Teacher as

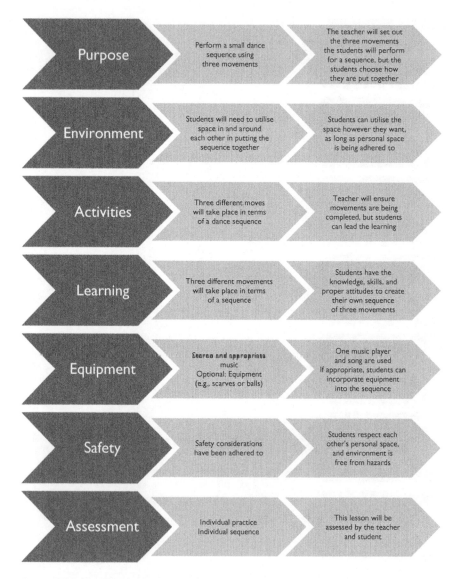

Figure 14.3 The Teaching Continuum – Shared Guides

a Guide style provides limited opportunity for the teacher to provide specific, individual feedback to students. As shown in Figure 14.2, the teacher chooses the music, directs and informs students of what they will be learning, and chooses the movements in which students must do. The teacher acts as a 'mirror' so students can 'copy' the exact movements related to flow, time and energy with the teacher-chosen music. Similar to The Spectrum's

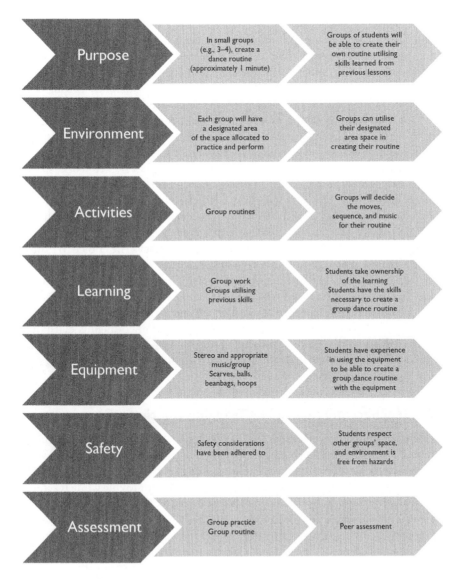

Figure 14.4 The Teaching Continuum – Student Self-Guide

post-impact set (Mosston & Ashworth, 2008), in Teacher as a Guide style, teacher decisions are required by comparing, contrasting and making conclusions about the performance against pre-determined criteria. In Figure 14.2, effort, participation and spatial awareness are the main types of assessment the teacher focusses on with no student input.

Shared Guides. Unlike the Teacher as Guide, where the teacher facilitates the entire learning experience for students, Shared Guides (Figure 14.3) has the teacher introducing the task, yet there is greater emphasis on student input. Here, the teacher presents the task or problem (i.e. 3-step movement sequence) and remains accountable for encouraging students to learn. Students however, have greater choice in how the task is to be performed. Similar to The Spectrum, in Shared Guides style, the shift in decision making from teacher to learner provides students with a greater responsibility throughout the lesson. In Figure 14.3, the teacher 'sets the stage' by providing the task (i.e. 3-step movement sequence), but now students are afforded opportunities to determine how the movement sequence is to be performed, the space utilised and co-assess the learning process with the teacher.

Student Self-Guide. Here, the students have the opportunity to work, share, create and assess their learning. The teacher can either set-up the learning outcome, or share the responsibility with the students. Beyond that, the students have the freedom to explore. The example in Figure 14.4 shows that the teacher has limited the choice of music for each group through an approval process. Beyond this however, the students have the choice to utilise the designated space, create a routine any way they choose and assess their learning. Similar to The Spectrum, in Student Self-Guide style, learners are provided with opportunities to experience the discovery process. In Figure 14.4, although students are given a lot of choice throughout the lesson, the teacher still retains an active role by moving around encouraging, clarifying and answering any questions students may have. It must be noted that teachers need to ensure that their students are responsible enough to *self-guide* their learning experiences.

Why teachers should use The Teaching Continuum

Evidently, as shown in the three lesson examples, there are appropriate times when one teaching style can be a more effective choice than another. Invariably, many teachers develop a particular teaching style that they perceive to be most effective or that they are the most comfortable employing while teaching physical education. In such circumstances, it can be challenging for teachers to realise that a single approach to teaching may not support the learning of all students, and to accept that change would help establish a more conducive learning environment. The difficulty in this may be convincing teachers who wholeheartedly declare their lessons already provide students with opportunities to imitate, practice, communicate, explore, discover, self-initiate, etc.

(Bradford & Hickson, 2014). Hence, the reasoning for a simplified theoretical understanding of available teaching styles to choose from and one that might resonate with GT teachers tasked with teaching physical education in elementary schools. In order to lessen the extent of teacher resistance when introducing The Teaching Continuum, specific concrete examples can be shared (see examples in Figures 14.2, 14.3 and 14.4). Providing teachers with concrete examples of how certain teaching styles play a part in the development of environments that are conducive to learning, and ultimately promote intentional learner success, should help lower teacher resistance (Bradford & Hickson, 2014).

Through the use of different teaching styles, students are afforded opportunities to reproduce and produce knowledge consistently in environments that are conducive to learning. And, as previously mentioned, The Teaching Continuum has been developed to offer a simplified, easily-understood theoretical framework for GT teachers to make appropriate teaching style choices that support student learning. As well, it is hoped that The Teaching Continuum enables GT teachers to become more confident in their teaching of physical education.

Choosing appropriate teaching styles for the teaching of physical education can impact student learning. Although several learning outcomes in the physical domain can be achieved by employing the *Teacher as a Guide* teaching style, when other educational objectives emerge, other styles should be chosen (Bradford & Hickson, 2014). For example, when teaching forward rolls in a gymnastics-type learning opportunity, the Teacher as a Guide style should be called upon for reasons such as safety considerations. To obtain the skills required to successfully and safely perform a forward roll, students require opportunities to imitate the teacher's correct directions and observe demonstrations, as opposed to creating and discovering their own that may be incorrect and possibly unsafe (Bradford & Hickson, 2014).

Further, with a new emphasis and foci in physical education curricula on such understanding and appreciation of; problem solving, citizenship, cooperation, etc., the use of Student Self-Guide may be most appropriate for student learning in specific learning environments (Bradford & Hickson, 2014). Hence, it is hoped that teachers employing *The Teaching Continuum* will expose their students to the most conducive learning environments, whilst, simultaneously, increase their own levels of teaching confidence by observing their students reaching higher levels of success in physical education (e.g. skill development, social skills, problem solving, enjoyment).

Conclusion

Considering the different teaching styles available to GT teachers can potentially assist in enhanced levels of teacher ideas, which may, in turn, enhance student learning. The purpose of this chapter was to discuss how to enhance confidence levels for GT teachers, whilst teaching elementary school physical education, in choosing from an easy-to-understand and available teaching styles theoretical framework to support student learning. Based upon the foundational framework of The Spectrum that can help build success for non-specialist (GT) teachers' understanding of physical education teaching, The Teaching Continuum is not an attempt to replace The Spectrum. Rather, it was created in recognition of the immensity of tasks facing GT teachers in elementary schools and to support their successful teaching of physical education.

When teachers employ different teaching styles, students can benefit. And, contrarily, it is detrimental for student learning when a teacher consistently chooses the same teaching style from lesson to lesson without considering student learning (e.g. learning outcomes, learning needs). For example, depending on the learning context, the use of Teacher as a Guide can provide a learning environment that is either more or less effective as opposed to the use of Student Self-Guide.

Evidently, learning more about how teaching styles can impact the learning process can significantly affect teachers' overall views towards the learning environment. Hence, The Teaching Continuum is a fitting initial step for GT teachers in developing a broader scope of knowledge and understanding of available teaching styles for the teaching of elementary school physical education. The Teaching Continuum is a beginning and helps introduce GT teachers to The Spectrum while developing further understanding of exemplary teaching of elementary school physical education. Additionally, it may also prove to be of worth to those that provide professional development opportunities to teachers and teacher educators. The sharing and the utilisation of this work will hopefully provide greater success in the gymnasium and on the playing field for both students and GT teachers.

References

Almond, L., & Whitehead, M. (2012). Physical literacy: Clarifying the nature of the concept. *Practice Matters, Spring,* 68–71.

Beni, S., Fletcher, T., & Ní Chróinín, D. (2016). Meaningful experiences in physical education and youth sport: A review of the literature. *Quest, 69*(3), 291–312.

Bradford, B., & Hickson, C. (2018). Impacting student learning: An introduction to the teaching continuum in elementary school physical education. *Active + Healthy Journal, 25*(1), 41–48.

Bradford, B. D., & Hickson, C. (2014). Teaching Styles in elementary school physical education: The effect on children's learning. *The International Journal of Pedagogy and Curriculum, 20*(3), 1–17.

Fishburne, G. J. (2005). Developmentally appropriate physical education for children and youth. University of Alberta: Ripon Publishing.

Gleddie, D., Hickson, C., & Bradford, B. (2018). *Physical education for elementary school teachers: Foundations of a physical literacy journey.* Victoria, BC: Ripon Publishing.

Haywood, K. M., & Getchell, N. (2014). *Life span motor development (6th ed)*. Champaign, IL: Human Kinetics.

Iannotti, R. J., Kogan, M. D., Janssen, I., & Boyce, W. F. (2009). Patterns of adolescent physical activity, screen-based media use, and positive and negative health indicators in the US and Canada. *Journal of Adolescent Health, 44*(5), 493–499.

Jaakkola, T., Yli-Piipari, S., Huotari, P., Watt, A., & Liukkonen, J. (2015). Fundamental movement skills and physical fitness as predictors of physical activity: A 6-year follow-up study. *Scandinavian Journal of Medicine & Science in Sports, 26*(1), 74–81.

Jenkinson, K. A. & Benson, A. C. (2010). Barriers to Providing Physical Education and Physical Activity in Victorian State Secondary Schools. *Australian Journal of Teacher Education, 35*(8), 1–17.

Lander, N., Eather, N., Morgan, P. J., Salmon, J., & Barnett, L. M. (2017). Characteristics of teacher training in school-based physical education interventions to improve fundamental movement skills and/or physical activity: A systematic review. *Sports Medicine, 47*(1), 135–161.

Liong, G. H. E., Ridgers, N. D., & Barnett, L. M. (2015). Associations between skill perceptions and young children's actual fundamental movement skills. *Perceptual and Motor Skills, 120*(2), 591–603.

Mosston, M., & Ashworth, S. (2008). *Teaching Physical Education* (1st Online ed.). Retrieved from https://spectrumofteachingstyles.org/assets/files/book/Teaching_Physical_Edu_1st_Online.pdf.

Pangrazi, R. P., & Beighle, A. (2013). *Dynamic physical education for elementary school children*. (17th ed.). New York, NY: Pearson.

ParticipACTION. (2018). *Canadian kids need to move more to boost their brain health. The ParticipACTION Report Card on Physical Activity for Children and Youth.* Toronto, ON. Retrieved from https://participaction.cdn.prismic.io/participaction%2F5e923384-b01a-4680-a353-60b45c271811_2018_participaction_report_card_-_highlight_report_0.pdf

PHE Canada. (2019). *Physical Literacy*. Retrieved from https://phecanada.ca/activate/physical-literacy.

Sport for Life. (2018). *Physical Literacy*. Retrieved from https://sportforlife.ca/physical-literacy.

Syrmpas, I., Digelidis, N., & Watt, A. (2015). An examination of Greek physical educators' implementation and perceptions of Spectrum teaching styles. *European Physical Education Review, 22*(2), 201–214.

SueSee, B., Pill, S., & Edwards, K. (2016). Reconciling approaches – a game centred approach to sport teaching and Mosston's spectrum of teaching styles. *European Journal of Physical Education and Sport Science, 2*(4), 2501–2535.

Whitehead, M. (Ed.). (2010). *Physical literacy: Through the lifecourse*. New York, NY: Routledge.

Chapter 15

Future considerations on The Spectrum

Mitch Hewitt, Shane Pill
and Brendan SueSee

The paper by Chatoupis (2010), *Spectrum Research Reconsidered*, gave two specific suggestions "for conducting sound SR (Spectrum Research) and expanding the field" (Chatoupis, 2010, p. 34). First, a significant limitation of early research involving The Spectrum (Mosston & Ashworth, 2008) was the lack of observation of teaching styles being used. According to Silverman (1985), the effects of teaching styles on students (treatment) is not verified if observations are not employed. The implementation of observation demands the development and promotion of legitimate and dependable observational methods that conform to The Spectrum (Mosston & Ashworth, 2008) theory. In the absence of these methods "SR (Spectrum research) will be idiosyncratic and unreliable" (Chatoupis, 2010, p. 91). An idiosyncratic approach means that personal biases and interpretations are applied to the teaching styles and creates inconsistencies in the style being researched. A second consideration by Chatoupis was to ensure that future research involving The Spectrum (Mosston & Ashworth, 2008) achieves appropriate measures of validity and reliability by reducing deficiencies that have been evident in many studies. These deficiencies include:

- Non-compliance to The Spectrum (Mosston & Ashworth, 2008) theory (ignoring the decision patterns, comparing the landmark objectives of one style against a different style);
- Inappropriate style comparison (reproduction styles against production styles);
- Inappropriate subject matter selection (teach dribbling in basketball with the command style); and
- Short duration of the fieldwork (Chatoupis, 2010, p. 91).

In light of these recommendations, there have been a number of research initiatives aimed at addressing the deficiencies outlined by Chatoupis (2010) and also in further development of The Spectrum (Mosston & Ashworth, 2008). We discuss a number of these in the next section: canopy designs, the inventory, the model illustration and interrogating other teaching models using The Spectrum.

Canopy designs

Located between the 11 Landmark Teaching Styles on The Spectrum are many teaching and learning experiences called 'canopy designs' (Ashworth, 2010). Canopy designs highlight in differing proportions a segment or combination of "the decisions, the learning objectives, and the developmental focus of the two landmark styles they are in between" (Ashworth, 2010, p. 2). Canopy designs are delineated by a set of decisions that correspond with specific learning objectives. However, canopy designs do not promote significantly diverse decisions or learning objectives from the Landmark Teaching Styles that they exist between (Ashworth, 2010). Canopy designs highlight and share approximate, but not precise, learning objectives, decision structures and the developmental focus of the Landmark Teaching Style(s) that they are located near or between, however, they cannot be assessed or labelled as the exact same behaviour (Hewitt, 2015). Canopy designs are a useful addition to The Spectrum theory as research in the field of pedagogy requires the capacity to identify and reliably differentiate one teaching style from another (Ashworth, 2010). Learning experiences are generally shaped by instigating different teaching styles. It is therefore vital that the information and skills required to differentiate various teaching styles observed during a learning experience be constant and dependable (Ashworth, 2010).

The labels assigned to canopy designs are determined according to the Landmark Style(s) they most support, and the decision(s) that distinguish them from the Landmark Teaching Style. The labels also highlight the central developmental focus that differs from the Landmark Teaching Style(s) (Ashworth, 2010).

> The symbol located above the letter is like an umbrella – a canopy over a larger area. The pole is the landmark teaching style and the distance from the pole to the edge of the canopy (umbrella) represents a range of options that are associated with, that represent, that carry, in varying degrees, the decision structure of the landmark teaching style.
>
> (S. Ashworth, personal communication
> with M. Hewitt, 17 August 2014)

For instance, B+socialisation can be read as a canopy design of Practice Style plus socialisation. This labelling means that this particular teaching episode adheres to the decision structure of the Landmark Teaching Style Practice Style. The central characteristics of Landmark Teaching Style Practice Style consists of: "individual and private practice of a memory/reproduction task with private feedback" (Mosston & Ashworth, 2008, p. 94). In this style, the coach or teacher make all the decisions in the *pre-impact set* (i.e. decisions relating to planning and content preparation) and *post-impact set* (i.e. decisions relating to assessment and feedback). With the *impact set* (i.e. decisions relating to the implementation, execution and performance of tasks), a change occurs in relation to who makes certain decisions. The following nine decisions listed are shifted from the teacher or coach to the learner in the impact set of Landmark Teaching Style Practice Style. In other words, the learner now makes all the decisions in the impact set related to:

1. Location
2. Order of tasks
3. Starting time per task
4. Pace and rhythm
5. Stopping time per task
6. Interval
7. Initiating questions for clarification
8. Attire and appearance
9. Posture. (Mosston and Ashworth, 2008)

The canopy design that approximated the decision structure of Landmark Teaching Style Practice Style is labelled canopy design Practice Style-B plus (+) a social partnership to complete the task (**B+socialisation**). The assigned labelling means that this specific teaching episode follows the decision structure of Landmark Teaching Style Practice Style while adding the element of socialisation (i.e. interacting with other learners during the task). The decision of socialisation or interacting with others while performing a task is not part of the decision structure of landmark teaching style Practice Style. Rather, individual and private practice of a task is a requirement during the *impact set* of this Landmark Style. This canopy design is labelled with a 'plus' (+) (i.e. canopy design **B+socialisation**), as the addition of socialisation moves the learning experience towards the next Landmark Teaching Style. The next landmark teaching style on *The Spectrum* is Landmark Reciprocal Style. A key feature of this Landmark Style is social interaction and partnerships that develops feedback, observation and communication skills.

In essence, a canopy design recognises that a learning episode may be predominantly delivered through one teaching style, but include elements of another. Some canopy designs are labelled with a plus (+) and others with a minus (-). If the set of decisions move the experience towards the next Landmark Teaching Style on the continuum it is assigned a plus (+). If, however, the set of decisions move the experience away from the Landmark Teaching Style's set of decisions it is assigned a minus (-). Therefore, in the first example, the addition of socialisation moves the experience towards the next Landmark Teaching Style – which is Reciprocal, therefore a plus (+) is included.

A study by Hewitt (2015) that explored the instructional practices and insights of Australian tennis coaches provided the first account of research investigating canopy designs. It also provided empirical evidence of the existence and employment of canopy designs during sport coaching sessions. This study identified two canopy designs during the coaches' observations. The canopy designs were:

1. Canopy design Command Style minus (-) pace and rhythm.
2. Canopy design Practice Style plus (+) a social partnership to complete the task.

The abbreviated notation for canopy design Command Style minus (-) pace and rhythm is recorded as A-P&R. The abbreviated representation of canopy design Practice Style plus (+) a social partnership to complete the task consists of B+socialisation. The assigned labelling for A-P&R means that this particular teaching episode follows the decision structure of Landmark Teaching Style Command Style while omitting the decision of pace and rhythm (P&R). In this case, the learner made the decisions with regard to speed or how quickly or slowly they decided to perform the task or activity. A common teaching episode or scenario of this variation during the coaches' observed sessions consisted of the following:

*   The coach demonstrated the serving action to the players in the group; and
*   The players then copied or reproduced this action, imitating the cues and performance of the coach.

In this teaching scenario, the coach made all the decisions relating to: subject matter, location (where the task is to be performed), posture, starting time, stopping time, duration and feedback. The only decision the coach did not make was the pace and rhythm (P&R) of the task or activity. The players decided how quickly or slowly they performed the serving activity. The labelling for B+socialisation means that this teaching episode adheres to the decision structure of Landmark Teaching Style Practice Style while adding the element of socialisation. The added decision of socialisation does not form part of the decision structure of Landmark Teaching Style Practice Style. Instead, individual and private practice of a task or activity is a requirement of Landmark Teaching Style Practice Style. An example of this variation frequently observed during the coaches' video-recorded sessions (Hewitt, 2015) consisted of:

1. The coach explained the activity that involved the practice of the forehand and backhand groundstroke; and
2. The players then practised this task with a partner.

In this teaching scenario, the coach made all the decisions regarding the subject matter and logistics of the task, as well as providing private and individual feedback to the players. The players made the decisions relating to:

location, the order in which the task is to be practised, starting time, pace and rhythm, stopping time and initiating questions for clarification. The added decision in this scenario was socialisation. Rather than practising the task privately and individually, the players practised the task with a partner.

This study extended the theoretical conception of The Spectrum framework by describing the difference between Landmark Teaching Styles and canopy designs. This development allowed the researcher to establish with increased accuracy the level of congruence between what the coaches believed they did pedagogically and what they actually did. Further research is needed to verify the concept of canopy designs in physical education and sport coaching. We stress that canopy designs cannot be assessed or labelled in the same manner as the Landmark Teaching Styles. Canopy designs only share approximate learning objectives, decision structures and the developmental focus of the Landmark Teaching Style(s) they are located near or in between (Ashworth, 2010; Mitchell, 2015).

An inventory of Landmark Teaching Styles

An important aspect of the 2004 review on The Spectrum (Mosston & Ashworth, 2002) was to identify methods used to collect data on how often teachers had implemented certain teaching styles from The Spectrum to teach physical education. The *Teacher's Perceptions of Teaching Styles* (Cothran et al., 2000) was an inventory used to record the teaching styles used to teach physical education in Queensland (Australia) from Years 1–12. After methodically reading the scenarios from this instrument for each of the teaching styles, these scenarios were compared with definitions and descriptors about The Spectrum (Mosston & Ashworth, 2002). It was concluded that some of the scenarios by Cothran et al. did not accurately reflect the Landmark Teaching Styles intent or behaviour. Therefore, it was decided that an instrument that more accurately reflected The Spectrum definitions was needed.

In 2005, SueSee, Ashworth and Edwards developed new scenarios they considered would more accurately reflect each of the teaching styles. Items 2–4 (of Cothran et al., 2000) instrument which related to the factors not relevant to teaching styles from the *Teacher's Perceptions of Teaching Styles* instrument were omitted. Through the process of identifying critical aspects of each teaching style, short scenarios were written. This process created the *Spectrum Inventory*. The instrument – *Instrument for Collecting Teachers' Beliefs about their Teaching Styles used in Physical Education: An adaptation of the Description Inventory of Landmark Teaching Styles: A Spectrum Approach* (2006) is available on *The Spectrum of Teaching Styles* website. The instrument is useful in the self-assessment or reflection by teachers of their teaching and the application of The Spectrum. In using the Inventory of Landmark Teaching Styles (Spectrum Inventory), users will have a much clearer understanding and focus of both understanding and observing teaching styles identified by the very useful Spectrum (Mosston & Ashworth, 2002). The design, development and refinement of The Spectrum Inventory added for the first time an instrument that accurately provides "unambiguous teaching descriptions that most closely capture the individual image of each Landmark Teaching Style along The Spectrum" (2010, p. 8). This means curriculum writers can now draw conclusions about how well a curriculum document is pedagogically implemented. For example, if a curriculum document contained aims such creating 'new movement' or 'solving previously unknown problems' then teacher's completing The Spectrum Inventory would report using styles from the production cluster. If they were not, then professional development to support teachers in achieving these goals through the appropriate teaching styles is necessary in order to ensure teaching that aligns with the curriculum expectation. In support of an understanding of The Spectrum and as a training instrument for the use of The Spectrum Inventory we suggest that development of an online resource and App showing the teaching styles and how to use the inventory to observe and record these for verification of teaching alignment to curricula standards, outcomes or competence statements is required. Additionally, the Spectrum Inventory has the potential to evaluate sport-coaching instruction as an educational endeavour to the planned objectives of the coaching session. This is an area for future research endeavours.

The Spectrum model

Currently, The Spectrum is represented as a linear model with the teaching styles evenly spaced on a continuum Style A through to K, shown in Figure 15.1.

The model shown in Figure 15.1 illustrates that the interaction between the teacher and learner always reflects a teaching behaviour, a learning behaviour and a teaching objective or objectives. This interaction is described as the T-L-O relationship (Mosston & Ashworth, 2008). As each Landmark Style is defined by the behaviour and decisions of the teacher, the behaviour and decisions of the learner, and the teaching objectives that the relationship addresses, each style has its own T-L-O (Figure 15.2).

To explain Figure 15.2, Mosston and Ashworth (2008) suggested that the objectives of a learning experience affect the teaching behaviour which then influences the learning behaviour by requiring the learner to behave in a specific way. These interactions result in an outcome. We suggest that a different (but not contradictory) model or view can be offered. To use a metaphor to illustrate why we think a new model illustration is necessary, when a tradesperson decides to build something he does not ferret through his/her toolbox first and then decide what to make. The tradesperson decides what to make and chooses tools according to what action is necessary and according to the characteristics of the task. With this metaphor in mind, we argue that

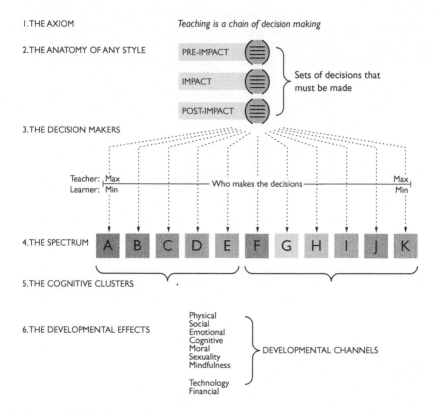

1. THE AXIOM — *Teaching is a chain of decision making*

2. THE ANATOMY OF ANY STYLE — PRE-IMPACT / IMPACT / POST-IMPACT — Sets of decisions that must be made

3. THE DECISION MAKERS

Teacher: Max / Learner: Min — Who makes the decisions — Max / Min

4. THE SPECTRUM — A B C D E F G H I J K

5. THE COGNITIVE CLUSTERS

6. THE DEVELOPMENTAL EFFECTS — Physical / Social / Emotional / Cognitive / Moral / Sexuality / Mindfulness / Technology / Financial — DEVELOPMENTAL CHANNELS

Figure 15.1 The Spectrum Model

Source: Reprint from Teaching Physical Education First Online Edition, 2008 are used with permission from Dr. Sara Ashworth, Director of the Spectrum Institute. Free Digital Download Available at: https://spectrumofteachingstyles.org/index.php?id=16

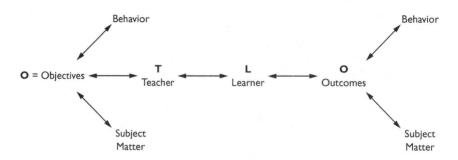

Figure 15.2 The Pedagogical Unit

Source: Reprint from Teaching Physical Education First Online Edition, 2008 are used with permission from Dr. Sara Ashworth, Director of the Spectrum Institute. Free Digital Download Available at: https://spectrumofteachingstyles.org/index.php?id=16

teachers need to ask 'what is it I am trying to achieve?' That is, what is the objective? This is illustrated in Figure 15.2 by showing the O-T-L-O as a pedagogical unit. The lesson objective is a major factor determining the teacher's behaviour with regards to the choice of teaching style. A teacher will focus on what is the goal of the learning experience. The goal of the learning experience will lead to the choice of teaching style. However, the objective is not considered in isolation to the student, rather it should also include the student's characteristics that they bring to the learning experience. Just as a tradesman may consider the type of wood they will be working with to achieve the task. Based on this consideration of the students' characteristics we suggest that the learner should be placed in the centre of decision making and The Spectrum placed around the learner. The Spectrum with the learner at the centre of teacher pedagogical decision making is shown as Figure 15.3.

In Figure 15.3, we place the student at the centre indicating that the teacher chooses the teaching style based on what they wish the student to

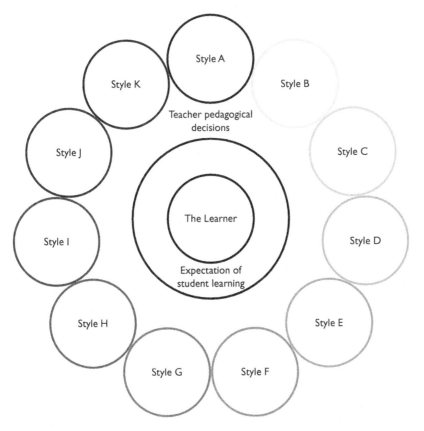

Figure 15.3 The Learner and learning outcomes at the centre of The Spectrum

achieve (aims/objectives/outcomes) and because the teacher also considers the learner in terms of their development and placement in the developmental channels (see Ashworth's Chapter 1 for more on the developmental channels). For example, if the learner has never done Reciprocal Style before, they may have no experience or knowledge about receiving or giving feedback. Therefore, if the teacher used a canopy version of Reciprocal Style with a lengthy criteria sheet and not directly teaching the skills of giving and receiving feedback the episode is likely to be a challenge and not achieve the social interaction that Reciprocal Style is directed towards. The teacher may draw conclusions that Reciprocal Style does not work: however, this conclusion may be incorrect because the teacher has not considered the students lack of social skills and has not taught the skills through modelling what is required.

We argue that by presenting The Spectrum as illustrated in Figure 15.3, recognises the reality of the individual learner needs of the learning environment (that only the class teacher can know) sit together with and the realities of the Landmark styles on The Spectrum. Thinking about the learner first in the example previously used (low experience with Landmark Reciprocal Style and may struggle with pen and paper in PE), and the expectations of student learning (e.g. want student to develop social skills) would direct the teacher to choose to modify Landmark Reciprocal Style. The modification will create a Canopy Reciprocal Style where the students are asked to watch the partner perform a movement skill and give feedback (which could be based on 'thumbs–up' and 'thumbs–down'). We are not arguing that this would be a Landmark Reciprocal Style episode. It is clearly a canopy design as the episode includes an additional step for the teacher and students to develop the social skills of giving feedback and move towards a Landmark Reciprocal Style.

A teacher is required to make judgements about their students and subject matter, and plan for challenge with eventual success. Choosing styles from The Spectrum is therefore derived from the expectation of student learning (Figure 15.3). It is argued that teachers need to consider the desired learning outcome when choosing both Landmark Styles and Canopy Styles. For example, if a teacher did not consider the learner's characteristics and the desired learning outcomes and chose a Landmark Style then the result may not achieve teaching effectiveness and learning opportunities are potentially diminished. The teacher may reject The Spectrum (or the individual style). We suggest the necessity of placing the learner at the centre to make it clear that teaching style decision making starts at the point of understanding the learner and their needs before choosing a style (whether Landmark or Canopy). Further, the representation of The Spectrum we present in Figure 15.3 is consistent with the idea of a canopy design, which we propose is a closer approximation to the realities of the classroom than the lens of Landmark teaching styles.

Using The Spectrum to in fields other than physical education and to interrogate other teaching models

To date, the only application of The Spectrum to sport coaching is Hewitt's use of The Spectrum to interrogate the perceived and actual teaching styles of junior club tennis coaches (Hewitt, 2015; Hewitt, Edwards, Ashworth & Pill, 2016; Hewitt, Edwards & Pill, 2016; Hewitt, Edwards, Reid & Pill, 2018). Sport coaches and physical education teachers have a common concern with pedagogy and learning, therefore, the application of The Spectrum to research in sport coaching is an area where more work can occur. Furthermore, the central concern of The Spectrum with teacher pedagogical decision making means The Spectrum can be used as a research tool or theoretical framework in any area of education – school, higher education or community settings.

Another possibility for future work with The Spectrum is to consider teaching models, or models-based practice, using the lens of The Spectrum. Some work has already begun in this area. SueSee, Pill and Edwards (2016) examined the Tactical model (Metzler, 2011) called the Game Sense approach (Australian Sports Commission, 1996). Tactical models for games and sport teaching have been associated with guided discovery, which is also associated with Guided Discovery Style from The Spectrum. Other than Dyson, Griffin and Hastie (2004), synergies between multiple pedagogical approaches or teaching models is rare in the extant literature, with researchers and practitioners mostly advancing the cause of their preferred approach (SueSee et al., 2016). This results in pedagogical competition in scholarly literature. We agree with Stolz and Pill (2014) that the result is often pedagogical confusion for PE teachers. However, SueSee et al. (2016) using The Spectrum to consider the Game Sense approach showed that a model can be seen as not one instructional style, but a canopy of teaching styles. SueSee and Pill demonstrated another application of The Spectrum lens to a teaching model in Chapter 7. They used The Spectrum for the purpose of showing "the specific decisions, who makes them, how they are made and for what purpose they are made, leads to insights into the structure of the possible relationships between teacher and learner and the consequences of these relationships" (Mosston & Ashworth, 2008, p. 20). For example, when The Spectrum lens is applied to a Constraints Led Approach (CLA), it allows the viewer to see who is making the decisions, the intent of these decisions and when these decisions are being made and illuminates the numerous teaching styles occurring in CLA episodes. The two episodes outlined in Chapter 7 (taken from Chow & Atencio, 2014; and, Renshaw, Chow, Davids & Hammond, 2010) viewed through The Spectrum lens identified specific teaching styles based on the assumed teacher decision making.

Conclusion

This chapter has outlined the initial work by Hewitt (2015) discussing Canopies and the need for their further development and use in research. The development and use of The Spectrum Inventory (SueSee, Ashworth & Edwards, 2006) in identifying teaching styles was outlined and its value to curriculum writers, syllabus writers, teachers and teacher educators was suggested. The Spectrum Inventory requires further development if it was to be used to identify Canopy Styles. Finally, we introduced a new model of The Spectrum placing the learner and the learning outcomes at the centre to represent a 'student-centred' view for teachers when choosing styles. This is a significant suggestion as to date; The Spectrum has been focussed on the teacher. We have also argued for The Spectrum journeying outside the subject matter field of physical education as The Spectrum defines teaching as a chain of decision making. All teaching styles, regardless of the subject matter, can be viewed through The Spectrum lens.

References

Ashworth, S. (2010). *Description inventory of landmark teaching styles: A spectrum approach.* Retrieved 12 September 2011. Retrieved from http://spectrumofteach ingstyles.org/assets/files/articles/Ashworth2004_Description_Inventory_Of_Land mark.pdf

Australian Sports Commission. (1996). *Game sense: perceptions and actions research report.* Belconnen, ACT: Australian Sports Commission.

Chatoupis, C. (2010). Spectrum research reconsidered. *International Journal of Applied Sports Sciences, 22*(1), 80–86.

Chow, J. Y., & Atencio, M. (2014). Complex and nonlinear pedagogy and the implications for physical education. *Sport, Education and Society, 19*(8), 1034–1054.

Cothran, D., Kulinna, P., Banville, D., Choi, E., Amade-Escot, C., MacPhail, A., Macdonald, D., Richard, J., Sarmento, P., & Kirk, D. E. (2005). A cross-cultural investigation of the use of Teaching Styles. *Research Quarterly for Exercise and Sport, 76*(2), 193–201.

Dyson, B., Griffin, L., & Hastie, P. (2004). Sport education, tactical games and cooperative learning: theoretical and pedagogical considerations. *Quest, 56*(2), 226–240.

Goldberger, M., Ashworth, S., & Byra, M. (2012). Spectrum of teaching styles retrospective. *Quest, 64*, 268–282.

Hewitt, M. (2015). Teaching styles of Australian tennis coaches: An exploration of practices and insights using Mosston and Ashworth's Spectrum of Teaching Styles. Unpublished Doctor of Philosophy thesis. School of Linguistics, Adult and Specialist Education, The University of Southern Queensland.

Hewitt, M., Edwards, K., Ashworth, S., & Pill, S. (2016). Investigating the teaching styles of tennis coaches using the Spectrum. *Sport Science Review, 25*(5/6), 321–344.

Hewitt, M., Edwards, K., & Pill, S. (2016). Teaching styles of Australian junior tennis coaches. In J. Bruce & C. North (Eds.), *2015 Game Sense for Teachers and Coaches Conference Proceedings* (pp. 40–52). Christchurch, 19–20 November.

Hewitt, M., Edwards, K., Reid, M., & Pill, S. (2018). Applying the game sense approach and Mosston and Ashworth's Inclusion Style E to promote athlete-centred tennis coaching with junior novice players. In S. Pill (Ed.) *Perspectives on athlete-centred coaching* (pp. 93–103). New York, NY: Routledge.

Metzler, M. (2011). *Instructional models for physical education*. Scottsdale, AZ: Holocomb Hathaway.

Mosston, M., & Ashworth, S. (2002). *Teaching physical education*. San Francisco, CA: Benjamin Cummings.

Mosston, M., & Ashworth, S. (2008). *Teaching physical education* (1st Online ed.). Spectrum Institute for Teaching and Learning. Retrieved from www.spectrum ofteachingstyles.org/e-book-download.php

Renshaw, I., Chow, J-Y., Davids, K., & Hammond, J. (2010). A constraints-led perspective to understanding skill acquisition and game play: a basis for integration of motor learning theory and physical education praxis? *Physical Education and Sport Pedagogy, 15*(2), 117–137.

Silverman, S. (1985). Critical considerations in the design and analysis of teacher effectiveness research in physical education. *International Journal of Physical Education, 22*(4), 17–24.

Stolz, S., & Pill, S. (2014). Teaching games and sport for understanding: Exploring and reconsidering its relevance in physical education. *European Physical Education Review, 20*(1), 36–71.

SueSee, B., Ashworth, S., & Edwards, K. (2006). *Instrument for collecting teachers' beliefs about their teaching styles used in physical education: Adaptation of description inventory of landmark teaching styles: A spectrum approach*. Queensland University of Technology, Brisbane, Australia. Retrieved from www.spectrumofteachingstyles. org/literature

SueSee, B., Pill, S., & Edwards, K. (2016). Reconciling approaches – a game centred approach to sport teaching and Mosston's spectrum of teaching styles. *European Journal of Physical Education and Sport Science, 2*(4), 69–96.

Index